Sisters of the Shadow

Sisters of the Shadow

By Maxine Harris

University of Oklahoma Press : Norman and London

Library of Congress Cataloging-in-Publication Data

Harris, Maxine.
    Sisters of the shadow / by Maxine Harris.
      p. cm.
    Includes bibliographical references and index.
    ISBN 0–8061–2324–9
    1. Homeless women—Psychology. 2. Shadow (Psychoanalysis)
   3. Women—Mythology. I. Title.
   HV4493.H37   1991
   362.83′086942—dc20   90–49624

For my husband, Mark Smith, whose love and acceptance helped me to see my own shadow.

We are the myths. We are the Amazons, the Furies, the Witches. We have never not been here, this exact sliver of time, this precise place. There is something utterly familiar about us. We have been ourselves before.

—Robin Morgan, *Going Too Far:*
The Personal Chronicle of a Feminist

Contents

Acknowledgments

Above all others, I must thank the many homeless women who willingly shared their stories with me. Their experiences helped me to formulate and define my own thoughts and encounters with the shadow. Barbara Karpf assisted in collecting the interviews and also provided an atmosphere of trust that allowed the women to speak freely. The staff at Community Connections were personally supportive while I took time to write the manuscript. The many patients I worked with in psychotherapy shared their own struggles with the shadow as they worked to become more whole.

Friends Helen Bergman, Laura Munder, and Charles Bethel read an earlier version of the manuscript and offered suggestions, as well as encouragement and support. Paul Dixon and Jean Rather offered support and guidance. Leona Bachrach, my friend and mentor, encouraged me to find my own voice and guided my early attempts at writing.

Sybil Tudor Trader, my typist and first editor, carefully and lovingly prepared the manuscript, and Laura Farah with care and enthusiasm performed the tedious task of assembling the manuscript for submission to publishers. Kim Wiar and John Drayton, of the University of Oklahoma Press, handled my work with respect and professional concern.

I cannot thank my family enough for their support, tolerance, and encouragement throughout this process. My sisters, Janet Ennis and Karen Harris, offered suggestions, but mostly sisterly love during the many months when I agonized over whether this manuscript would find the right publisher. Karen has graciously allowed me to use her painting *Maelstrom* on the cover of this book. My mother, Sara Harris, has been there for me all of my life and was a support and strength for me throughout this process as well. Finally, my husband, Mark Smith, wore many hats during the writing of this book. He was my editor, agent, confidant, and companion. He listened to my ideas with respect and enthusiasm and never tired of helping and supporting me; most of all he continued to love me even when I found it hard to love myself.

MAXINE HARRIS

Chevy Chase, Maryland

Part One

Homeless Women and the Shadow

Chapter 1

Homeless Women and Non-homeless Women:
An Introduction to the Issues

One evening as I was visiting with several friends, the conversation turned to the predicament of homeless women. Washington, D.C., like many other large urban centers, has a highly visible and heterogeneous population of homeless men and women. The homeless population had been receiving media attention because, in an effort to prevent these people from using the city's subway stations as temporary residences, the mayor had decided to close the entrances leading to the subways each evening.

The mayor's decision had received mixed reviews within the city, and it also received mixed reactions from my friends that evening in my home. One woman acknowledged, somewhat timidly, that she was horrified by the sight of homeless people, especially disheveled, homeless, psychotic looking women. She confessed that she had such a strong, visceral reaction to the sight of these deranged and lost souls that she actually took a circuitous

3

route to work to avoid passing groups of homeless women congregating in front of a soup kitchen. While she was somewhat embarrassed to acknowledge her reaction, my friend was clearly uncomfortable and unnerved at the thought of having to encounter these unfortunate women.

Another woman was less tentative in her reaction. She was enraged at the sight of homeless people on the city streets. She asserted that she paid her taxes, that she deserved to live in a pleasant environment, and that if she wanted to see poverty and despair, she would rather see it at the movies where she could control the distance between herself and the images on the screen. She felt that she had a right not to be bombarded on her way to work by people whom she found repugnant and intrusive.

A third woman, who leads a somewhat nontraditional life-style, was appalled at the reactions of the other two. She felt that not only did homeless women have a right to be on the streets, but that those of us who were more economically fortunate had a moral obligation to acknowledge them, to see them, and to find some way to relate to them. She believed that, above all else, we should not be allowed to deny the existence of these less fortunate and less socially acceptable women.

As I listened to the conversation, I was struck by two things. First, it was predominantly the women among my group of friends who felt compelled to talk about this subject. Although there were occasional comments by the male members of the group, the men seemed less touched by and less involved in the problems of homeless women. I do not think that they were any less caring or any less socially concerned than the women in the group, but, the presence of homeless, disturbed women was not as alive and unsettling for the men as it was for the women.

Secondly, and perhaps more importantly, I was impressed by the passion with which these women expressed their opinions. There was vehemence to their words. These were not merely intellectual opinions, these were deeply felt emotional reactions. What started as a discussion turned into a debate, and by the time the evening ended, these women were literally screaming their different opinions at one another.

Such intense reactions are not limited to my group of friends; they are echoed throughout our country by civic leaders, journalists, and average citizens. Mitch Snyder, the former director of the Community for Creative Non-Violence, had on several occasions almost starved himself to death in an attempt to advocate for the needs of homeless people. One mayor in a southern city proposed to spray community garbage with poison to dissuade homeless people from eating out of public refuse cans. This mayor likened himself to an exterminator taking care of a population of vermin. In other cities bands of teenage hooligans have knifed and set afire homeless people sleeping in public parks. Each of these is an intense and extreme reaction to the visible presence of homeless men and women.

The intensity and irrationality of these reactions jar us and demand that we attempt to understand just what has aroused such powerful emotional responses. Clearly, these responses do not merely derive from an intellectual perspective on the shortage of housing among the nation's poor. When we look at homeless men and women, we see more than just people who must live without adequate shelter. We see the reflection of something that both frightens and shocks us and from which we must turn away.

Social scientists tell us that homeless people suffer from more than a lack of housing. Not only are they without a place to sleep, but they are also profoundly alienated and disaffiliated from the larger culture. Homeless people have been called urban nomads by mental health researchers; modern-day gargoyles by a homeless street poet; and our living nightmares by Jonathan Kozol, author of the much acclaimed book *Rachel and Her Children*, which is about homeless families.[1] For most of us, homeless people are faceless specters who haunt our city streets only to spook us if we encounter them as we go about our business.

Homeless women, in particular, present us with an image that is difficult for us to comprehend. These are women who in no way live a life that we expect of a modern woman. They are totally disconnected from the popular American dream: a home in the suburbs, a white picket fence, and two children. But more significantly, they remain outside of our understanding of how women are supposed to live. Part of our discomfort in viewing these women is that we cannot easily make sense of their lives; it is much easier for us to understand the homeless man. There is a long tradition of the vagabond male, the hobo, and we can more easily assimilate the image of the roving, wandering, disconnected man. The homeless woman, bundled in her overcoat, hunched over and clinging to the sides of city buildings, arouses so much dissonance in most men and women that we are unable to tolerate her.

In a psychological sense we can deal with her only if we define her as being fundamentally "other." She is different from us; she is that which we are not. One homeless woman described herself as both feeling like and being treated like she was from the moon. People could only relate to her if they thought of her as an alien—someone not from our planet, not from our culture, and not from our psychological world.

Jonathan Kozol reports, with some embarrassment, that after interviewing homeless families, he returned to his own lodgings and felt the need to cleanse himself physically.[2] While he knew that there was some logic to this bathing because he had in fact been with people who were infested with lice, he also knew that the cleansing served a ritual and metaphoric function for him. He needed to distance himself from the despair that he had experienced in the presence of these homeless families, almost as if he wanted to wash away the hopelessness that he had shared in their presence. While our rational minds tell us that homelessness and despair are not contagious, our preanalytic, more emotional selves urge us to disinfect ourselves thoroughly, lest our dealings with these urban untouchables contaminate us in some permanent way.

In the conclusion to his book, Kozol remarks that the graves in Potter's Field, a cemetery in which homeless people are buried, have no markers.[3] The graves have no markers by design, because city officials have decided that they do not want to glorify the lives of poor, homeless people. They do not want in any way to memorialize the death or life of a social outcast. The lack of a personal marker also says that we as a society are uncomfortable recognizing the individual humanity of these people. We do not want to believe that they are real people, separate, unique individuals like us. Rather, we want to continue the fantasy that they are aliens, that they are part of an anonymous, nameless horde that we can continue to keep at a safe distance from ourselves.

Shelter providers have noted that when people become homeless, their identity as homeless people seems so powerful that it tends to obliterate any previous identity. Project Help, in New York City, an outreach program to homeless people, reports that over 50 percent of the people they serve are listed merely as John or Jane Doe.[4] While some homeless individuals have personal reasons for not wanting to reveal their identities to authorities, there may be another determinant of the overwhelming anonymity of the homeless population: namely, that when one becomes homeless, one's previous identity seems not to count, not to matter. These individuals often refer to the events of their past lives as if those events were indeed part of the distant past. A woman might say "I used to be a mother," or "Once I worked in a store." All of these other identities take the form of "ex" identities with the only identity seeming to matter currently being one's identity as a homeless person. That the lack of permanent housing should become the core of one's identity suggests that homelessness is more than just the absence of a place to sleep or a place to live; homelessness comes to define an individual in a fundamental way, so much so that it becomes all that he or she is.

The desire to keep homeless women and men at a safe distance from the rest of the populace seems to be one of the considerations used when locations for shelters to house homeless people are selected. The city of Boston, for example, buses its homeless people to a shelter on a promontory that juts into Boston Harbor.[5] While the city has economic and logistical justifications for this policy, the result is that homeless people are placed almost out at sea, far from the rest of the citizenry. One cannot help but be reminded of the solution that New York City recently devised for handling its garbage. City sanitation workers put the garbage on a barge, set it out to sea, and searched for a site to dump it, a safe distance from the rest of the population.

In some states there is even a move to resurrect some of the abandoned old buildings at state mental hospitals to serve as shelters for homeless people. Many of these hospitals, which have been refuges for outcast members of society in the past, are located far away from downtown metropolitan areas. In a surprising act of advocacy, members of a neighborhood in Queens where homeless people were to be sheltered at a state psychiatric facility suggested that the presence of homeless men and women on the grounds of the state hospital might have an adverse effect on the psychiatric patients who were housed there.[6] Homeless people are thought of as so aberrant, so outside the mainstream of society, that we are even worried that they will harm or contaminate psychiatric patients, who have been traditionally defined as alien and other than the rest of us.

The most recent "humane" suggestion for sheltering homeless people came during the 1988 presidential campaign debates when then Vice-President George Bush advocated using empty barracks on some large army bases as temporary shelters. While the suggestion was intended to alleviate the tragic shortage of affordable housing, it was frighteningly reminiscent of past "humane" uses of internment camps during World War II for Japanese Americans.

What is it about homeless people, especially homeless and often mentally ill women, that repels us to the point of needing to place these people at a safe and extended distance from the rest of us? How is it that we have come to view other human beings as so much debris, needing to be packed up, shipped off, and hidden from view? It does seem to be true that our society has never been very good at knowing how to treat things or people that are damaged, broken, or no longer useful. We pollute our water and our air with the by-products of our consumption; we bury our nuclear waste and naïvely hope it will go away; and we tragically clutter our city streets with the living shadows of broken lives and shattered dreams. We want damaged goods out of sight and far away.

It is especially pertinent that homeless women are often referred to as "bag ladies." Taken literally, this name derives from the fact that many homeless women walk around the streets carrying all of their belongings in shopping bags, or pushing everything that they own in front of them in a shopping cart. These women are quite literally weighted down with baggage. When we come to know homeless women in a more personal way, we often discover that the contents of these bags have frequently been collected from garbage cans or from thrift shops. These women carry with them baggage that has been discarded by other women.

At a metaphoric level the bag lady, weighted down with cast-offs collected from the trash of wealthy matrons, is a disconcerting image. In the popular vernacular we describe our neuroses, those parts of ourselves that we would like to disown and with which we feel uncomfortable, as our "psychological baggage." Self-help books frequently admonish us to rid ourselves of the metaphoric and psychological baggage that we carry. It is doubly interesting that homeless women—bag ladies—carry with them baggage, baggage that is quite literally not only the leftover, discarded possessions of other members of the society, but also baggage that may, at a metaphoric level, represent those elements of our psychological selves for which we no longer have any use or with which we are no longer comfortable. I am suggesting that homeless women carry for us our literal baggage and our psychological baggage, and that some of our great need to distance ourselves from them represents our need to distance ourselves from our own psychological, disowned, or unused parts.

How then can we come to look inside the baggage that homeless women carry for us? How do we become more familiar with these cast-off and discarded elements so that we can free these women from having to carry our bags for us and, at the same time, come to know ourselves better?

This book is about homeless women, specifically the disheveled, slightly mad bag lady, the woman whose furtive glance makes us look away, who had she lived four hundred years ago might have been burned as a witch. Even as the population of homeless women changes to include more homeless mothers with children, economically marginal single women, and inner-city crack addicts, the bag lady continues to haunt our collective imaginations, signifying more than her individual life, resonating with images at the core of all women. Indeed, this book is about modern women and about personal and psychological integration. It is my hope that in coming to understand homeless women, we will also come to understand ourselves more fully. If we can repossess those parts of ourselves that we have cast off, we will not only become more whole and more fully human, but we will also unburden those who currently carry some of these discarded aspects of femininity and humanity for us.

In attempting to understand the lives of homeless women, we face an ethical and methodological problem. We want to allow women the opportunity to share their individual and personal stories with one another and with us; yet we want to respect their privacy. We want to understand the significance their stories have for all of us; yet we want to avoid turning them into objects of inquiry. We want to understand the transcendent significance of certain patterns; yet we want to avoid mythologizing and reifying the tragedy of their lives.

These women certainly deserve to be understood as unique individuals and to have their personal stories recorded. All too often when we speak of homeless men and women we use the collective noun, "the homeless." It is easier for us to remain distant from an anonymous horde of homeless people. When we select out of this undifferentiated mass a particular homeless woman, she gains a personal identity for us, making it much more difficult for us to view her as an alien creature. She becomes a real woman, with a real name and a real life story, and we have to treat her and respect her as such.

We are obliged to rescue homeless women from the anonymity into which they have been cast and to restore their own particular lives to them. In the telling of their personal stories, they reveal to us that, while the content of their lives may be very different from the lives most women lead, the structure and rhythm of their experiences are not very different from the ups and downs most of us encounter. These women have their successes as well as their failures; they have their triumphs as well as their defeats; and they have their hopes as well as their disappointments. It is important for their reaffiliation with the larger society that we allow them to recount their personal histories.

In reading or hearing these stories, however, it is hoped that other women, more fortunate women who have not experienced the profound disenfranchisement of homelessness, will recognize aspects of themselves that perhaps they have been unwilling to acknowledge. Consequently, the process of acknowledging the personal reality of a group of homeless women will serve a twofold purpose. It will rescue these particular women from the anonymity of homelessness, and will also allow other women to rescue their vulnerable and disowned psychological parts from the trash bags into which those parts have been cast.

I have chosen, in part, to recount the stories of homeless women by allowing them to tell their own stories. Storytelling has always been a particularly female activity. Women have a history of talking with one another over the backyard fence and over the coffee table in the morning, talking with their daughters and with their sisters. While this conversation has often been denigrated and devalued as idle gossip, it has been not only a way in which women have connected with other women, but also a way in which women have imparted their particular philosophies or world views to one another.

Because women have traditionally been preoccupied with the everyday tasks of managing a home and managing a family, their stories are often interwoven with the mundane details of their lives. Women do not impart their world views directly, and are less likely than men to write philosophical treatises. Their views of the world are conveyed rather indirectly, almost as distractions or asides in the telling of a particular tale.

The rhythm of women's stories may be seen as parallelling the texture of a woman's life.[7] In the process of going about her business or in the process of telling her story, a woman often interjects a piece of wisdom that she has garnered from her life experience. Writers have commented that in the sharing of stories, women can come to form a community—a spiritual community perhaps somewhat akin to that which develops in churches when people testify and share their religious experiences with one another.

Sheila Collins, a feminist theologian, suggests that in the process of collective storytelling women may begin to discern patterns—similarities among their separate lives—that allow them not only to bond with other women, but also to offer validation to the individual woman who is telling her story.[8] For many of the women who contributed to this book, the telling of their stories was a profoundly moving experience. They discovered aspects of themselves that they had forgotten or ignored. Some refined and retold their stories several times. Having their stories heard and valued allowed them to value and reown their experiences.

As stories are told and retold, the inessential details fade, and women are left with images that carry a mythological or transcendent message. In telling the stories of individual homeless women, it is my hope that I will not only provide a cathartic experience for those women who tell their stories, an experience that will aid in the reintegration of these women into the larger community of women and men, but that I will also reach out to other women who will resonate to aspects of these stories. Stories often touch us in a way that objective and intellectual material does not. Perhaps in the hearing of another woman's story, we will have our defenses sufficiently relaxed so that we will gain access to parts of ourselves that we have kept hidden for a long period of time.

In the early days of the women's movement, women often discovered a feeling and experience of sisterhood as they heard one another tell their stories. The experience of affective resonance that we have when listening to another woman describe her life experience has been called the "yeah yeah" experience.[9] We say "Yes," at a deep emotional level to what we hear. Each woman listening knows that the content of the story has a personal meaning and relevance for her beyond a mere empathic connection to the woman who is telling the story.

During the solicitation of stories from homeless women, the project was described to them and they were asked if they would agree to tell their stories and to have them taped and prepared for potential publication. A number of women readily agreed and were enthusiastic about sharing their experiences, not only as homeless people, but their experiences prior to becoming homeless. One woman in particular spoke for the group when she said, "I would be glad to talk about my life if it would help other women to learn from my experiences." When she first stated those words, I took her quite literally, and I assumed that she was talking about other homeless women and that perhaps she would be providing some concrete advice for how someone should cope with life on the streets. In fact, her story had very little to do with life on the streets and contained no helpful hints for survival. I concluded that her words of well-wishing to other women were merely a conventional way of being accommodating. I later came to realize that her story did contain valuable material for other women, but not necessarily for other homeless women. Her story and the story of her life spoke to all of us if only we were available to listen.

Chapter 2

Understanding Homeless Women

Many practitioners, sociologists, psychologists, and public-policy analysts have tried to describe or to explain the current wave of homelessness that has engulfed vast numbers of men and women. These analyses are so varied that we may well question whether different researchers are in fact looking at the same problem. I am reminded of the story of a group of scientists who are each asked to write a description of an elephant. Each scientist is blindfolded and placed at one spot along the body of the huge beast. Based only on what he or she can feel, each is to extrapolate a description of the elephant. The resulting descriptions bear little resemblance to one another. Analogously, we may legitimately ask whether those who write about the problems of the homeless are aware of each other's piece of the elephant.

In an attempt to sort through these different analyses, some researchers have suggested that these disparate approaches may represent different levels of conceptual analysis. One psychiatrist, for example, postulated that we might look at the characteristic pattern of wandering from place to place, evidenced by many homeless women, at several different levels.[1] At a biological level, for example, we might explain her constant walking as having to do with hyper-motor activity. At a psychological level, however, the same behavior might be understood as having to do with her desire to flee anxiety-ridden relationships. At a sociological level, the analysis might focus on the lack of affordable housing and other economic realities that forced the woman to keep moving from place to place. The author suggests that an analysis of each of these levels may contribute ultimately to our understanding of the problem of homelessness.

While there may be a number of ways in which we can examine and understand the current epidemic of homelessness, the metaphor of levels of analysis may not be the most precise. In talking about different levels of understanding, we employ a metaphor that is both spatial and linear. Levels are assumed to exist in a hierarchical relationship to one another along a real or imaginary vertical axis. When, for example, archaeologists excavate a prehistoric site, they dig from the most recent level of civilization to the most distant or primitive. The different levels of excavation are organized simultaneously on several axes: how far workers had to dig in order to reach them, how long ago their civilizations flourished, and how modern their societies were. In each case the linear metaphor of levels demands that we organize the levels in some hierarchical and mutually exclusive relationship to one another. While such organization does bring some order to the various analyses, it forces us to make evaluative judgments among the levels and to limit our inquiry to one level at the expense of others.

For the purpose of analyzing the problems of homeless women, I would prefer to employ a somewhat less mechanistic and more contextual metaphor, namely that of successive filters applied to the lens of a camera. A photographic filter allows only certain wave lengths of light to enter the camera while screening out or rejecting others. By changing the filter, one can highlight certain aspects of the visual field at the expense of other aspects, gaining different perspectives on the scene at hand. It would be foolish and unnecessary to evaluate one filter as more true or more sophisticated than others. Once a particular filter is applied, it is possible to aim the camera in a myriad of directions. The filter does not determine in which direction the camera will be aimed; rather it determines what aspect of the field will be highlighted once the target has been chosen.

Applying this metaphor to various discussions of homelessness, it is possible to view different approaches as resulting from the application of different contextual filters to the camera of inquiry. For example, when we place a sociological filter over the lens, we view all elements within the field from a sociological perspective. Once the filter is in place, we can then aim the camera in multiple directions permitting discussions of description, causality, and solution all to emerge with a sociological tint.

For this investigation into the lives of homeless women I have chosen to survey the landscape primarily with the lens of metaphor on the camera. From a perspective of metaphor, the problem of homelessness, indeed the very existence of profoundly disenfranchised and homeless women, assumes a relevance not only for the women who must survive without adequate shelter, but for all of us who have incorporated homeless women into our mythological consciousnesses.

The filter of metaphor, while capable of profoundly altering our perceptions, often goes unnoticed by most of us. We are frequently unaware that someone or some group of people have assumed metaphoric or symbolic status for us; we may only know that a person arouses intense and often uncanny feelings in us. In general, we are more cognizant of and more willing to acknowledge the use of clearly objective and analytical perspectives. Most of our current analyses of homelessness and homeless women employ either a sociological or psychological filter. In some instances a second, modifying filter, an economic one, for example, is added to the primary filter, further altering our perspective.

I will begin by scanning the field with the two most commonly used filters, those of sociology and psychology (the latter being the preferred perspective of many of the homeless women interviewed). Ultimately the metaphoric filter will be snapped into place, becoming the predominant perspective for the remainder of this inquiry.

The Sociological Filter

With the sociological filter applied, the camera can be aimed in a variety of directions. We can describe homeless women, explain the causes of their homelessness, and offer solutions, all from the perspective of societal forces and social institutions.

In a descriptive mode, several social scientists have observed that homeless women tend to be profoundly disaffiliated from the larger society. Often these women are no longer connected to family members, no longer connected to religious communities, and no longer connected to societal norms and values. Not only are they perceived as being outside the mainstream by those of us who observe them on the streets, but they also experience themselves as being disconnected from other people. Homeless women in Great Britain who were interviewed by two social scientists frequently referred to themselves as outcasts, nameless wanderers, people who did not really exist.[2] These women thought of themselves as being no longer human, referring to themselves as objects, rubbish, monsters, industrial waste. The extent to which many homeless women have ceased to think of themselves as viable human beings speaks to the extent of their disaffiliation from the human community.

Social scientists have coined the phrase "social margin" to describe the distance that exists between an individual and his or her economic or social disaster and collapse.[3] Our social margin is populated by all those individuals who might be available to help us if we were to experience either economic or emotional trouble. If, for example, we have a large extended family that consists of many members who can provide economic support or can provide temporary housing or are available to lend an ear to listen if we have problems, then our margin is fairly deep. Presumably, we can weather any storm that comes along.

In considering the population of homeless and often mentally ill women, what we find is that their social margin is extremely narrow. These women have very little buffer between themselves and social or economic collapse. When one observes homeless women on the streets, one is often struck by how they seem to carry so much with them. They have several changes of clothing, often a bag or two of groceries, and not infrequently, several overcoats. A casual observer might be inclined to question why these women need to carry so much with them. Employing the concept of social margin, we might conclude that homeless women carry all the social margin that they have around with them on their backs. They have no hidden reserves stored away some place and consequently need to guard assiduously what little buffer they do have. Tragically, the only margin that remains between them and the coldness of the outside world consists of the literal layers of clothing that they wear on their backs.

Despite the fact that many homeless women have moved outside the bounds of conventional society, their need for a community does not cease. For many women the shelters function as a surrogate family where women are able to come together and experience some sense of belonging. Even on the streets some women form part of a fringe subculture in which they coexist with other homeless persons in a pseudosociety.

I recently heard a young homeless woman, who labeled herself as a street tough, describe a relationship she had forged with a much older and more vulnerable homeless woman. The older woman, tired of being intimidated and harassed for money, approached the younger woman and asked if she could hire her as a bodyguard. The younger woman, an alcoholic, agreed to trade her services for a quart of wine. Thus began a somewhat tenuous relationship between the two.

It would be misguided to think that these subcultures possess the same emotional and instrumental support that other social groupings have. They are more often anonymous clusters of individuals only loosely connected to one another by virtue of a shared space on the streets. Nonetheless, for many homeless women these loosely organized groupings are the only community to which they continue to belong.

Moving beyond description, other social analysts examine the combination of forces that have led to this condition of disaffiliation and homelessness. In so doing, they frequently add a second filter to the sociological one. These combinations shade the sociological perspective with economic, political, and policy overtones.

From an economic perspective, analysts see homelessness as being inextricably tied to poverty and the lack of affordable housing. Jonathan Kozol, after studying homeless families for two years, concluded unequivocally that the number one cause of homelessness was a lack of affordable housing.[4] In many large cities urban neighborhoods have changed dramatically in the last twenty years. Marginal areas of the city have been transformed by urban renewal into chic neighborhoods for upwardly mobile young professionals.

The economic analysts maintain that we are increasingly becoming a society with an underclass, a society that has a large population of working poor individuals who just barely maintain themselves, and who are always one paycheck away from economic disaster. Regrettably, women, especially single women, make up a large portion of the working poor and are consequently especially vulnerable to homelessness when their already imperiled economic status takes a turn for the worse.

In surveys that have been done of the homeless population, many homeless people agree with the economic analysts that homelessness is for them the reflection of economic deprivation. These individuals cite a lack of money, lack of a job, and lack of affordable housing as being the primary determinants of their homelessness.[5]

Continuing to focus on causality, but with a political filter added to the sociological one, Sophie Watson and Helen Austerberry, two British sociologists, argue that homelessness among women results when a patriarchally organized society, such as Great Britain, emphasizes and economically supports the male dominated nuclear family as the primary unit of social organization.[6] This unit, they argue, not only determines social relations and social interactions within the larger community, but it also favors certain housing patterns. If a society is committed to promoting the nuclear family, then that society will make available housing resources to male-dominated nuclear families at the expense of other social units. Women who are disconnected from this primary social unit because of divorce, widowhood, or single status do not participate in the society's primary social unit. Consequently, they are more likely to experience disaffiliation and disconnection from social intercourse.

In an attempt to explain increased numbers of homeless men and women, some social scientists have applied the filter of public policy and have specifically cited recent shifts in mental-health policy. Although the estimates vary widely, observers continue to note that a high percentage of homeless people also suffer from some major mental illness. This observation has led a number of social analysts to consider the impact of the recent deinstitutionalization movement on homelessness.[7] Deinstitutionalization was a complicated social, economic, and treatment initiative that mandated the release from public mental hospitals of thousands of men and women. While the majority of these individuals have found homes either with family members or in group and supported residential arrangements, a number now make their homes on city streets. These individuals were either discharged without adequate preparation or failed to follow through on the discharge plans that were made. The portrait of a deranged man or woman wandering city streets, isolated, unmedicated, unfed, is so appalling that journalists have been quick to bring this kind of story to the public's attention. While we as a society need to be aware of the casualties of current mental-health policy, the frequency with which these stories are reported might inadvertently lead us to believe that all homeless people are merely displaced former mental patients. This is not the case, and we need to be mindful lest we overemphasize the role that deinstitutionalization policy has played in creating the problem of homelessness.

Retaining a sociological filter, some researchers have been bold enough to aim their inquiry in the direction of possible solutions to the problem of homelessness. Economic solutions, while difficult to implement, are easy to articulate. If we build more affordable housing and if we provide people with rental subsidies or housing vouchers, we will satisfactorily address the problem of homelessness. Once again, many homeless people find themselves in agreement with the economic analysts. When asked what they needed most to remedy their housing problems, homeless men and women consistently asked for more economic resources.[8]

The solutions put forth by the political analysts are both radical and vague. They call for a fundamental restructuring of hierarchical relationships within the society and a movement away from patriarchal and class-conscious values. While such a reorganized society might indeed be more humane and just, it remains unclear how we are to get there from here. These analysts may be more effective at describing the problem than at providing solutions.

Finally, most of those who suggest that deinstitutionalization may have contributed to the problem of homelessness are adamant that reinstitutionalization is not the solution. Indeed they maintain that it would be a mistake to turn the clock back and return thousands of men and women to institutional care. Rather these authors advocate better aftercare and community support programs for discharged patients.

Regardless of whether we describe the characteristics of the population, attempt to discern underlying causes of homelessness, or suggest possible solutions, as long as we employ a sociological filter, our analysis will highlight and emphasize social and often impersonal policies, institutions, and relationships at the expense of other aspects of the field of inquiry.

Psychological Filter

By contrast, a psychological filter highlights the personal, intrapsychic, and interpersonal aspects of the lives of homeless women. Before we apply this particular filter, however, some caveats are in order. Employing a psychological perspective, we can describe the inner world of many of the homeless women who were interviewed. We do need to be careful with issues of causation and with trying to find a particular psychological profile that predisposes people toward homelessness. Some researchers argue that if there is indeed a causal connection between homelessness and psychological dysfunction, it may well be that it is homelessness, with its consequent physical and psychological burdens, that causes psychological symptoms, rather than the other way around.[9]

It should also be noted that many of the homeless women who were interviewed came to adopt a psychological perspective when describing their experiences. While that perspective was not aimed at articulating the causes of their homelessness, it did carry implications for eventual reaffiliation and return to more mainstream society. More important, a psychological perspective provides a context in which to hear the personal stories of homeless women as well as a bridge for connecting their experiences to the lives of other women; the intrapsychic and interpersonal dilemmas they experience are felt at some level by all women.

Perhaps the most startling psychological characteristic of many homeless women is their profound sense of alienation. These women are not merely alienated from their own personal support networks and from the larger culture in which they live, but they are often fundamentally alienated from their own core selves. Many of the women interviewed had lost large portions of their own life stories. It seemed almost as if they had fallen asleep or ventured into some enchanted land in which time stood still. They either could not remember things that had happened to them or had disassociated themselves from particularly painful elements of their personal histories.

Many of the women displayed an almost quizzical stance toward the fact that they had arrived at middle age. It was as if the last time they had stopped and taken a look at their lives, they were teenagers, and somehow, without their knowing what had happened, years had gone by and they now found themselves in their thirties, forties, and fifties, unable to account for lost decades. Some of these women seem akin to characters in fairytales who drink some magic potion and forget their own identities. They wander endlessly, unable to reconnect with the self that they were before the magical intervention occurred. Not coincidentally, these fairytale characters are often found wandering deep in a dark forest, disconnected from the community from which they came, lost not only to themselves, but to their own societies.[10] We can speculate that our city streets have become the modern equivalent of the dark forest, and that many homeless women wander like lost souls in this modern-day woods.

While the physical realities of homelessness—lack of clean clothing, lack of a place to bathe, lack of consistent nutrition—contribute to a woman's losing contact with her own body, it is surprising how many women remain alienated from their physical selves even after they are no longer living on the streets or in shelters. Many of these women seem not only to neglect their bodies, but also to lack a fundamental understanding of how their bodies work. They complain about physical ailments almost as if they were magical curses that have been cast by external demons. Despite their having the intellectual capacity to make such logical connections, they exhibit no understanding that certain behavior might result in their getting an infection. If the body is the home of the self, these women demonstrate an even more profound disconnection from home than just their lack of external shelter.

In her book *All Sickness Is Homesickness,* Dianne M. Connelly, an acupuncturist, put forth the thesis that all illness, all dysphoria, and all dysfunction are really a reflection of one's alienation from one's own core self; that if home is a metaphor for the place in which one is centered, the place where one can come to rest and find peace, then when we are ill we have somehow drifted away from home, from our own inner core.[11] This metaphor seems especially apt for homeless women who are literally homeless, but more important many of whom are also spiritually homeless in that this fundamental connection to self has been severed. It is surprising to note how many of the women who were interviewed did not have a strong sense of who they were, what their interests were, or what their skills and strengths were. Some of them came to discover themselves in the process of telling their stories to other women.

In American Indian mythology, the character Spider Woman admonishes her people that those who forget why they came to this world will lose their way.[12] Many homeless women who indeed seem to be lost souls have in a literal sense forgotten why they came to this world. They have lost the sense of meaning and purpose in their lives, and they often wander aimlessly from one shelter to the next. The very life-style of a homeless woman cuts her off from the everyday activities and rituals of life. She cannot be concerned with or involved in the rhythm of waking, preparing for the day, engaging in activity, preparing a meal, and closing the day down, because she is without a base or stable environment. Despite how they may have arrived at the place of homelessness, homeless women often find themselves alienated from the everyday activities that allow other women to define themselves more easily.

Alienation from self is not the only recurring theme in the psychological profiles of homeless women. Equally important is the almost pervasive history of abuse. Many of these women were victims of child abuse, of incest within their homes, of abuse by spouses, and once they became homeless, of physical abuse and rape on the streets. Abuse and violence are so much a part of the lives of many homeless women that it is almost impossible to talk about their everyday existence without including these tragic and frightening realities.

While the reality of violence exists for all homeless women, their responses to their victimization vary. Some women clearly and consciously build a barrier around themselves that prevents anyone from gaining access. They make sure that they stay distant from other people, never allowing anyone to get too close. Some women even keep themselves dirty and smelly so that they will be unattractive to would-be attackers. Some women who were the victims of incest refuse to sleep within the confines of a bedroom because it was in a supposedly "safe" bedroom that the crime committed against them years ago occurred. Still other women will not sleep lying down because they fear being attacked. Their night's rest, even in a shelter, is spent sitting up, always vigilant, always on guard. Moving from shelter to shelter or apartment to apartment, never getting too close to anyone, never allowing anyone to know them too well is a pattern many women adopt to guard themselves from potential violation. It seems that when they begin to make connections to other people, they need to move on because interpersonal relationships have in the past been so dominated by abuse, violence, and betrayal that they do not dare trust that new relationships might be any different.

While some women cope with their histories of abusive relationships and with the ever-present threat of violence by distancing themselves from all relationships, others adopt a different and more personally damaging stance: they internalize and, in essence, concur with the voice of the oppressor. Many homeless women carry with them what analyst Demaris Wehr has called an internal self-hater.[13] These women feel that they are to blame for the victimization that they have experienced and consequently identify with the view that others have of them, namely that they are evil, or ugly, or defective in some way. Women in the sample frequently referred to themselves as the bad one in their family; the outcast of the family; as one woman poignantly put it, "I am the ugliest black woman alive." Tragically, many women who have been abused and denigrated come to the conclusion that they must deserve to be beaten down, and consequently they beat themselves down even further for being unworthy wretches. Thus, many homeless women have to contend not only with the actual abuse and victimization that threatens them every day, but also with the internalized oppression that has now become a part of their self-concept. Clinicians who work with sexually abused children report that it is not uncommon for these children to self mutilate.[14] They have come to think of themselves as people who deserve punishment and mistreatment, and when they are not mistreated by some external agent, they deliver the punishment themselves.

Other women, perhaps more fortunate, turn their rage and hatred outward. One woman described herself as a boiling kettle of hate, just waiting to overflow and burn anyone who came near. Clearly there are homeless women who look fierce on the streets. They have managed to perfect the outward appearance of a raging tiger so that anyone with any sense at all will stay far away, and those people foolish enough to try to get close will come to regret their decision soon enough. One woman asserted rather dispassionately, "I'll kill anyone who messes with me." It was un- clear whether she actually meant this threat or if this was her own version of the tiger's growl, designed to frighten any foolhardy attackers and to assert her preeminence in the jungle of the streets.

A number of the women who were interviewed had a history of violence. They were perfectly nice, gentle, and accommodating one moment, and then almost as if in a flash they switched into being hateful and rageful. Even in retrospect the women did not have a good explanation for what had triggered their verbal or physical outbursts. All they knew was that something seemed to well up from inside and explode outside of their control.

This combination of fearfulness, depression, and self loathing with episodic violence resembles the picture that has been painted of returning war veterans. In a very real sense, homeless women may be suffering from their own version of posttraumatic stress disorder, the syndrome that psychiatrists have developed to ex- plain the often erratic behavior of returning Vietnam veterans.[15] Many homeless women have indeed been engaged in fighting a war of their own, and they continue to be the combatants of the streets.

A psychological perspective on the lives of homeless women would not be complete without some attempt to record the nuances and images of their internal fantasy lives. These women, like all of us, have daydreams and aspirations. They are infused with the same storybook mythologies that nonhomeless women share. Yet, two distinct patterns emerged as these women shared their innermost wishes and dreams. First, these myths of family harmony and idyllic love stood in sharp contrast to and had to compete with the often harsh and brutal realities of their lives. And second, these women had seen their fantasies battered and smashed more times than most of us could endure. Despite these dual sources of disappointment, however, most of the homeless women with whom I spoke continued at some level to cling to the fantasies with which they had grown up.

It should be noted that these fantasies or mythologies are in no way synonymous with delusions or psychotic perceptions; rather these are the shared idealizations of our culture, and they influence the longings of many of us who grew up before the upheaval and disillusionment of the 1960s. These are the stories of Walt Disney and the Grimm brothers and the romanticized families from the situation comedies of the early days of television. Together these cultural gurus have bequeathed us a fantasy world peopled by damsels in distress, fairy godmothers, heroic princes, and Donna Reeds (a woman whose name has almost come to epitomize the ideal family of our dreams).

Many of the personal mythologies of the women interviewed begin with stories of idyllic family life. Repeatedly, these women described their childhoods in idealized language. Pictures emerged of perfect families and almost utopian existences in which there was enough love, food and nurturing for everyone. One woman fondly recalled a time when she and some girlfriends snatched a pie from a neighbor's windowsill and took it into the field, rejoicing in their stolen treat and their shared adventure.

Despite these memories of wonderful childhood times, and a current desire to regain this "paradise lost," most of these homeless women endured a childhood that was less than an ideal time.[16] In fact, many of them were products of broken homes with parents either being divorced or with one parent dying at an early age. Some of the women were sent off to be raised by distant relatives, and others found their way into foster care. A number of them had parents who were abusive and either alcoholic or drug addicted, and many of the women grew up in poverty. The reality of their lives is in such dramatic contrast to the families of their imagination that one may have cause to wonder if they did not, as small children, invent or imagine a family life that was more to their liking than the one they actually had.

Not only have many of these women blurred the details of their past to avoid the pain of remembering what growing up was in fact like, but many of them continue to look for the ideal nurturing family that they never had. The search for the good family is perhaps crystallized in the search for the good mother.[17] Many of these women talked explicitly about their continued longing for the mother of their dreams. They sought an all-good, all-nurturing woman who not only would take care of them, but also would intuit and tend to their needs without their even having to ask.

A surprising number of the women that were interviewed had lost their biological mothers either in early childhood or during their early teenage years. Consequently, they had no opportunity to develop and refine a relationship with a real mother. Their relationships with a mothering person had abruptly stopped before they reached adulthood, and in some sense their own development stopped at the same time. Consequently, many of these women appeared to be child-women. They had the bodies of adults, but the longings of little girls, still looking for the mother they had lost years ago.

Having not been mothered well themselves, many of these women seemed incapable of being mothers to their own children. None of the women who told their stories was currently raising her own children. Most of them, however, had given birth to at least one child and often several children. It was surprising how many of the women could not remember the ages of their children and in some cases did not know where their children were. Some of them had lost their children in custody fights with the families of the child's father; others had had their children taken away by child protective services; and still others had dropped their children off at some relative's house hoping that someone else might do a better job of raising the child than they thought they would.

More than wanting to be mothers, many of these women desired, at a deep psychological level, to be mothered. One woman even articulated her desire to have a child as her desire to become involved once again in a mother-child relationship. She seemed unaware that this time she would be the mother and not the child.

Unfortunately, there are no perfect, ideal mothers in this world; consequently, the search for the good mother frequently ends in failure and disappointment. Repeatedly, women searching for this idealized caregiver find a special friend or someone who seems capable of providing the nurturance that they need, only to be disappointed at some point down the road when the mothering falls short of the ideal fantasy. Some of the rage that homeless women display seems to be derived from their unbearable hurt and disappointment at once again not having found the good mother for whom they continue to long. In most cases the disappointment is short-lived, however, and the women move on to the next relationship, keeping the hope and the search for the perfect mother alive.

As adult women, the search for the good parent often gets transformed into the search for the good husband, the Prince Charming who will rescue them from their lives of despair and disappointment. Regrettably, this particular fantasy often has dire consequences for homeless women. Several of the women with whom I spoke went from one man to the next, each time hoping that she had found Prince Charming, the "ghostly lover" who would transform her life.[18] More often than not these women found men as vulnerable as they, who would only use them or abuse them for a time. One woman, desperate for a hero to rescue her from despair, sent her name in to an overseas lonely hearts club and received a pen pal from China. This man proposed to her through the mail, and she was elated, believing that she had finally found the man of her dreams.

Just as with the search for the good mother, the search for Prince Charming invariably ends in failure. A number of the women interviewed had become homeless after being thrown out of an apartment that they had shared with one of these potential knights in shining armor. A number of women had been beaten by men that they had trusted, and still others had had their entitlement checks taken by men who promised to take care of them forever. There were even women who chose to give up their own apartments once they had finally secured permanent housing to go off with some man who was promising them romance and happiness.

Given the realities of their past and present lives, it is paradoxical that many of these women continue to cling to the fantasies of feminine mythology. They still want the perfect family, the good mother, and the Prince Charming. It would seem that they would have abandoned these unrealistic desires given that they have, for the most part, failed to get even a small part of the American dream. Yet they cling to these fantasies even more desperately than women who have received more in terms of emotional and material benefits. To accept that these dreams are in fact dreams and that Cinderella is not going to go from rags to riches is painful. To come to terms with the extent of the deprivation of their lives requires a degree of honesty and acceptance that would be extraordinarily difficult for anyone. Sometimes the only hopefulness that homeless women express is their allegiance to the unrealistic dream that they will be rescued magically from despair. Unfortunately, their attachment to this fantasy deprives them even further of any chance for real happiness. Many of the women continue in a position of passive waiting, hoping, and praying rather than taking action that might actually change the circumstances of their lives. Unrewarded by their real lives, these women continue to cling to and uphold the fantasies of our shared childhood mythologies.

The psychological filter reveals a picture of homeless women that is both highly personal and transpersonal. In describing personal realities, these women have shared not only their day-to-day interpersonal lives, but also their more intimate internal fantasies and wishes. It is difficult for us to keep homeless women as anonymous aliens when we know about their personal psychological pain and suffering. More than merely humanizing and personalizing our portrait of homeless women, a psychological perspective aids us in reintegrating these women into the human community. As we explore their intrapsychic and interpersonal dilemmas, we can see all too clearly that they struggle with many of the same complexities, aspirations, and disappointments with which the rest of us must contend. Rather than representing a radically different life experience, the lives of many homeless women may simply represent an extreme point on the continuum of our shared reality.

Metaphoric Filter

The filter of metaphor provides both the simplest and the most complicated perspective from which to view the plight of homeless women. Metaphor allows us to summarize succinctly and powerfully a great deal of information in a relatively compact form. Metaphor, however, has the potential to distort the reality of any situation and to seduce us into substituting emotional power and resonance for cognitive complexity.

When we employ metaphor, we take an abstract idea, a concept that exists only in our imagination, and concretize or materialize that concept outside of ourselves. Many of our religious and political symbols are concretizations of abstract ideas. For example, the flag is a symbol of patriotism and love of country; the blindfolded woman who holds the scales in her hand is a symbol of the abstract idea, justice. When we see these tangible symbols, they conjure up for us the complex and emotional abstract ideas which they represent. By using concrete symbols, we are able to convey a great deal of information in a relatively concise way.

Similarly, poetic metaphor allows us to compare two very different situations by bringing them together in an unexpected juxtaposition. William Shakespeare, who was a master of metaphor, uses this technique repeatedly throughout his sonnets. His second sonnet begins, "When forty winters shall beseige thy brow, and dig deep trenches in thy beauty's field."[19] The concrete image of aging as deep trenches in a field allows the author to describe subtly and powerfully the ravages of old age, evoking an emotional reaction that might have remained untouched had he just begun the sonnet with, "When you are old and wrinkled."

Susan Sontag in her essay *Illness as Metaphor* describes the way in which various illnesses, specifically tuberculosis and cancer, have become modern metaphors for certain incomprehensible life events.[20] If we were asked to draw a concrete picture of the abstract notion of death, we might well depict the dissipated and drawn victim of cancer or tuberculosis. These illnesses then, over and above their biological reality, have a symbolic meaning, representing death and destruction itself. Sontag argues quite persuasively that it is dangerous for us and for the victims of certain diseases to make the conceptual error of taking our metaphors literally.

A distinction should be drawn between constructing a metaphor and taking that metaphor as a literal fact. In art and poetry it is not uncommon to rely on a visual image to materialize an abstraction for us. It would be foolish, however, to assume that these concretized abstractions are the literal representations of events. Take, for example, the Shakespearean sonnet; we in no way assume that actual trenches are being dug; we would be out of touch with reality if we were to suggest that soil be brought in to fill the trenches and restore the field to its previous beauty. One of the markers of a psychotic illness is the patient's inability to distinguish reliably between metaphoric and literal events.

While the foolishness of taking a metaphor literally is obvious in the above example, it is not so obvious when we talk about metaphors that have been materialized in the person of living beings. Sontag laments that many tuberculosis and cancer victims have been seen as literal representations of death and despair and that we have often shunned them and cursed them because we do not see them as suffering from a merely biological illness, but as truly being the agents of death. We can and must employ a metaphoric analysis and attempt to see how certain tangible events or external objects can represent abstract, internal ideas without falling prey to the error of literalizing the metaphor.

Within psychoanalytic discourse the process of projection is somewhat akin to the process of metaphor-making. When a projection is formed, an internal, often-abstract concept, frequently a part of the self that is currently disowned or unwanted, is taken and projected outside the self. The particular psychological quality finds a resting place in another person so that an individual other than the self comes to carry or to represent a part of the self that has been projected outward and disowned. Psychologists argue that we engage in the process of projection because there is some psychic content that we are unable or unwilling to integrate or absorb into our own concept of self.[21] While we may not be able to acknowledge the existence of certain abstract qualities in our own person, we can readily acknowledge those same qualities if we project them out and lodge them securely in the person of another.

It is possible to view the process of externalization and projection as one step on the road to eventual acceptance of parts of the self, since in this process we are at least able to acknowledge the existence of those shadow parts of human nature in another. Eventually, by coming to know in the person of another those aspects of ourselves that make us uneasy, we might begin to feel more comfortable with them and perhaps eventually to accept them into ourselves once again.[22]

Regrettably, we often make the same conceptual error of literalism with regard to psychic projections as we do with regard to conceptual metaphors. Once our psychological baggage is projected outside the self and concretized in another person, we often assume that the other person does in fact contain our own discarded psychological contents. What belonged to and troubled the self now rests securely in another person. If, for example, an individual is unable to acknowledge or integrate his or her own rage, then that individual might project that rage out onto another person. The rage now appears to be written across the other person's face, and he or she is described as an angry, violent, hostile individual. We are in serious psychological and social danger, however, when we assume that the individual onto whom we have projected these unwanted parts of ourselves is literally rageful. When we forget from whence the projection came and assume that it belongs irretrievably to the other, we begin to treat the other as if he or she is literally an angry person, a criminal, someone needing to be locked up and kept under watch. This is the same error we make when we take any metaphor literally. It becomes both more dangerous and more seductive to make when we are dealing with projected psychological content—more dangerous because we jeopardize the autonomy of another person and more seductive because it protects us from having to acknowledge undesirable or conflicting psychological content ourselves.

Jean Baker Miller, a psychiatrist, in her book *Toward A New Psychology of Women,* argues that it has traditionally been the role of women to carry the undesirable or unwanted psychological content of the male members of society. Men routinely project onto women those psychic attributes that make them uncomfortable and uneasy.[23] Specifically, she argues that men project qualities of weakness and vulnerability onto women who then carry those characteristics for the entire society. The danger, of course, is that women then come to be seen as weak and vulnerable and consequently have certain rights and privileges taken away from them because of their supposed inadequacies.

The tendency to literalize an embodied metaphor or an embodied projection is so strong that some authors argue that we should stay away from metaphoric analysis completely.[24] The potential is just too great to do damage both to the person who is the carrier of symbolic content and also to the individual who projects that content out.

Metaphor making and projection allow for the possibility of powerful emotional experiences. Some authors argue that we can identify a projection by reading our own emotional response; we characteristically respond to individuals who carry projections for us with intense affect that is often out of proportion to the person or situation with whom we are interacting.[25] Metaphors have the power to evoke strong feelings in us as well. When we respond to the concrete symbol of the flag with tears in our eyes, we are not responding to the literal flag, a piece of cloth with stars and stripes on it; rather we are responding to the concretization of our love of country. We may recognize that a metaphor is at work by monitoring our own emotional responses. When we respond deeply and powerfully to tangible and commonplace objects, we can assume that we are responding to some as yet unarticulated abstract idea or emotional content. Therefore, when we respond to homeless women with powerful emotional reactions—with rage or despair or horror—we can assume that we are responding to them not only as flesh-and-bone women, but also as symbols of our own disowned and unwanted psychological selves.

From the perspective of metaphor, we might conclude that homeless women carry in their bags and shopping carts more than just the cast off clothing of other women. They carry the disowned and unwanted aspects of modern woman's psyche. Homeless women have become the concretization of the feminine shadow.

Chapter 3

The Shadow

The shadow represents the dark underside of the conscious personality. It is that part of the self that is either disowned, denied, or devalued.

In the development of his system of psychology, Swiss psychoanalyst Carl Jung identified what he called archetypes of the collective and personal unconscious.[1] Jung suggested that these archetypes were the categories or basic structure whereby we understand or process intrapsychic and emotional events. Just as philosophers had identified categories of intellectual understanding, such as cause and effect, that allow us to link events in predictable ways, Jung believed that there were similar inborn categories of interpersonal and emotional functioning that would allow us to make sense of our everyday life experience.

The archetypes, while part of the structure of our internal psyche, frequently make themselves known in our personal and collective mythologies. They constitute the recurring motifs of personal and interpersonal interaction that have shaped the way in which we understand what it means to be human. It is central to the concept of an archetype that the term be reserved for big events, big categories. A purely personal or a trivial event is not designated as archetypal; rather archetypes are universal categories of interpersonal understanding to which all of us can resonate. Moreover, they are categories that transcend the conventional boundaries of space and time. Specifically, archetypes are usually not limited to a particular generation or to a particular culture, but instead have relevance and significance across generations and across different social and political milieus. Jung was quick to point out that the modern dress or modern appearance of the archetypal image might change with successive generations; however, the basic structure and possibility of the archetype remained constant over time.[2] This consistency and continuity allow us to respond to archetypal images with a deep emotional recognition that may seem out of proportion to the actual image being presented.

Some psychologists have commented that archetypes exist as pure structure. They are the potentials of our interpersonal understanding and our emotional organization.[3] As potentialities, they remain ready to be filled by the personal experience of our interactions with others and with ourselves. Yet these potentials, these structures, are similar for diverse groups of individuals.

Perhaps an example will serve to illustrate the modus operandi of archetypes. One of the most common archetypes is the myth of the hero. Hero mythologies exist in diverse cultures, and they have existed for centuries, from primitive times up until the present.[4] The universal and routinely repeated pattern of the hero's life is what constitutes its archetypal structure. Several authors, most notably Joseph Campbell, have attempted to explore the archetype of the hero and to unveil the many different faces that the hero has worn in different cultures and in different times.[5] Regardless of the external dress, the hero tends to be someone whose birth is shrouded in mysterious and often miraculous events and who rises from humble origins through some superhuman power to a triumphant attainment of prominence. The hero invariably struggles with the forces of evil, and while he usually triumphs, he occasionally succumbs, almost always as a result of some prideful act.

We can recognize this archetypal pattern in the lives of such diverse characters as the Greek warrior Achilles and the more modern film and cartoon character Superman. The archetypal structure of the hero's interactions with others allows us to have predictable relationships with and responses to anyone who occupies the role of hero. As with all of the archetypes, the archetype of the hero remains an ever present potentiality within ourselves. It is not always filled, but it is always available to be filled when an appropriate object comes along.

Most archetypal patterns are identified by a generic human type: the good mother, the wise old man, or the trickster. The archetype that is the subject of this book is far more enigmatic and insubstantial. It is the archetype of the shadow, and it exists in the transitional space between the human and the nonhuman environment. Jung described the shadow as the unlived part of the personality.[6] It is in some sense the opposite of the conscious ego. Rather than manifesting itself in the full light of day and being part of an individual's conscious interactions with others, the shadow stays hidden, containing those parts of the personality that either will not or can not be made known.

Not surprisingly, the combination of factors that results in certain parts of the personality being split off and being forced to go underground is a complicated one. It has been suggested that certain combinations of social and cultural forces may make parts of the individual less acceptable to the public world.[7] When we consider the public lives of women, we know that different cultures demand either explicitly or implicitly that women suppress or deny parts of their personalities. Different societies have forbidden women from expressing alternately their sexual, assertive, or independent selves. These unowned or unlived aspects of the self become relegated to the realm of the shadow. When the culture or the social milieu cuts off possibilities for conscious actualization, the shadow grows in size and comes to contain the options of human interaction that are not allowed to surface publicly.

Although the shadow does contain those elements of the self that are denied, it is not totally dissociated from the conscious self. Jung maintained that the shadow is most likely to be projected out on to people of the same sex, people who are different enough from the self so that we can continue the process of disowning the shadow characteristics, but similar enough so that we can recognize our shadow and reown it when we are able.[8]

As with much projected content, authors have suggested that we can recognize our shadow in others by the response that we have to those other individuals. Marie Louise Von Franz, a follower of Jung's, asserted that we can locate the shadow by recognizing our own nervous and agitated response to another individual.[9] When a particular person or a particular set of qualities make us nervous, edgy, or uneasy, then we can reasonably guess that our shadow is projected onto that individual.

While the shadow side of the personality has often been associated with the evil, bad, dangerous part of the self, this does not always have to be the case. It is equally possible that certain valued, desirable qualities become split off, disowned, and unlived. The essential characteristic of the shadow is that it contains that which has been forced underground, which is not allowed to see the light of day and to flourish as part of the conscious personality. Unfortunately, the equating of the shadow with the evil part of the self has been rather ubiquitous. In the early history of radio in the United States there was a popular detective program entitled "The Shadow," and the lead-in to this production was the following: "Who knows what evil lurks in the hearts of men? The Shadow knows." While this declaration ostensibly referred to the detective, the character the Shadow, who would in the course of the broadcast discover and bring to justice any perpetrators of evil, it is possible to give an archetypal interpretation to this same sentence. The psychological shadow does indeed know what evil lurks in the hearts of men and women behind their conscious public personalities, for the shadow contains all elements of the dark side of the self.

While the shadow represents those parts of ourselves that we are unable or unwilling to own consciously, we must remember that these disowned parts of the personality are just as integral to the development of the total self as are aspects of the conscious ego or the public personality. It is only when we take the shadow elements of the self and the public elements of the self and combine them or integrate them that we have a picture of a total, fully formed person.

Consequently, it is impossible for an individual to fully disown or disavow his or her shadow. We can project the shadow out and temporarily ascribe it to another individual or group of individuals, but we can never fully rid ourselves of this part of our personality. Indeed, it could be argued that the fundamental task of our psychological development is to come to terms with our shadow side, and to come to know it and perhaps even to embrace it as a necessary and equal partner in the development of our personality.

I am reminded of the childhood rhyme: "I have a little shadow that goes in and out with me, and what can be the use of it is more than I can see." This rhyme embodies the intimate, yet paradoxical, relationship that many of us have with our own shadows. Try as we might, we are unable to avoid the shadow or shake it off. It does indeed go in and out with us as an integral part of who we are. Yet, unfortunately, many of us fail to see the purpose of the shadow. It often seems like unwanted baggage, like something that we should and would rid ourselves of if only we could. It is, however, just as impossible to disown our literal shadows as it is to rid ourselves of the psychological shadow that constitutes a fundamental component of our interpersonal and intrapsychic structure.

The English translation of the German proverb "you can't jump over your shadow" expresses the necessity of accepting the shadow side of ourselves. Try as we might, we cannot get away from the shadow side of the personality. Despite the inevitability with which shadow aspects of the self manifest themselves, people have tried for centuries to rid themselves of these unwanted and unlived parts of the self. Indeed, the ritual phenomena of sending a scapegoat into the desert may well have been a primitive way of ridding oneself of the shadow. The scapegoat, originally called the escape goat, was one of two goats presented to the altar for ritual sacrifice.[10] One of the animals was indeed sacrificed. The other, however, was symbolically loaded with the sins of the community and then allowed to escape into the desert, presumably taking those sins or those unwanted, disowned parts of the self far away from the main body of the population out into the desert where it would eventually be lost or killed.

The archetype of the shadow thus represents or embodies those aspects of the self, the personality, that are disowned or not allowed to reach conscious expression. While the particular aspects of the self that are disowned may vary across different generations, what remains constant is that there is always a part of the personality that we feel must be hidden and must remain out of sight. When that part of ourselves is projected onto and embodied in other people, those people come to represent the shadow for us.

Shadow Metaphors and Mythologies

The lore and metaphor that surround physical shadows may be examined as a way to enhance our understanding of the psychological shadow. Keeping the concept of the archetype of the shadow in mind, it is possible for us to reexamine some of the language that surrounds literal shadows and to give new psychological meaning to those factual definitions. For example, the *Dictionary of Contemporary American Usage* defines the word "shadow" as designating "a partial darkness; an area in which brightness and the heat of the sun or some other source of light does not fall."[11] While this definition is intended to be specific to the physical property of shadows, it has implications for the archetype of the shadow as well. One of the primary characteristics of the archetypal shadow is that it too lives in darkness; it is the underside, the hidden part of the personality that is not illuminated. The light of investigation or the heat and brightness of psychological reality do not fall on the shadow; rather, the shadow remains in the murky and dark world of the unconscious.

Furthermore, it is the singular property of physical shadows that they are cast forth from an individual or from an object. One does not see the shadow on the object itself; the shadow is only visible as it is projected out from the individual or from the object at hand. Similarly, the psychological shadow is made visible when we project it on to the person of another. Only as personified or embodied in another individual do we come to see the elements or characteristics of our shadow side.[12]

Shadows vary in their size and in their direction depending on the angle and the height of the sun. For example, at the noonday shadows are relatively short, if they exist at all. As the sun sets, a bigger shadow is cast. When we think about the psychological shadow, it is possible to say that there are times when an individual casts a particularly big shadow and other times when the shadow is relatively small. If an individual needs to disown many parts of his or her personality, then we might expect that the shadow projected outward will be a large shadow, a long shadow. On the other hand, when the individual owns much of who he or she is, then we might expect that the shadow will indeed be relatively small or short.

It is also possible, depending on the direction of the sun, for physical shadows to be cast in front of the individual or behind the individual. Applying this physical property metaphorically to psychological shadows, we might say that there are times when a person is led by his or her shadow. The underside of the personality may assume such power that it actually determines the ways in which the public personality will act. On the other hand there may be times when the shadow follows the individual. In such cases most elements of the personality are integrated as part of the public self, and the shadow seems to trail along behind in a more secondary role.

Finally, we find that physical shadows often have a fuzzy or indistinct quality. We can make out the broad outlines of the object or the broad outlines of the individual, but we often cannot discern particular features or individual characteristics. A viewer might not be able to tell whose shadow he or she is viewing. Individuals of relatively similar size and shape may indeed cast very similar physical shadows. Taken from a psychological perspective, this suggests that the archetype of the shadow is indeed a collective archetype rather than a personal or an individual one. We might argue that instead of each individual casting his or her own shadow, groups of individuals at a particular time in history or in a particular culture cast a collective shadow, the shadow containing those elements that are collectively disowned or disallowed by a large group of people.

Because they are such mysterious objects, shadows have captured the imagination of many storytellers. Physical shadows are clearly visible and seem to be substantial and real, yet they contain a quality of insubstantiality and elusiveness that makes them especially intriguing. Our fascination with shadows begins when we are small children. It is comical and charming to watch a young child turn in circles trying to catch or confront his or her shadow. Similarly, it is not uncommon for children to create a whole pantheon of creatures by projecting shadow puppets onto the walls of their bedrooms. Interestingly, these projected characters of our childhood imagination are often monsters, murderers, and beasts. Children seem much more interested in projecting out bizarre, dangerous beings whom they can control with just a flick of their wrists or a movement of their fingers than in creating the more benign birds and bunnies that teachers and parents encourage them to form. In a psychological sense it could be argued that this early shadow play is the child's first attempt to come into some relation with his or her shadow; the child does indeed project out those monstrous elements that are not allowed in polite society. Yet the child becomes familiar and often comfortable with these creatures of his or her imagination. Part of the shadow play involves the child's learning how to control these dangerous characters since it is the child and his or her own hands that make and manipulate the shadow embodiments. This early play, then, is our first experience that the shadow has some connection to the self and is even more fundamentally a part of the self.

We also find images of the psychological shadow in formal folklore and fairytales. While the shadow is not mentioned by name, it is easy to see the uninvited guest in Sleeping Beauty as a representative of the female shadow. In the story of Sleeping Beauty, the king and queen give birth to a beautiful daughter, and to celebrate her birth, they have a huge party in which they invite everyone in the kingdom. Through some oversight, however, one of the fairy godmothers is not invited to this event; she is left out; she is disowned and denied.[13] As the party is proceeding, this uninvited guest makes a surprise appearance; she is the evil godmother who delivers the curse to Sleeping Beauty that will eventually determine her fate. This uninvited guest is a potent image of the female shadow. She is that part of feminine reality that we do not like to acknowledge. She represents death and destruction rather than birth, nurturance, and affirmation.

The evil godmother does indeed make her presence known. Once recognized, she erupts with venomous power and full force, and she curses the young princess to an early death. There is yet another godmother who is able to lessen or ease this curse a bit, but the curse cannot be eliminated completely. The power of the shadow will be manifested and will have some impact on the young princess's life. The psychological message here is an important one: when we deny or disown parts of ourselves for too long or with too great a force, those parts invariably erupt in some destructive and powerful way. The story would have been quite different if the king and queen had invited the evil godmother to the party in the first place. If they had owned her and acknowledged her as part of the community, she would not have had to behave in a wicked and violent way.

In a less well-known story, the Navajo story of Changing Bear Maiden, the image of the shadow is used more explicitly.[14] This is the story of a young woman who experiences a series of losses and tragedies and goes berserk, engaging in a wild killing spree. To subdue this maiden, magic has to be invoked, and her younger brother, who is also her eventual killer, is instructed on how to subdue her. He is to shoot an arrow into her shadow. It is illuminating that in this story the shadow is considered to be both the vulnerable part of the individual and that part of her that contains destructive and rageful elements. By destroying her shadow, the young warrior will destroy the maiden herself. From a psychological perspective this shadow is inextricably tied to the woman herself; it is a part of her, a disowned part, a part that is split off and consequently more vulnerable to attack. Yet it is the part of herself that contains those undesirable, dangerous elements that have been causing the rest of the tribe difficulty. By destroying the shadow, the disowned and evil part of the woman, the warrior is able to destroy her.

We get a different perspective on shadow mythology from some of the Egyptian stories in which the shadow is seen as the most valuable part of a tree; indeed, the shadow provides much-needed relief from the heat of the desert.[15] For many of us raised in a western culture, we might not think to value the tree because of its shadow. Somehow the shadow is not seen as being such an intrinsic part of the tree itself. The wood or the fruit of the tree are seen as being essential to the tree. The shadow is somehow considered to be incidental. In Egyptian lore it is just the reverse. It is the shadow that is essential to defining the essence and, more important, the value of the tree. Whether the tree has fruit or a particular kind of bark may be irrelevant, but the bigger shadow that the tree casts, the more esteemed and valued the tree is. Such mythology suggests to us that we might be wise to look to the shadow as containing some valued and lost parts of the self. Shadows are not only evil, as depicted in the first two stories, but they are potentially valuable, worthy parts of objects and, in a psychological sense, of the self. Our task becomes to recognize the shadow aspects of the self and to reintegrate them into the core personality.

The archetype of the shadow represents the collective disowned, devalued, unwanted parts of the self. We can become familiar with our shadow side if we look at those individuals onto whom we project our shadow characteristics, for it is in the face of another that we see our own other and unwanted side.

Chapter 4

Aspects of the Feminine Shadow

Each individual's public conscious self evolves over the course of his or her life. This evolution reflects the unique combination of dispositions, circumstances, and occurrences that determines each individual's particular life story. The development of the personal self also reflects the relationship of each individual to the culture's prevailing view of what constitutes the good life and how the ideal man or woman should go about living it. We thus form our sense of who we are from a combination of individual factors and from our relationship to society's ideal images.

While much has been written about the development of the public self or a personal sense of identity, the development of the shadow side of the self often goes unnoticed by both psychologists and individuals themselves. Yet the shadow undergoes an evolution across the life of an individual and the life of a culture that parallels the evolution of the public persona. The development of the shadow is affected by events in an individual's personal history as well as by the values and ideals of the culture at large, for societal values will often determine what parts of the self need to be hidden or disowned.[1]

In his discussion of the concept of archetypes, Jung was careful to maintain that archetypes existed as vessels waiting to be filled, but never permanently filled and never constant for all time.[2] An archetype existed as a potential organizing and containing structure, and it remained for each culture or each generation to fill that structure with relevant content. There is a famous quote from Jung that it is "the obligation of each generation to dream the myth forward," which means that we must give the archetype a modern form, a modern dress, so that it evolves parallel to the evolution of the society itself.[3]

The mythologist Joseph Campbell, in discussing the relationship between current events or current content and enduring archetypal structure, used the analogy of a bird building a nest.[4] He maintained that the structure of the nest is akin to an archetype and is inherent in the mental apparatus of the bird. The bird somehow knows how to form the nest, but the particular materials that it uses in the construction of any particular nest are taken from the immediate and surrounding environment. Thus, while a nest in one place or at one point in time will have the same shape and form as a nest from another place or another point in time, it will consist of different materials, the materials being gathered from the immediate environment.

Taking this analogy and applying it to the archetype of the shadow, we can say that the structure of the shadow and the existence of the shadow are inherent parts of human development. We will always have a shadow side of our conscious personality, but the particular content of the shadow will be built up from the relevant and existing materials in our environment, changing as the environment changes and as the available raw material alters over time.

In the course of its evolution, the content of the shadow evolves in two distinct but related ways. It changes in terms of its particular content, reflecting the underside of whatever the conscious personality might be at that time, and it also changes in terms of how it becomes materialized in the environment. Susan Sontag in her work *Illness as Metaphor* commented that the archetype of the exile or the wanderer was at one point in time projected onto the victims of tuberculosis.[5] The image of the exile and wanderer still exists within our collective consciousness. The victims of tuberculosis, however, no longer provide an appropriate hook for that archetypal image. Instead, I would argue, homeless men and women are now the carriers of that archetypal projection. Consequently we have a case in which the content of the archetype remains relatively constant, but the bearer of that archetypal projection has changed with the cultural context.

In the case of the female shadow we see an evolution in which particular women carry the archetype of the shadow, and also an evolution in the content of the feminine shadow. Prior to the sexual revolution of the last twenty years, and prior to the Freudian revolution within psychiatry, it was reasonable to assume that the feminine shadow was a sexually wanton and libertine woman.[6] The public persona of women was to be sexually repressed, demure, somewhat inhibited, and as a result the shadow side carried the more sexually assertive, sensual part of a woman. As women have come to reown certain aspects of their sexuality, there is no need for the shadow to contain all of the sexually expressive parts of the self. It is not surprising that this sexual assertiveness was often projected on to the woman gone astray—the prostitute—who carried that aspect of the feminine shadow for those who were uncomfortable with the sexual part of themselves. As sexuality has become an acceptable part of conscious feminine development, women no longer need to relegate their sexual selves to the shadow underside. Since the shadow continues to be a vibrant and necessary archetypal image, we must ask ourselves what the current content of the feminine shadow is.

Just as modern women play many roles and lead complex and complicated lives, so too does the feminine shadow lead a complicated and complex life. The shadow is no longer a single embodiment, a single representation of just one part of woman, but instead contains the complex of disowned and disallowed images of feminine possibility. The disowned parts of modern woman are her vulnerability, her alienation, her aggressiveness, and her rebelliousness. And so, in this the latter half of the twentieth century, I would argue that the feminine shadow consists of a combination of the victim, the exile, the predator, and the rebel.

The Victim

Women's relationship to the role of victim or vulnerable member of the society is a complicated one with a long and established history. Many psychologists have argued that it has often been the woman's role to carry those characteristics of weakness and vulnerability that men do not feel comfortable carrying, so that women have been identified with vulnerability, both their own and that of their strongseeming fathers, husbands, and sons.[7] Women have traditionally been referred to as the weaker sex. Vulnerability, at least in the past, has been associated with a woman's public self.[8] A woman's weakness did not live in the shadow(s), but rather she carried it openly for all to see. Despite this past willingness on the part of their mothers and grandmothers to be the public victim, women in recent years are less willing to own consciously their weak and vulnerable selves.

The advent of the women's movement marked a time of self-assertion for women and a desire on the part of many women to cast off consciously the role of victim and the role of weak and vulnerable member of the society. We have seen a proliferation of assertiveness training and self-defense groups for women as women consciously want to reown their strength and power. This change in the public selves of many women has not gone unnoticed by the shadow. The shadow is nurtured and sustained by the cast-offs of public women. As vulnerability and victimization become unacceptable emotional attire for women to wear in public, these characteristics are relegated to the realm of the shadow.

Indeed, some feminists have argued that the public presentation or the preferred archetype of the women's movement is either the Amazon, the powerful woman warrior,[9] or perhaps the goddess Artemis,[10] the independent, self-contained virgin. Both of these embodiments deny weakness and vulnerability, and at the same time they applaud the outward show of strength and power on the part of women. Women, especially in the professional and corporate world, are encouraged to don the same power suit that their male counterparts wear, to dress for success, and to present themselves, publicly at least, as being powerful and invincible. Such a public presentation has caused at least one psychologist to speculate that perhaps the shadow side of this Amazon-like woman is indeed the vulnerable victim of our past.[11] A role that was once owned publicly and was considered part of the conscious life of most women has now been relegated to the underside, to the shadow. Despite reports of real victimization of women and real physical abuse of women, we would like to believe that most of us are no longer really threatened, really vulnerable, or really weak.

Once this part of human development has been consciously denied, it must find some place to live. Since these disowned parts of the self take root in the shadow, it is reasonable to assume that at least one face of the feminine shadow is the victimized, vulnerable, and weak woman whose characteristics women no longer care to own publicly.

In an attempt to deny their own potential for victimization and vulnerability, many women engage in blaming victims for the fact of their victimization. Women do this every time they assert that an abused woman is at fault for being abused or that a woman who is raped on the street provoked the attack. These explanations help women to deny that such an event could indeed happen to them. Vulnerability only happens to those who want to be vulnerable or those who in some way bring it on themselves. The rest, by learning how to walk assertively or avoid dangerous neighborhoods or not look a potential predator in the eye, can avoid abuse and potential violence.

While these myths of self-protection might indeed allow women to venture forth more assertively and aggressively, and might be soothing and comforting, these illusions also help to deny the vulnerability that continues to be part, not only of female existence, but of all human existence. No matter how many self-defense courses we take, no matter how strong or powerful we make ourselves, each of us finally is flesh and blood, mortal, and vulnerable to some kind of assault and injury. Part of being human is coming to terms with one's essential vulnerability and fragility in the face of the various onslaughts that the world might deliver.

It is regrettable that as women become more powerful and more assertive and strong, they follow too closely in the footsteps of their male predecessors, denying, as men have always done, the weak and vulnerable side of themselves. This denial serves to relegate vulnerability to the realm of the shadow.

Paradoxically, many women are especially vehement in their disavowal of vulnerability. Perhaps they are intolerant of vulnerability because they only too recently had to own more than their share of weakness. As new converts to the faith of strength, women are zealous in their adherence to the canons of power and unforgiving toward those who still display vulnerability. Indeed, it is often women within a group who are angry at a woman who is abused or victimized or raped. They do not want her to show this kind of vulnerability, and they do not want her to remind them that they too might be vulnerable. They are perhaps too inclined to make her vulnerability her fault, so that they can continue in their assurance that they do not have to be vulnerable unless they want to be.

The Exile

Modern society has been described as an alienated society.[12] As both men and women become increasingly busy and preoccupied with the demands of family and career, individuals pass one another like ships in the night, never really touching or engaging each other in a meaningful way. This experience of alienation, described not only in sociological literature but also in popular literature, is easier to discuss when we think about alienation as a property either of the collective society or as a property of other individuals in the society. It is much more difficult for each of us to personally acknowledge his or her own alienation and sense of outsiderness with respect to others. It has been said, particularly of modern women, that one of the great fears that women have as they become increasingly autonomous and independent is that they will also be alone and isolated.[13] We may even have second thoughts about how independent we want to be if independence becomes a euphemism for loneliness and alienation.

While some writers comment that it is the fear of isolation and loneliness that characterizes modern women, other more radical feminist authors have proclaimed that women are in reality outsiders.[14] This is nothing to be feared. This is the reality of feminine existence; woman is the quintessential outsider. She exists at the periphery of mainstream society, looking on, looking in, but never really being included in a fundamental and meaningful way.

To accept one's isolation and aloneness is a painful process, however, and we go to great lengths as a society to deny our individual aloneness. We are a society of joiners. We belong to clubs and organizations, fraternities, sororities, anything that might allow us to be part of something and to be included rather than excluded. Even within our political process we hear politicians repeatedly talking about the politics of inclusion with the implicit promise that there is room at the center of power and decision making for all individuals, not just for a select few.

In the 1988 presidential election, several minority politicians demanded an end to their exclusion from the seat of power. They wanted to sit at the table where decisions were made and policies were decided. For centuries insiders, primarily men, have sat around the table both in a literal and a metaphoric sense and made important decisions. Not only have they shared in the position of power, but they have also shared one another's companionship. Such images are reminiscent of the stories of King Arthur and his knights who sat at the Round Table and shared not only power and status with one another, but also friendship, loyalty, and cama- raderie. These current-day politicians then were not only asking to be part of the decision making, but they were also asking to be part of the club, to be included with other men in the fellowship of male bonding.

Taken in this light, women have always been excluded from the table. They have been allowed to stand at a respectful distance and watch the work that goes on. They have been allowed to wait on the men at the table and to take care of their various needs, but they have not been included in a meaningful way in either the decision making that occurs or the fellowship that flows from being a member of the group.

Feminist Carolyn Heilbrun argues that modern women are en- gaged in a collective, albeit unconscious, attempt to deny their status as outsiders.[15] Repeatedly, women want to believe that they are included in the mainstream, and they ignore evidence to the contrary. Some women, Heilbrun argues, borrow the insider status of their husbands and believe that that status and that inclusion pertains to them as well as to their husbands. In the role of "Mrs.

so and so" they can gain temporary admission to the "in" group. Unfortunately, many women find that their valued inclusion disappears if their husbands die or leave. I recall one elderly woman, following her divorce, lamenting that she missed being able to go to the club. While she was talking very specifically about a country club whose membership she had lost in the divorce settlement, her words could be taken symbolically to indicate the larger "club" in which she was no longer included.

For other women who function in the corporate or professional world, denying their outsider status takes another form. Often these women are the sole females in their group, and they are tacitly encouraged to accept status in the group as honorary males.[16] Paradoxically, it is only when they deny their femaleness and become "one of the guys" that many women can move into the inner circle of corporate or professional life. They allow themselves, by virtue of being token females, to pass as honorary men. Since they cannot at the same time be both female and be included, they give up their status as women in exchange for inclusion in the male club.

It is sad and probably inevitable that the few women who become included and cease to be on the outside looking in hoard and guard their new status vigilantly. They do not open the doors to others and allow them to come in as well. Rather, they frequently disown their previous relationship to those who now remain as outcasts. They rationalize that because they have been allowed in, anyone can be allowed in, and the belief that women are left out, exiled, or alienated, is really a myth. Some even go so far as to suggest that it is a myth perpetuated by women who either really do not want to come in or do not have the skills and the capabilities to come in. As a result of this rationalization, women who have been allowed in no longer must believe consciously in the reality of their previous outsider status. Consequently, the position of exile or outcast no longer belongs to their conscious or public self and becomes the province, once again, of the feminine shadow.

In addition to the inclusion into the mainstream of society that a few women have felt, the sense of sisterhood that many women experienced during the height of the women's movement in the 1970s also allowed for a denial of the role of exile or outsider. Women came together and formed their own club of outsiders.

Interestingly, the idea of a club of outsiders was suggested by Virginia Woolf many years ago.[17] She challenged women to form a group of outsiders, a group whose very existence would paradoxically negate their outsider status.

The experience of collective sisterhood and shared purpose allowed many women to disown the outsider role, pushing the exile out of consciousness and further into the darkness of the shadow. For most women, however, the denial of personal aloneness is accomplished by inclusion in a nuclear family. Surrounded by a brood of demanding and loving children, a woman can postpone, if not deny, her own sense of alienation. Consequently, many women, whether because of their participation in the women's movement, their inclusion in mainstream corporate and working America, or their enmeshment within a family group, no longer want to consider themselves as being outside, alienated, or exiled. Once again modern women need to find appropriate others on to whom they can project this disowned and unwanted part of themselves.

While the discussion to this point has been about the feminine shadow, it can be argued that men, who have traditionally been at the center of power and have had the experience of being part of the majority, equally have had to disown or disallow their own aloneness. Regardless of how included a person may be, aloneness is an essential part of the human condition. It is often said that we all die alone, that at fundamentally important moments in our lives we must experience the emotion and the power of the moment as a separate, alone individual. Existential philosophy acknowledges the essential aloneness of each person. Consequently, a denial of one's alienated self has relevance not only for modern women, but certainly for men as well who have felt for an even longer time the need to disown the exile within them.

The Predator

Rage, violence, and hostility have, perhaps more than any other affects, been disowned and disallowed by women.[18] As young girls women are taught to mind their manners, to behave, to avoid fighting back. They are reminded that it is unladylike to be overly aggressive or angry. Many of the same behaviors that are applauded in boys and young men, such as physical aggressiveness, assertiveness, and loudness, are actively discouraged in girls and young women. This socialization is often so effective that by the time women reach adulthood many no longer experience anger, or if they do experience the unwanted affect, they often feel troubled and guilty because of it. Indeed, psychologists working with women patients have reported that many women feel that their anger and bitterness are unacceptable and they come to therapy because they are either guilty over such feelings, or depressed because they are suppressing so much unacceptable anger.[19] The angry side of woman thus becomes consigned to the realm of the shadow—not acceptable in polite society, and certainly not valued.

Some psychologists have maintained that the societal stereotype of the demure female is powerful even for post-feminist era women.[20] Femininity and anger continue to seem antithetical to one another, and consequently many women feel that they cannot be women or cannot be feminine if they are rageful or angry. Indeed, the image of an angry woman is a very unattractive one, and society portrays an angry, rageful woman as being hysterical, sometimes crazy, often castrating and cruel. The standards we apply to men and women concerning what constitutes acceptable aggressive behavior are startlingly different. A man who does not get angry when he is criticized may be described as impotent or wimpish. A woman who gets enraged or angry when she is criticized is frequently labeled as defensive or hysterical.

Unfortunately, for many women, the prohibition against aggressiveness and anger is so complete that it often generalizes to any kind of assertive or forceful behavior. Even verbal assertiveness is discouraged, and women are frequently subtly encouraged to play down their autonomy and power and to act inept or incompetent rather than tough and forceful. It is no wonder then that the angry, hostile, rageful woman—the predator capable of inflicting injury on another—is an image that most women want to remove from their conscious persona.

It is curious, but not really surprising, that we allow ourselves to value the female predator within the animal kingdom. The proud lioness is an admirable symbol of strength and power. Yet, she is an animal, and thus exists at a psychologically safe distance from the conscious psyche of most women. Within the human community the predator must be disowned and actively denied, attaining power only in the dark world of the shadow.

The Rebel

Sharing the action orientation of the deadly predator is the raucous and assertive rebel. The rebel is that part of the human psyche that says "no." It refuses to conform or to do that which is expected. For most women a premium is put on conformity. Women are identified as the carriers of a society's traditions and of family values. They are the ones who participate most faithfully in religious organizations and who uphold and keep together family systems. Furthermore, women are often entrusted with the task of transmitting and retaining the history and heritage of previous generations. As keepers of the familial, societal, and religious faith, it is not surprising that women frequently must disown their more rebellious selves.

While it is not uncommon during their teenage years for women to rebel and break the rules that their parents set for them, as they grow up and attain adult status, they frequently fall into line as the champions of tradition and the prevailing social order. Especially as women strive for social and professional acceptance, fighting to avoid the status of outsider, it is doubly important that they not make waves or call attention to themselves by being overly rebellious. If, for example, a person feels that his or her status as an insider is precarious, he or she is hardly in a position to risk that status by openly defying the established order. Consequently, women and other newcomers to any inner circle need to be especially careful to control their rebellious sides.

It might be argued that the phenomenon of the super woman or the super mother, recently written about in the popular press, is a result of modern woman's denial of her rebellious side. As women have expanded their roles and their opportunities, they have taken on new responsibilities. Yet, they continue to maintain their previous responsibilities within the home for homemaking, family life, and child care. To these preexisting responsibilities many women have added new responsibilities outside the home— responsibilities of career, and also of community. It might be assumed that if increasing responsibilities were heaped on a particular group that eventually someone would rebel, someone would say, "No, stop. We've had enough. We can't do any more."

What is so intriguing about the situation of modern women is how few women have said stop; instead, many women continue to accept good-naturedly the additional responsibilities that they are asked to bear. It is perhaps a testament to how in check women have their rebellious sides that even when they have good cause to rebel and to defy the demands that are made of them, they refuse to assume the role of rebel.

Anyone who has raised children or understands child development knows that the oppositional rebellious self is a part of each of us. From the screaming two year old who refuses to do what his or her mother says to the misbehaving teenager, we all contain an element of rebelliousness. Moreover, there is a history within male mythology of the glorified rebel, the single individual who refuses to accept the existing order, who defies authority, and usually triumphs. Female mythology, in contrast, is devoid of the heroic rebel as an acceptable embodiment of the feminine spirit. If they exist at all, rebels within female mythology—women who refuse to do what is asked of them—are portrayed as outcasts and as evil wrongdoers, or more recently as fools. We need only remember the popular, societal response to the feminist movement. Cartoonists and journalists seized on the bra-burning radical not only as a symbol of the movement, but as an object of derision and scorn. She was not seen as a righteous rebel, but rather as a silly or out-of-control woman.

Women have a long tradition of putting aside their rebelliousness, a tradition that has been reinforced by the larger society. Women should mind their manners and stay in their place, and that place is not out causing trouble and challenging the established order, but rather maintaining the social order and its traditions and values. It is no wonder then that there is little room for the image of the rebel in the public persona of most women. The rebel is forced to live with other unwanted and disowned parts of the feminine psyche in the realm of the shadow.

Summary

Modern woman, like the women who have gone before her, exists as a complex combination of different human possibilities. She can be gentle and kind; she can also be vicious and hostile. While certain aspects of the feminine self manifest themselves frequently in one's conscious personality, there are other aspects of femininity, equally important in defining the total woman, that seem to be relegated to the underside of the feminine self. This shadow sister of the conscious personality contains those elements that women need to disown or disallow.

The feminine shadow is a combination of the victim, the exile, the predator, and the rebel. For each individual woman, depending on her personal development and her personal life history, different aspects of the self will be relegated to the realm of the shadow with varying amounts of force.

Because the conscious personality is ever changing and developing both in the life of a single woman and also in the collective lives of women in our time, the shadow side of woman is also changing. Those aspects of the feminine psyche that are currently relegated to the shadow have not always been submerged in the shadow and may not always need to be denied or disowned in the future. When we speak of the content of the shadow, we need to be mindful that this content is always relative, relative to a particular woman and also relative to a particular society and to a particular point in time. At this point in our development, women seem most unable to accept those parts of themselves that are weak and vulnerable, that are isolated and alone, that are violent and aggressive, and that are rebellious and nonconforming. Just because women are unable to own these parts of themselves consciously, these unwanted elements of feminine development do not go out of existence; they continue to survive underground in the realm of the shadow. Furthermore, in an attempt to make the shadow known, women continue to project those parts of themselves out on to other people in their environment.

The question then remains, who is it among us who wears the garb of the shadow?

Chapter 5

Homeless Women and the Shadow

When we project unwanted parts of ourselves out into the universe, they float free until they meet an appropriate object on which to settle. Some authors have likened this readiness of a particular object to accept a projection to the role that a hook plays; one sends things out and they only get caught if the object in the environment has a hook on which to snare them[1]. Homeless women, hunched over, haunting our streets like anonymous specters, have the appropriate hook to snare the projections of the shadow. In an almost macabre way these women actually resemble shadows. They are often dirty, dingy, huddled in corners, lurking in the darkness. Often the physical features that might mark their individuality are undiscernible. Homelessness and the ravages of living on the streets have rendered them anonymous and almost ghostlike.[2]

When we look at the real lives of homeless women, we can see their stories present an appropriate hook for our projections. Many of these women have experienced victimization. They have been economically victimized, often losing housing and jobs. They exist in a marginal position in our society with respect to economic resources. They have also often been victimized physically by family members, by friends, by lovers, and as homeless people they have experienced further victimization on the streets. A high percentage of homeless women have been mugged or raped as they make their way from shelter to shelter.[3]

These women also live lives of exile. In many cases they have been cut off from the mainstream of society. They may no longer have contact with their own families, and many of them have lost an even more basic contact with the larger human family, existing very much on the periphery of society. They wear cast-off clothing and eat cast-off, leftover food, whether foraged for in garbage cans or made available at soup kitchens. Many of these women wander like nomads within the city. Some leave their cities of origin and wander again like exiles from town to town trying to find some respite from their own alienation and loneliness.

A number of these women, to be able to survive, have become predators. Many women describe the shelters as dangerous places where the strong do indeed prey on the weak, intimidating them and extorting from them what little resources they may have. Brian Kates, in his book *The Murder of a Shopping Bag Lady,* describes some women who have become evil and violent in response to the lives they have had to lead.[4] To protect herself, one woman in particular came to radiate a kind of evil and dangerousness so that people on the streets would stay away from her. For many homeless women the conventions of polite society have broken down, and they have had to resort to a more primitive and often violent way of interacting. A number of the women who were interviewed have engaged in street brawls, have carried weapons, and have been violent with one another in a desperate attempt to survive.

Many of these women live the lives of rebels. They have left family and friends, often gone off on their own, and have defied the expectations that family and society had of them. None of these women was leading a life that she herself might have expected or certainly that society would expect of a female. While some have consciously chosen the role of rebel, others have inadvertently fallen into it and found themselves in a defiant stance toward society's rules and regulations. By virtue of the kind of lives they are leading, many homeless women indeed constitute a likely hook on which to catch the shadow projections of other women.

Before there were homeless women, other shadow sisters carried the unacceptable aspects of the feminine self for all women. In colonial New England, angry and rebellious women who defied and violated social role and gender expectations were labeled witches and were frequently burned for their outspokenness.[5] These carriers of the feminine shadow often lived out the assertive and independent lives about which their meeker sisters dared not even dream. We can speculate that in restrictive and patriarchal colonial America the relationship that women had to their shadow sides was of necessity a violent and hateful one. To survive, struggling communities defined acceptable behavior along narrow and rigid lines. Deviance was denied in the average woman; willfulness was repressed and consequently grew in intensity and scope; and shadow content was projected onto older, somewhat litigious, and outspoken women whose very presence became so hateful and noxious that the community denied them not only membership but life itself.

The painful experience of seventeenth-century witches and twentieth-century bag ladies demands that we understand the process by which certain women come to carry the shadow for all of us. Certainly the chosen individuals must have experiences, thoughts or feelings that make them likely candidates for the projection. Feelings of vulnerability are not projected onto kings and queens, nor are feelings of anger and rage projected onto the Virgin Mary. Moreover, the object must, even at an unconscious level, accept the projection. This acceptance of other people's disowned psychological content occurs either when the projected content resonates with a view the individual has of him- or herself or when the individual is in a confused and vulnerable state and ready to accept any definition of self, albeit a harmful one.

An analogy to physical medicine might help explain this readiness to accept projected content. Individuals with AIDS are unable to ward off pathologic organisms that routinely exist benignly in the environment, but become life threatening to the individual whose immune system is weakened. Similarly, the individual who takes in psychological shadow projections does not have a sufficiently stable sense of self, the equivalent of a psychological immune system, to ward off the projections. He or she is consequently vulnerable to a host of free-floating projected content.

Once the particular projected content has been accepted, it may become the core of a stable and regrettably dysfunctional sense of self. The individual identifies with the projected content, making it his or her own and relating to others within the role defined by the projection. This role allows one to know oneself in a particular and definable way and to be in relationship to others in a particular and definable way. In some cases the individual is only able to relate to others if he or she wears the mantle of the projection. Some women, for example, have remained in abusive relationships with domineering and patriarchal husbands because these women identified with the projected image of the vulnerable and weak wife. They became the empty-headed, dependent, and needy wife in part as a way of being in relationship with their husbands, the much-needed protectors.

It is also the case that some homeless women maintain a loose sense of community as part of a predatory street society by identifying with the projection of evil and rageful shadow content. Violent behavior becomes the ticket for admission to a community of street hustlers and dangerous characters. Thus, one may accept a projection because it serves to constellate a sense of self, it defines how to be in the world, and it guarantees some kind of relationship to others.

Once a projection has been incorporated into a sense of self, it may become the essential defining characteristic of the self. The individual who had some characteristics of the victim, when identifying with the projections of victimization, becomes the quintessential victim. His or her other characteristics may be lost, obscured, or disconnected from the sense of self. He or she now exists only in his or her role as victim, not only for others but for him or herself as well. The identity that is constellated around the projected content is not only a relational one but a personal one, defining the individual's relationship to him or herself as much as it defines the relationship to the world.

The relationship between an archetypal image or projection

and the literal or real person who carries that projection is a complicated one. While the archetype and the individual clearly have an impact on one another, the relationship might best be described as one of mutual influence or reciprocity rather than cause and effect. The archetype in no way causes the reality of the individual who carries its power, nor does the individual cause the archetype to appear. They do, however, mutually influence one another.

Such a dialectical relationship is often difficult for us to understand; we may be tempted to lapse into a more easily comprehendible relationship, namely that of cause and effect. As in any case in which the relationship is reciprocal rather than causal, this would be a dangerous error. The existence in human consciousness of the shadow archetype in no way created the problem of homelessness, nor does the existence of homeless people create particular unconscious archetypal images; rather these two have a mutual and reciprocating effect on one another. The archetype of the shadow exists and has existed prior to its materialization in the form of homeless people, and homeless people exist independent of the archetype of the shadow. A particular confluence of forces occurs when these two exist in the same psychological space, for then we do find homeless people materializing the image of the shadow for us. In so doing they give a vibrancy and a life to this archetypal projection, both influencing its expression and being influenced by it.

Whenever we have real individuals who embody particular archetypal projections, we are in danger of making the error of literalism, that is, assuming that these individuals are in fact the people that we have made them by virtue of our projections. As we look at society's response to the problem of homelessness, we can discern solutions that seem reasonable and rational given the nature of the problems at hand. We can also, at a metaphoric level, read some of these solutions as reflecting our relationship to our own psychological shadow. Each time we devise a solution for homeless men and women, we must ask ourselves whether those solutions are in response to real needs of homeless people or whether those solutions merely address our own relationship to our shadow selves. When we mistakenly attempt to address the internal relationship that we each have with our shadows by devising programs for homeless individuals, who embody the shadow for us, we are treating homeless men and women as if they were literally our shadow selves.

Much has been said about the distancing that goes on between an individual and his or her shadow projections.[6] By virtue of the very process of projection itself we remove certain aspects of ourselves from our immediate psychological reality. We project these images outside; we distance ourselves from that which makes us uncomfortable. This psychological distancing of the self from the shadow parallels the physical distancing that many would like to impose between homeless people and the rest of society. Jonathan Kozol, in particular, has talked about our apparent need to put homeless people at a great physical distance from the rest of society.[7] When we establish shelters, we often put them on the periphery of main urban areas, and we have even set up mechanisms whereby homeless people can be bussed out of the city to available housing elsewhere.

We also desire to hide or conceal our shadow elements. These are disowned parts of the self, and we would like to keep them disowned, denied, and hidden from view. Similarly, there is a desire to conceal the homeless. Several authors have commented that the problem of homelessness becomes more of a public problem when homeless people are more visible.[8] When their numbers are reduced or when they find ways to keep themselves inside or out of our sight, we are less troubled by them even though their lives may be just as impoverished or difficult. When homeless people sit in our subways or block entrance to our office buildings and we have to see them on a daily basis, we become much more horrified and overtly concerned about the problem of homelessness. If shadows were meant to be seen, to some extent they would not be shadows. If we could look certain parts of ourselves directly in the eye, we would not need to relegate them to the realm of the shadow. The very nature of shadows and the parts of ourselves that we relegate to the underside is that they should not be seen.

Individuals act out their relationships to their own psychological underside by overt and conscious relationships to the carriers of shadow projections. This tendency is not new. In her discussion of madness during the Victorian age, Elaine Showalter identifies asylum inmates as carriers of certain aspects of the human shadow.[9] She maintains that these individuals, and in most cases the women among them, stood for the alienation and fragmentation of the times. Given then that many of these individuals were materializations of the Victorian shadow, it is interesting to see how these people were presented and treated.

Certainly they were confined and contained within the bounds of the asylum so that both they and the shadow they carried were held in and removed from discourse with the general population. Moreover, in many of the photographs that were taken of mad women during that time, we observe that these women were dressed up for the camera in a particular way. Many of them are seated politely with hands folded in a prayerful gesture looking demure and pious. They are almost always wearing neat little bonnets, and their hair is arranged in a somewhat juvenile but prim way. This suggests and reflects a desire to make the shadow presentable, to tidy it up, and to deny its unwanted and undesirable aspects. How similar this is to the way in which many homeless people are treated. We are often quite concerned with cleaning them up, tidying them up, disinfecting them in some way. There is a reality to this response, and many of these individuals do indeed need a new dress, a new suit of clothes, and a hot shower. Some of our fervor in these efforts, however, may well reflect our relationship to our shadow more than our concern for homeless people. We can confront the shadow more easily when it has been packaged and presented in an acceptable and refined way.

During a National Institute of Mental Health demonstration project in which homeless women were assisted in moving into apartments of their own, some of the women were visited by community observers who wanted to see how the women were progressing. On more than one occasion these visitors commented how nice it would be if the apartments could be fixed up with pictures on the walls and matching curtains and bedspreads, making them more presentable and more homey. While the sentiment involved in these suggestions may well have been a laudable and charitable one, it also reflected the desire on the part of these observers to make the picture of homeless women more genteel.

In an interesting aside, Showalter comments on the reaction of one particular visitor to the Victorian asylum.[10] The young man was an actor and was coming to the asylum, he thought, to observe the raw, deranged, and exhilarating inmates who lived there. Needless to say, he was disappointed to find that the inmates lived a rather mundane, pedestrian, and unexciting life. The assumption that there is something dramatic and exciting about the lives of deranged, or in this case homeless, people again speaks to a particular relationship that the individual may have to his or her shadow. It is not uncommon for us to romanticize our shadow and to assume that somehow that which has been denied conscious expression is more magical, more powerful, more creative, and more artistic than the everyday routine expressions of our conscious lives. If we romanticize the life of the shadow, we are certainly in danger of romanticizing the lives of homeless people who embody that shadow for us. I have occasionally heard people speak somewhat enviously about the freedom and daring that homeless people must possess, given that they do not have to be bound by the nine-to-five workplace strictures that constrain the rest of us. This romanticization may bear little relationship to the real lives of homeless people who are often frightened, disheveled, and cold; it says more about our relationship to our own shadow side.

Because our relationship to our own shadow is a complicated one, the relationship to those who embody the shadow may be similarly complicated. In addition to those responses already described, it is not uncommon for an individual to want to stamp out, banish, or attack his or her unwanted parts.[11] Indeed, we have observed vicious attacks directed toward homeless people, attacks that seem out of proportion to anything these individuals may have done. Uncontrolled violence toward one's shadow and consequently toward those who embody the shadow for us is tragically not uncommon.

Perhaps the most violent relationship between the conscious personality and the shadow in recent history occurred in Nazi Germany. Many scholars have endeavored to understand the brutality that the Nazis displayed toward Jews. Although the present comments are in no way intended to be a thorough analysis of that complex relationship, it is possible to use the concept of the shadow to suggest a function that the Jews may have served for the Germans before World War II.

If the German people indeed experienced, as has been suggested, the full humiliation of their defeat in World War I,[12] then they would have needed to integrate their collective sense of shame and vulnerability into their existing self-concept of strength and superiority. I suggest that this integration did not occur, but rather that weakness and victimization were consigned to the shadow and that the shadow of the German people was ultimately projected onto the Jews. The Jewish people were seen as weak and inferior, and the "ultimate solution" was designed to rid the Aryan race of all defective elements.[13] One might conclude that in destroying the Jews, the Nazis were really attempting to destroy their own vulnerable shadow side. The present example is intended less as a commentary on the rise of Nazism but rather more as an illustration of the disastrous consequences that can accrue when unconscious archetypal projections are taken literally and then acted on with a vengeance.

It is possible to understand some of the remedies for homelessness at a metaphoric level and to view them as embodying our turbulent and misguided relationship to our own shadow selves. Specifically, if we feel that the shadow is out of control and potentially dangerous, we might be likely to try to contain it, to build walls, to build shelters, to build some kind of barrier to hold the shadow in and to keep the shadow safely contained, controlled, and at arm's length from us. Conversely, if we understand the shadow to be the defective part of the personality, the part that is damaged or impaired, then we might well decide that it needs to be treated and set up various kinds of treatment programs to engage the shadow in rehabilitation. And finally, if we believe that our shadow is really the dirty, unclean, or smelly part of our personality, then we might work quickly to try to clean up or disinfect that part of ourselves. Each of these psychological relationships to the shadow has an obvious correlate in some of the proposals that are being put forth for working with homeless people.

Currently, suggestions exist to provide housing and shelters, to render psychiatric and psychological treatment, and to cleanse, disinfect, and delouse people who have lived on the streets. Again, these solutions need to be considered from two different perspectives. Concretely, we need to consider how these proposals impact on people who do not have adequate housing. At the same time, however, we need to be cognizant from a metaphoric perspective as to how these solutions influence our psychological relationship to the shadow. For example, even some of the more benign and charitable interventions with homeless people may reflect our relationship to the shadow. Specifically, if we feel especially care-taking or gentle toward our shadow self, we might well engage in volunteer work with those people who materialize the shadow. We might be gentle and nurturing and reach out in some compassion-ate way to those individuals, just as from a metaphoric perspective we might want to reach out in a compassionate way toward our own disowned self.

As the stories of actual homeless women are recounted, it is important that we continue to think about their stories as having not only personal validity, but also archetypal or metaphoric sig-nificance. Similarly, particular solutions or remedies to the prob-lem of homelessness should be considered in the same way. We need to acknowledge the real problems of homeless people, but we also need to differentiate real, reasonable solutions from solu-tions that are really literalizations of our psychological relationship to our own shadow self. When we make this important differentia-tion, we can then proceed in a humane way with those solutions that address the real problems that need to be addressed and perhaps leave aside those solutions that are really metaphors for the relationship we currently have to our own disowned shadow.

Part Two

The Stories of the Shadow

The stories of living victims, exiles, predators, and rebels were constructed from interviews with homeless women in Washington, D.C. In each case, the woman's name has been changed and certain identifying details have been altered to safeguard individual privacy. In some instances, the details of two separate stories have been merged. In all cases, the spirit of the woman's story has been preserved.

Chapter 6

The Victim

Just as it takes two to tango, it can be argued that it takes two separate individuals to produce a victim. Generally the victim emerges when an interpersonal relationship is dominated by the dynamics of prey and predator. One individual, the weaker or more submissive of the two, becomes the victim, while the other, the stronger and more dominant one, becomes the predator or master.

For a relationship to produce a victim, the relationship must be hierarchical; that is, it must manifest a difference in power between the two individuals, one being bigger, stronger, or more powerful; the other being smaller, weaker, or more vulnerable. In a relationship so defined, the more powerful individual causes the weaker—the victim—to suffer, to die, or to be demeaned in some fundamental way. Traditionally, men have often assumed the dominant position in hierarchical relationships, while women, children, ethnic minorities, or slaves have occupied the bottom rung of the hierarchical ladder thus rendering them more likely to serve as victims[1].

A difference in power between two individuals is a necessary but not sufficient condition for victimization to occur. A person cannot be victimized if he or she is not in a weakened position; however, a person does not automatically become a victim just because he or she is in a weakened position. There are parents who do not victimize their children and men who do not victimize their wives.

It should be noted that as society becomes more psychologically sophisticated and as we become more prone to label and differentiate distinct parts of the psyche or different parts of the self, writers of popular psychology increasingly have come to describe a type of victimization in which the same individual simultaneously plays both the role of victim and the role of perpetrator. In such cases, the individual is said to be the victim of some internal desire, impulse, or wish of his or her own. One part of the individual's personality, often felt by the individual to be alien and out of control, victimizes or damages another part of the self. Indeed, when an individual speaks about being the victim of a particular desire of his or hers, he or she might well describe that desire as an external brute who exerts a powerful dominance over a weaker and more vulnerable part of the psyche.

Returning though to the more usual case of victimization, in which the victim and the perpetrator are two separate individuals, we find that victimization can take many different forms. For example, the victimization can be of a psychological nature. In such a scenario, the perpetrator criticizes, demeans, and verbally attacks the very worth of the victim. In his book *People of the Lie,* psychiatrist Scott Peck labels as evil those individuals who dominate and control the lives of others.[2] Psychological dominance and abuse may be just as debilitating as repeated beatings and just as entrapping as ropes and chains.

The dynamics of predator-prey may manifest themselves in the economic or social arena as well. Marxist economists and theoreticians have described the economic victimization of one class by another, in which the labor of one group is exploited for the benefit of another group. Slavery is the most egregious and obvious example of such economic tyranny.

Yet while psychological and economic victimization do occur, they are each more difficult to prove than physical victimization. Depending on his or her particular point of view, one observer might decide that economic or psychological victimization is occurring; another might argue just as vehemently that no such phenomena is taking place. Physical and sexual abuse, however, leave the observer with no such ambiguity. It is difficult to argue about whether physical or sexual victimization has occurred when an individual presents with broken arms or a bloodied nose, or the obvious signs of a brutal rape.

For most of us, our relationship to specific individuals who have been victimized or to the victim in general is an ambivalent one. On the one hand, we may want to reach out to the victim and provide him or her with some kind of assistance or sustenance. On the other hand, the plight of the victim may be so frightening and disconcerting that we may be inclined to impose real physical or at least psychological distance between ourselves and individuals who embody the victim for us.

One way in which this distancing occurs is when we deny that victimization has actually happened. In fact, statements made by ex-President Reagan on the plight of homeless people reflect such a strategy of denial. Mr. Reagan maintained that homeless people were homeless by choice. They were on the streets because they wanted to be. Such a statement denied that economic, social, or psychological victimization had taken place or that these individuals were really abused and denigrated by the rest of society. By arguing that men, women, and children choose homelessness, Mr. Reagan was saying in effect that it may look like victimization, but it is really just a choice of eccentric life-style.

In many marriages in which a wife is victimized or psychologically abused by her husband, it is common for the husband to rationalize his treatment of his wife by declaring that "she does not mind," or "it does not bother her." In extreme cases the husband may even maintain that his wife enjoys being demeaned and denigrated, and if she is sufficiently vulnerable, she might even agree. By assigning responsibility and even choice to the victim, the perpetrator relabels abuse as personal preference and thereby denies that victimization has occurred.

Another strategy for distancing oneself from a victim is to acknowledge that real abuse has occurred but to assign culpability for the abuse to the victim. The explanation offered by some rapists, "She asked for it," is an example. In fact, one of the definitions of "victim" is an individual who suffers as a result of a voluntary act.[3] Consequently, we may be lulled into believing that only those who invite attack or set themselves up to be abused are likely to suffer victimization.

Such a distancing strategy serves two functions. First, it relieves any guilt or responsibility that bystanders observing the prey-predator dynamic might feel. After all, if the victim causes his or her own victimization, there is no need for anyone to feel responsible. But perhaps more importantly, if we impute willfulness to those who are victimized and assume that they are abused because at some level they want to be abused, then we may feel safe from potential victimization ourselves. As long as we do not want to be violated, we do not have to worry that someone else will force torture or suffering upon us. This reasoning allows individuals to remain in a relatively safe position, smug with the belief that they are in control of their own destinies perhaps more than is realistic.

Susan Brownmiller in her now classic book on rape and male/female relationships, *Against Our Will*, describes having to confront her own denial of vulnerability, and she challenges other women to acknowledge that they too are perpetually vulnerable to abuse and assault.[4] One cannot hide behind the assumption that only the willing are abused; abuse and victimization may potentially strike any who are in a weakened or one-down position.

Finally, we can deny that victimization has occurred by denying that the intent of the victimization was to injure the other person. In many abusive child-rearing practices, it is not uncommon to hear the perpetrator declare that the practice is for the child's own good. In such a rationalization, the speaker may acknowledge that abuse has occurred, or that some kind of violation or suffering has taken place, but he or she may deny that it was inflicted with any evil intent. Rather, the hurtful, humiliating, or painful experience was inflicted so that the individual might learn some lesson and be ultimately strengthened in some way. Regrettably, many abusive interpersonal interactions are tolerated under the guise "it's for your own good."

In addition to denying the impact or even the reality of victimization, one can gain distance from the figure of the victim by asserting the victim's difference from one's self. The experience of the victim can then be dismissed as having no personal relevance for the individual. Such distancing is usually accomplished by viewing the victim as very different from one's self; the victim may be of a different sex, a different race, or possess a range of contrary characteristics. In the most extreme form of distancing, the victim is denied his or her humanity and seen as being a subspecies of the human race.

The psychiatrist James Grotstein, in discussing the psychogenesis of evil, uses the example of the Nazi treatment of Jews during World War II.[5] To justify the victimization of the Jewish people, the German hierarchy rationalized that the Jews were scum, pestilence, and a genetically inferior race. By labeling Jews as being subhuman, the Germans could distance themselves not only from the Jewish people but also from the abuse and victimization that the Jews experienced. They could also in a somewhat perverse twist of reasoning declare that the Jews, being such contaminated, inferior people, might corrupt the innocent and pure German race. Consequently, their total elimination was justified in the same way that eradicating a population of cockroaches so that it does not contaminate the food supply might be justified. In this way it is possible for people to acknowledge that victimization does indeed occur and that there are people who become victims without acknowledging that the role of victim has any relevance for them. Inherent in this formulation of victim is the notion that victimization happens to someone else.

Why the need to deny so adamantly, and at times deviously, our own potential to become victims and to be fundamentally vulnerable? When we acknowledge that we have the potential to be victimized, that we might be abused or dominated, we also tacitly acknowledge that we are mortal. In so doing, we must confront our own inherent weakness and fallibility and accept the limits of our personal power.

At an unconscious level, each of us would like to believe that adulthood brings with it a freedom from vulnerability and victimization. As we join the ranks of the "big" and "strong" grownups, we no longer need worry about being dominated and abused. While this may be a comforting fantasy, and one in which we all indulge to some extent, it is nevertheless a fantasy. The reality is that each of us is a potential victim and each of us contains some element of weakness, of dependency, or of submissiveness that might well be exploited by a more dominant other.

One may further understand the role of the victim and its place in our collective psyche by looking at the history of victimization as it has been recorded both literally and mythologically in our cultural and folk heritage. Not surprisingly, the mythological and literal history of victimization is often the history of women. Women being weaker are more likely to be cast in the role of victims. We can also turn our attention to the lives of some modern-day victims as we listen to the stories of homeless women.

The Historical Victim

An historical analysis of victimization reveals a host of anonymous victims and relatively few identifiable, named victims. In the process of raping, abusing, or even murdering another human being, the predator can deny his or her action more readily if the victim is just some unnamed woman or some anonymous child. In fact, victims of vicious slaughter are often dumped en masse in unmarked graves, allowing the perpetrators to deny that real people with unique identities and personal histories have been massacred. Indeed, memorial services commemorating the deaths of helpless victims of war often make a point of reading aloud the names of victims, returning some element of humanity to those who have been killed.

Despite the fact that we may be unable to identify many of the victims, we can certainly name the crimes of abuse. Specifically, the economic, political, or social victimization of one group by another has often included the rape and violation of women in the vulnerable or defeated group. It could indeed be argued that the subjugation of one group by another is concretized or symbolized by the physical abuse inflicted on women. Rape and sexual plunder seem to be as much a part of warfare, not only historically but in modern times as well, as confrontation on the battlefield.[6] It has been common for victorious soldiers to assume that it is their right to rape and violate the women of the defeated nation.

Throughout history, we find accounts of women being abducted, raped, and violated following the defeat of their countries. Paradoxically, even the ancient Trojan War, a conflagration ostensibly initiated to secure the return of Helen, a woman abducted against her will, to her native land, culminated with the victorious Argives kidnapping and violating the Trojan women.[7] Epic accounts describe the sobbing and frightened Trojan women and girls as they were herded onto enemy ships to be taken from their native land to be used and abused on foreign shores.

More recently, officials of the United States government, as well as private citizens, have had to contend with their collective shame and guilt over the behavior of some American soldiers who raped and violated Vietnamese women during the Vietnam War, women they were ostensibly sent to defend and protect. The history of the Vietnam War is replete with stories of casual rapes and abuses compounded by more dramatic tales of group rape and devastation.

Even during times of relative peace, economic hegemony often gave men of the ruling class the right to rape and violate women. In Europe it was not uncommon for the wives or sisters of serfs to be sexually available by force to the overlord, and it was the custom for peasant brides to be raped by the baron of the manor before being turned over to their bridegrooms.[8] In the United States it was commonplace for overlords to rape the women of slaves, and for the master of the house to force his will on any woman he owned without fear of reprisal.

In England, as late as the seventeenth century, rape was a means by which a man might obtain a woman's property.[9] English law allowed that if a man raped a woman who was an hieress or a property owner, her property would automatically go to the rapist, who would also become her legal husband. So, not only did the violator escape punishment, he was rewarded by officials who gave him property and conjugal rights over his victim and all that she owned.

Thus, women of all classes, wealthy and landed women as well as serfs and slaves, share a history of victimization by more powerful and dominant men. Indeed, it may be impossible to think about being a woman without also contemplating the possibility of being violated and subjugated.

Mythological Victims

Stories of rape and violation pervade classical mythology. In surveying the Greek myths, one is impressed by how many of the stories contain the rape or violation of a woman. Even those stories that are concerned with other matters often recount, in passing, some minor episode of abuse.

While the victim of these stories is often a mortal woman, she is sometimes a goddess; the perpetrator, however, is almost always a powerful god. These stories inform and shape our collective psyche in several ways. They illustrate the myriad forms in which female victimization can occur, and they serve to define more clearly the role of victim in its many and varied permutations. More specifically, these mythologies define a particular subservient role for woman and suggest her place in relation to man. The message is quite clear: women are in a position of vulnerability and weakness relative to men.

Themes of feminine victimization occur with regularity and have been made widely available through popularizations of specific myths. Consequently, it becomes difficult for either men or women to grow to maturity without having rape mythology incorporated as part of the psyche. For example, even individuals only minimally exposed to the history of art have probably seen one of the many paintings that depict the rape of Europa by Zeus or the rape of the Sabine women. These powerful visual images leave an indelible imprint on our consciousness and serve to remind us of the continued and ever-present vulnerability of women.

While rape and violation are indeed common themes in classical mythology, a few specific stories deserve close attention because they elucidate important aspects of the role of victim.

Perhaps the most famous story of rape and abduction is the kidnapping of the young maiden Persephone by Hades, the Lord of the Dead.[10] Persephone, daughter of the powerful earth goddess Demeter, is a naïve maiden, an embodiment of the eternal girl. At the time of her abduction, she is frolicking in a meadow with a group of young nymphs. Attracted by an especially lovely flower, she wanders off on her own. As she reaches down to pick the blossom, the earth opens up and she is wisked off by the waiting Hades.

In this first part of the myth the reader is struck by Persephone's apparently carefree naïveté. She is a young girl so safe in the love and protection of her powerful mother that she is actually unaware of her own potential vulnerability. It does not occur to Persephone to be wary or on guard as she plays with her friends on a beautiful spring day. Indeed, many women who have been abused or violated report that it never occurred to them that they might be in any danger. In fact, when the abuse or the victimization actually occurred, it came as a surprise, something unanticipated and terrifying. One might speculate that such naïveté is in itself a defense against the full realization of personal vulnerability.

Returning to the myth of Persephone, we find that the horror of her violation is compounded by the fact that the abduction occurs with the complicity of her own father, Zeus. Zeus, the king of the gods, is the brother of Hades and agrees to allow his brother to abduct Persephone. This aspect of the myth certainly suggests father/daughter incest, and, in reality, we find that sexual abuse is often initiated by a parent or a family member. Sexual abuse of female children is shockingly frequent. It has been documented that almost one-third of female children experience some form of sexual abuse before they reach the age of eighteen.[11] Thus, for Persephone, as for many women, her father, whom she might naturally expect to be her protector, is an accomplice to her violation.

During her abduction, Persephone screams, cries, and weeps, calling for her father to help her. Of course, her cries go unanswered. In the myth, it is Persephone's mother, Demeter, who anguishes over the loss of her daughter. She searches far and wide for her missing child. Because Demeter is the goddess of the seasons, controlling growth and fertility on earth, her personal agony results in her withdrawing her support from all living creatures.

As she searches for her missing daughter, Demeter falls victim to the second rape in the myth.[12] She is raped by the god of the sea, Poseidon. This rape of both mother and daughter points to an interesting aspect of victimization. It is not uncommon for victimization to occur in families. Abused mothers seem to bequeath victimization to their daughters along with the family china. For some women victimization becomes a way of life, and they not only do not know how to recognize potential predators, but they also do not know how to protect their daughters from the abuse that they themselves have experienced.

There is another lesson to be learned from the rape of Demeter. Demeter is not a naïve, young nymph, nor is she a vulnerable and powerless young woman. She is one of the most important and powerful goddesses, yet she, too, is raped and violated. This story seems to suggest the shared vulnerability of all women; even the most powerful goddess is not immune from violation and victimization.

The story of Persephone concludes with the young goddess's eventual reunion with her mother. The world cannot sustain Demeter's anguish, and men and women cannot survive as long as she continues to withdraw her life-affirming energy from them. Consequently, Zeus orders Hades to return the young woman to her mother. Persephone returns, however, a different woman. She is not the same young, naïve maiden that she was before her abduction, and indeed she must return to the underworld for three months each year because she has been transformed or changed by her experience, the transformation being symbolized by the pomegranate seeds that she ate while in the underworld.

The devastating impact of rape and child sexual abuse on the victim is similarly profound and long-lasting. It is a delusion to assume that the victims of such abuse are healed just because they can get up and walk away. Clinicians who work with survivors of sexual abuse report that two-thirds of child victims are found to be emotionally damaged by the sexual violation and that at least 14 percent are severely disturbed and impaired following their experiences.[13] One might speculate that the victim is not only changed in superficial ways by the abuse, but she is also transformed in a deep, inner way. Just as the earth grows cold and barren when Persephone must return to the underworld each year, so, too, does an alive and vibrant part of the self grow cold and die following victimization. Again, returning to reports of clinical work with child-abuse victims, we find that many of them do in fact become cold and stonelike in an attempt to harden themselves to any additional violation.[14] One young incest survivor even described herself as building a hard shell around herself, like a turtle, so that she might crawl inside and be safe.

While the story of Persephone's rape and abduction contains many of the core elements of victimization, there are other aspects of the victim's saga that are emphasized in other myths. The story of the rape of Europa begins much the same way as Persephone's story.[15] Europa, the daughter of a king, is out with some of her friends frolicking in the field, picking flowers. She is gay and lively and unaware that any potential threat looms. As the daughter of a king, she feels safe and protected. What she does not know is that Zeus himself is plotting to rape her.

The story does not proceed as a simple rape, however. Zeus, being married to the goddess Hera, cannot appear to Europa in his own form; rather he must disguise himself in order to seduce the maiden. In actuality then, the story contains two different and distinct forms of victimization. The god Zeus does indeed have his way with the young maiden, but in so doing he must deceive his wife. Thus, while Europa is the victim of an assault, Hera is the victim of a betrayal.

In his attempt to seduce the virtuous Europa, Zeus appears to her in the form of a beautiful bull, whose outward appearance both enchants and intrigues her. The bull is so charming and so humanlike that Europa is duped into trusting him. In her naïveté she reaches out for the bull, and before she knows what has happened, he flings her onto his back and runs away with his captive.

The bull takes the young woman to a far-off land and then disappears, returning to her in the form of a young man, the self-declared ruler of the island. In this human form Zeus bargains with Europa, telling her that if she will submit to his desires he will protect her from all harm. This segment of the story reveals another aspect of victimization. Many women submit to abuse and victimization out of fear. They may be fearful of surviving on their own, or just generally fearful of unknown and vague dangers. A close look at women who submit to abusive marriages or allow a pimp to offer them protection often reveals that they are trading, sometimes consciously, a known evil for other unknown and perhaps greater dangers. Similarly, in the myth of Europa, Zeus takes advantage of the young woman's vulnerabilities and fears and offers her protection in exchange for her submission; if she gives in to him, he will guarantee that no harm, other than that which he inflicts himself, will come to her.

When Europa awakes from her violation, she is plagued by guilt over what has happened to her. She blames herself for her victimization, believing that she was remiss to trust the bull and to venture out of her safe environment. Further, she is convinced that she should be punished and castigated for her failings. As she calls for her father, the young woman berates herself saying, "How dare I even utter the word father; I who have not taken care for my own maidenhood." Europa beats herself and psychologically torments herself believing that death would be a fitting penalty for her failing. Europa begs that a wild beast come and devour her so that she does not have to endure the pain of her own failure. Indeed, she contemplates suicide as the Furies taunt her and suggest that she hang herself rather than remain the concubine of a barbarian lord.

Regrettably, this tendency for victims of rape and sexual abuse to blame themselves is quite common.[16] Often victims of child sexual abuse feel guilty; they feel that the abuse has damaged and impaired them and they wrongfully conclude that they must be responsible for what has happened to them. Because they feel that they are to blame for having been victimized, many victims of abuse subject themselves to further victimization either at their own hands or at the hands of others. Self mutilation, suicide attempts, and other self-destructive behavior are not uncommon among survivors of childhood abuse. Equally devastating is the more subtle abuse to which survivors subject themselves. Often, in a desire to be punished for the original abuse, women will allow themselves to enter into abusive relationships, feeling that because of their original and earlier sin they deserve whatever abuse or punishment they might receive.[17]

Unfortunately, many of our societal attitudes toward the victims of rape and abuse reinforce this tendency of victims to blame themselves. It has been noted that the standard defense strategy in rape cases is for attorneys to attempt to blame the victim.[18] Victims of rape are often portrayed as either mentally unbalanced, sexually frustrated, or sexually promiscuous. In each case, there is the implication that the victim invited the attack; and indeed women often ask themselves, "What did I do to bring this on myself?" Such self-recriminations reinforce the societal attitude that it is the victim who is the guilty one.

The myth of Europa concludes with the goddess Aphrodite comforting the young woman and telling her that she will become famous because of this rape. An entire continent, Europe, will be named for her because she was the beloved of a god. Aphrodite, who is attempting to soothe Europa, provides us with an early example of the psychological process of reframing; the goddess tries to define what is essentially a victimization and an abuse as something positive. To be able to accept the violation that has happened to them, some women do attempt to find and highlight whatever good may have come from the act. Some women conclude that they are stronger, more independent, tougher than they were before the abuse. Just as Aphrodite's redefinition of the rape of Europa was a distortion of the reality, so, too, do we distort reality when we attempt to define abuse and violation as anything but a negative and destructive act.

The myth of Io, another young maiden who was raped by the god Zeus, expands the view of the victim presented in classical mythology. Most of the action in this myth takes place after Io has been raped and seduced by the god.[19] Her victimization does not end with the rape itself, and she suffers greatly because she has been victimized. First, Io is transformed from a young woman into a heifer. This is done by Zeus ostensibly to protect Io from the wrath of his jealous wife, Hera. Yet this intended protection has the result of dehumanizing Io. She loses her human form and becomes an animal.

Once she has been transformed, Zeus furthers Io's humiliation by giving her as a gift to his wife, Hera. Hera, realizing that the heifer is in fact her rival, takes Io and gives her to a hundred-eyed monster whose task it is to guard her. Thus Io adds imprisonment to her list of trials and torments. In her banishment, she is isolated and lonely and longs for the company of her sisters and her father. Thus she must endure not only the personal estrangement from her own human form, but also the more social isolation from the human community.

At the midpoint of the story Zeus is moved by Io's suffering and contrives for her to be released. She maintains her animal form, however, and is plagued by a stinging fly, sent by the goddess Hera, who pursues Io all over the world. Io is never free from the biting and stinging of this evil gadfly, a constant reminder of the abuse she has suffered. At the end of the myth Io is finally restored to her human form, but her life of wandering and isolation does not end. Returned to her womanly form, she wanders the earth in search of her young son who has been kidnapped by an emissary of the still jealous goddess Hera. In Io's story we see a woman who not only experiences the initial victimization of being raped, but as a result of having been victimized, she experiences additional and even more devastating abuses.

In an attempt to understand the full impact of a disability, sociologists have identified three different levels.[20] The primary disability stems from the actual illness, trauma, or abuse itself; the secondary disability results from the individual's own reaction to his or her primary disability. In the previous myth, for example, Europa's guilt, personal anguish, and self-destructive thoughts would be examples of secondary disability. As devastating, however, and certainly contributing to an individual's persistent disablement, is what authors have termed tertiary disability. This is the level of disability resulting from society's response to the individual's primary victimization or deficit.[21] Tertiary disabilities include a decrease in an individual's social and interpersonal support network and the stigma that is attached to having been a victim (poverty, unemployment, and a general sense of not belonging or being outside the mainstream of society).

The maiden Io experiences a combination of these tertiary disabilities: the support of her friends and companions has disappeared; she is isolated and removed from her family and previous community; and she no longer is a young and beautiful woman, having been transformed into an animal and stigmatized by virtue of this obvious physical change. Moreover, she experiences a sense of not belonging and longs and mourns for the companionship of her family. Finally, she is tormented by a disapproving and hostile outside world, in this case represented by the goddess Hera.

It is ironic that for many victims the initial abuse may not be the most painful and devastating part of their ordeal. Certainly for many homeless women, the secondary disability that stems from their own self abuse and guilt as a result of having been victims and the tertiary disability that results from society's negative response to them are often more painful and more enduring.

When we look at the lives of many homeless women, it is often hard for us to know what now causes most of their distress. Frequently, the original abuse and victimization that may have set them on the path toward homelessness is an event in the distant past, and the person's current life reflects both her own desperate and ill-planned attempts to cope with the abuse and society's ambivalent or even negative response to her as a victim. Thus, many homeless women, the survivors of physical or sexual abuse, find themselves trapped in an ever-expanding circle of victimization that adds trauma on top of previous traumas.

One of the most difficult circumstances that people who have been victimized must endure is society's disbelief at their victimization. This disbelief is exemplified in the myth of the young maiden Cassandra. Cassandra was a young woman, daughter of one of the kings of Troy, who chose the life of a virgin priestess.[22] She was a noble and religious young woman and consecrated her life to service in the temple of one of the gods. While she was going about her daily devotions, she was visited by the god Apollo who had been attracted by her very dedication and simplicity. The god demanded that she succumb to him and allow him to ravish her. The young woman reminded him of her pledge to remain a virgin and to devote her life to religious service, but the god was unmoved by her requests and continued to demand that she submit to him. The young woman became desperate and pleaded for her chastity.

In this encounter the god Apollo engaged in a power play of intimidation characteristic of male/female encounters.[23] He told Cassandra that he was more powerful than she, that he knew her and what was good for her better than she knew herself, and that she should stop her protestations and submit. He attempted to use his position within the pantheon of the gods, as well as his physical power, to intimidate her and to bully her into relinquishing her position.

Eventually the god grew tired of Cassandra's resistance and decided to abandon his pursuit of her. He left her with a cruel gift, however. First, he bestowed upon her the ability to prophesy the future so that she was plagued by recurring images of disasters that were yet to come. In a sadistic twist, he added to her gift of prophecy the curse that her prophecies would never be believed. No matter how accurate, no matter how clear her visions, no one would ever believe what she had to say and she was seen as a mad and dangerous woman.

Indeed, Cassandra did accurately prophesy the fall of her city of Troy and the death of many of the members of her own family, yet she was put in a dungeon because these prophecies seemed ridiculous and dangerous. She even prophesied her own eventual rape by a warrior in the temple of Athena. The rape that she envisioned for herself was an especially brutal one in which she was taken while clutching the feet of the goddess, pleading without result for mercy or divine intervention. While the myth does conclude with Cassandra's restoration to a position of respect, she spent most of her life shunned and disbelieved.

It is often the case with many victims of abuse that they are not believed, not only by the legal system but often by their friends and families as well. Authors have suggested that one of the reasons that proof in rape cases must be so stringent is the implicit assumption that the woman will not be telling the truth.[24] Because she may well be inventing the story, the demands for corroborative proof are great. It is thus often the plight of women who have been raped or abused that they have to suffer the fate of Cassandra; that is, when they finally tell their tragic story, they are not believed, and they are seen as crazy, manipulative, vindictive women who are just inventing a destructive story out of a spiteful attempt to hurt a man who has spurned them.

For many women, to not be believed is as painful as the initial abuse itself. One woman who was interviewed for this book remembers vividly trying to tell people about her rape at the hands of her father. When her mother refused to believe her story, she in turn refused to speak for almost four years. During her time of silence, she would make her needs and desires known by pointing to things and remaining withdrawn and isolated. One can conjecture that this young woman felt so distressed at not being believed that it seemed to her that the gift of speech was indeed a useless gift, and she refused to exercise her capacity to talk as long as her words were taken as idle chatter. Despite the fact that she regained her speech, she never recovered from the hurt she experienced at not being believed by her mother. She has been unable to forgive her mother, almost forty years later, for refusing to hear the truth of her words.

The shame that many women experience at being victims, and especially at being sexual victims, is often so great that they retreat into silence rather than reveal publicly what has happened to them. This need to hide or to disguise themselves in some way after they have been made to suffer abuse manifests itself in other ways as well. The theme of women who hide, disguise, or transform themselves following an abuse or a rape is common in early mythology. We can speculate that the desire to hide from others and from themselves is connected both to the profound feeling of shame that victims experience and also the desire to deny the self who has been victimized.

The mythologies of several ancient civilizations contain stories of grain goddesses or young nymphs who escape violation by hiding in the fields.[25] These stories not only contain elements of impending violation and rape, but also themes of deception and trickery on the part of the young woman. Generally the stories begin as the young goddess is pursued by a group of men intent on overpowering and raping her. She flees into a field where she magically causes the grain to grow, quickly concealing her and safeguarding her from her attackers. Securely hidden among the crops of the field, she successfully eludes the men who are intent on ravishing her. There is usually a farmer who is asked by the pursuers whether or not he has seen the young goddess, and he is able to answer truthfully that no one has passed this way since he first put the seed into the ground. Of course, the reader of the story knows that the seed grew very quickly by the magical intervention of the goddess; however, the pursuers do not know this and take the farmer's word at face value, assuming that no one has passed that way for many weeks. Thus, by virtue of her own power and deceptiveness, the goddess is able to hide and save herself from violation.

The myth is interesting for several reasons. First, we can see an early precursor of the notion of feminine wiles. Women often believe that the only way in which they can overpower or outwit a man is by being sneaky and deceptive. And the goddess in the story does indeed use trickery to save herself. Despite the fact that she is safe for the time being, the story also points out the vulnerability of the woman. Because she does not have the strength to confront her attackers in a direct way, she can only defend herself by hiding, a relatively passive way of protecting herself.

In describing work with runaway children, many of whom were victims of abuse in their homes, clinicians have described the propensity of these children to seek safe places to hide.[26] Their flight to the cities is often a flight in search of a good hiding place. Frequently, these children live in abandoned buildings, huddling in little nooks and crannies that might provide some protection from potential intruders and violators.

When people feel weak, desperate, and unable to defend themselves in any direct or straightforward way, the only way to avoid future victimization may indeed be to hide. Some of the women who have retold stories of their early abuse as children describe hiding under the bed and hiding under stairwells, attempting to make themselves invisible so that an irate and often drunken parent would not find them. Hiding in a physical sense, however, is only the most literal form of disguise that homeless and abused women use to defend and protect themselves. Women have developed other more subtle methods for disguising themselves and hiding, not only from potential abusers, but from themselves as well.

The early Christian monastic tradition contains stories of women who went into the desert to pray and to find God and who disguised themselves as men to safeguard themselves.[27] Certainly it would seem prudent for women living alone in the desert to be disguised as men to protect themselves from potential marauders and interlopers. For a number of these women, however, the disguise became a lifelong transformation, and there are stories of women who died after years of living alone in caves or in the desert who were only discovered to be women at the time their bodies were prepared for burial.

While Catholic theologians argue that this obvious denial of femininity was not a denial at a deeper level but merely a transcending of sexual differences so that one might better enter into a single community of God's followers,[28] it does seem striking to the lay person that the way in which these women entered this community was to enter as men and not as women. Similarly, we find that many homeless women acquire an androgynous look to survive on the streets. They no longer dress as women; they no longer wear their hair in a feminine style; they attempt to look asexual, if not masculine, so that they might be safe from abuse and attack on the streets.

There are stories in the Greek mythological tradition in which women relinquish even their human forms to protect themselves from abuse. The story of the goddess Nemesis is one such example.[29] Nemesis was given to the god Zeus to be his bride. She protested against this union and actively resisted the god's seduction. In an attempt to escape from him, she transformed herself from a beautiful young woman into various beasts of the earth, the sea, and the air. She was finally overcome by Zeus while she was in the form of a goose and he in the form of a swan. This young woman, however, never forgave Zeus for his mistreatment of her, and despite his attempt to soften her with his overtures and his love, she remained bitter and angry, hence her name Nemesis came to mean one who inflicts retribution or vengeance.

It is not uncommon for homeless women, in an attempt to protect themselves from further abuse, to transform themselves into almost subhuman or inhuman characters. Seen at a distance, clothed in many layers of rags and discarded apparel, homeless women appear a grotesque distortion of the human form. It is hard to imagine that they are real people, not just heaps of clothing in the distance. Some women have even talked of intentionally dehumanizing themselves, making themselves unattractive and odoriferous, to stave off potential abusers; certainly this almost conscious attempt to deny their humanity can be seen as a protective and defensive device. For many people who have been treated as subhuman for a number of years, the tendency to identify with this projection and to believe that they are other than human may at times be overpowering.

Living Victims

While the stories of victimization both from historical accounts and mythological accounts present us with an overwhelming portrait of the systematic victimization of women, the most tragic stories are those of women who have lived the life of victim in reality. The lives of homeless women, just as the lives of any individuals, are complicated and complex, and it would be foolhardy to assume that any one theme can capture the complexity and the multifaceted nature of an individual's life. Even so, there were some women who told their stories who almost seemed to embody the victim. These were women whose lives not only contained multiple acts of victimization and abuse, but who had formed their essential sense of self and their very personal identities around the role of victim.

Trixie's Story

Trixie has experienced almost every kind of abuse imaginable. She has been raped twice, mugged several times, and beaten and left for dead. As a child she was fondled and sexually molested by a series of men who dated her mother. She also witnessed the repeated abuse of those close to her. She saw her mother dragged from church by an irate boyfriend who wielded a stick in one hand and a brick in the other. Trixie hid in the bushes while two white boys beat her brother, stole his bicycle, and threw him in a pond, drowning the young boy. Trixie can still remember the terror she and her family felt as they watched the Klan burn a cross on the church lawn. Yet none of these traumas compares to what Trixie calls the pain in her heart from not having a mother's love. She believes that her sense of being unwanted and unloved has influenced all the events of her life.

During the first twelve years of her life, Trixie was raised by a woman she believed to be her mother, a woman who, while she had eight children and lived in poverty, managed to nurture her children both materially and emotionally. Trixie believed herself to be part of a large family and felt secure that within her family she could at least find some respite from the abuse and confusion that went on around her.

When she was twelve years old, Trixie discovered that the woman with whom she lived was not her biological mother. Rather, Trixie's mother was the town drunk, a prostitute who was publicly scorned, ridiculed, and considered an outcast in the small community. Before Trixie learned that this woman was her mother, she remembers watching one time as a man stripped her mother naked, beat her, and dragged her across an old wooden porch until her back was bloodied and cut from splinters. At the time, Trixie thought to herself, "Thank God that woman is no relation to me."

Trixie's horror was overwhelming when she discovered this woman to be her true mother. First, she felt betrayed and deceived by the woman she called "mother." She could not understand how this woman had lied to her for so many years. Trixie also felt that she was no longer a part of her family. She felt illegitimate and as if she was not entitled to the fellowship and support of her brothers and sisters. Toward her birth mother, Trixie felt a combination of anger and hurt. Although she did not want to be reared by this woman, Trixie felt a sense of abandonment that her mother had just given her away many years before. Mostly, however, Trixie felt panicked, confused, and scared to know who her mother was. She believed the town's scorn and hostility toward her mother were now directed at her as well. For Trixie, the discovery of her mother's identity meant the loss of her own stable sense of who she was and where she belonged.

Trixie's world was shattered by her discovery, and she began to behave in reckless and self-destructive ways. Trixie remembers getting drunk for the first time at age twelve when she discovered who her mother really was. Her drinking continued, and she remembers staggering around town, aimless and confused. Her drinking marked her first unconscious attempt to form a public and a pathological bond with the mother who had abandoned her.

With the secret of her birth now public, Trixie's mother reclaimed her daughter. Their reunion had no pleasant storybook elements, however. Trixie's mother took her from school and sent her to work in the fields. Trixie's small paycheck now went to support her mother's drinking habit. Any hope Trixie had had for an education was now gone and any fantasies she had had about having a loving and caretaking mother were similarly destroyed.

Trixie worked for over a year in the fields before she became pregnant, something she purposefully engineered as a way out of her horrible situation. Her pregnancy was also, she now believes, an act of spite. She was furious with both her natural mother and her adoptive mother for deceiving her and for turning her world upside down, and she thought that she could punish them by becoming pregnant.

Her pregnancy gave Trixie a temporary respite from day labor and reunited her with her adoptive mother, who took her back and helped her to care for her young child. The family was not the same for Trixie, however. She now felt as if she were an outsider, as if she did not belong. By the time she reached age eighteen, she decided that she would take her daughter and move to another city to start her life again. At this point she again was betrayed by her adoptive mother, who told her that she could only take her child if she repaid all the money that had been spent to feed and clothe the baby. Of course, Trixie did not have the money, and she vowed to go off to New York City, make her fortune, and send money back home so that she could buy her daughter back.

Trixie describes her life in New York as pure hell. She was a young woman, untrained, unskilled, vulnerable, and felt unloved and unwanted. By the time she arrived in New York City, she was already addicted to alcohol and became an easy target for many of the predators who roamed the city. She had a series of unsuccessful sexual affairs with both men and women and describes herself as looking for a good mother, someone who would love her, care for her, and, most importantly, someone who would want to have her around.

Her relationships frequently involved physical abuse as well as betrayal. People she thought loved her and cared for her turned on her and left her. She remembers waking up in strange beds, not knowing whom she had been with the night before and drowning her sense of emptiness in another drink. She was involved in prostitution, drug abuse, and petty crimes, all part of the city's violent underworld.

At one point she was taken in by a household of lesbians who promised to care for her and look after her. Instead, they introduced her to heroin and turned her into a sexual and domestic slave. When these women grew tired of Trixie, they plotted to murder her by burning down the house in which Trixie rented a room. On the night of the fire, Trixie failed to return home because she was so drunk that she passed out in a bar, thus saving her life. Three small children whose family occupied the back bedrooms of the house were not so lucky. All three died in the fire intended to take Trixie's life. This event devastated Trixie. Not only was she abandoned and betrayed by her supposed friends and caretakers, but she felt responsible and guilty for the deaths of three innocent children. She became crazed and went after these women with a butcher knife, an aborted attempt at violence that eventuated in Trixie's first psychiatric hospitalization.

Trixie's story of victimization has continued throughout her life. She has been homeless, she has been betrayed and used in relationships, and on several occasions she has attempted to take her own life. Trixie is convinced, however, that all of her pain stems from the fact that she is an unloved and unmothered woman. She continues to miss and to long for the security and the comfort that one gets from knowing that one is loved.

Many of Trixie's self-destructive activities have been desperate attempts to find the good mother of her dreams. Her relationships are often a search for someone who will care for her. She realizes that she frequently misjudges potential lovers, overlooking obvious faults, but she says that she is often so desperate and so hungry inside that she will throw her love at anyone who promises to give her some affection, however temporary that affection may be.

Trixie has also attempted to fill her inner emptiness with drugs and alcohol, feeling less lonely and less abandoned when she is intoxicated. In this way she has also fashioned a pathological identification with the natural mother who never loved her and never reared her. Trixie has paradoxically become that woman. She is alcoholic, promiscuous, and victimized and destitute, the very mother from whom she has been estranged. By merging with this pathological mother who abandoned her years ago, Trixie desperately tries to find an end to her sense of emptiness.

Paula's Story

Paula is a sizable woman who certainly looks as if she could take care of herself, yet she is frightened all the time. It is hard for her to describe exactly what it is that frightens her; she is only aware of a constant sense of dread. She feels sure that something bad is going to happen to her; she is just not sure when.

Paula's role as a victim began when she first started having relationships with men. In each of her relationships she has been used and abused, sometimes physically, sometimes psychologically, but always with disregard for her own needs and desires.

Paula's first husband, a homosexual, married her because he needed some cover for his gay life-style. While Paula imagined that her husband was marrying her because he loved her, cared for her, and wanted to make a life with her, he was in fact using her with little regard for her feelings. Eventually, he was unable to live the lie of a heterosexual relationship, and he cast her out and abandoned her, leaving her feeling bewildered and inadequate.

Her second husband also married her because he had some particular use for her. He was a foreigner and needed to marry an American-born woman to establish his citizenship. Paula recalls that this marriage was nothing but heartache, pain, and tears for her. She says, "That man didn't want me. He only wanted me to help him stay in this country, and I did that for him." Even though she knew she was being used and knew that she was unloved, Paula seemed willing to accept this kind of psychological devaluation and abuse because she so greatly feared being alone.

Her third husband was a violent and abusive man who had spent some time in jail. He was a small-time crook who enjoyed intimidating his frightened wife. Experiencing himself as having little real power in the world, he used his wife as a dumping ground for his own frustrations. Despite the fact that she was frightened during much of her third marriage, Paula did not leave her husband. Once again she waited for him to find her no longer useful and to leave her.

As soon as the men in her life have used her to their own satisfaction, they leave Paula, and she experiences a pervasive sense of emptiness, believing that she has once again been found inadequate and unlovable. Indeed, she blames herself for the abandonments even though she does not really know why they have occurred; all that she knows is that she is alone again with no one to turn to.

Paula first became a mother when she herself was still a child. She gave birth when she was in the seventh grade and at that time was asked to leave school because she was considered by the teachers to be a bad influence on the other children. This early pregnancy seems to have robbed Paula of much of her adolescent development. She did not have the chance to grow from a child into a woman; rather she was shot from the cannon of her girlhood into the harsh reality of adult womanhood. In that sense, part of her remains the eternal girl looking for the good parent and trusting that she will be treated fairly and decently by the people in her life.[30] Unfortunately, her experiences have not validated this naïve trust. Instead of being treated fairly and humanely, Paula has been used repeatedly, treated not as a woman with needs and desires of her own, but rather as an object—someone suitable merely for serving a purpose.

Paula's homelessness began when a man with whom she was living burned down their apartment. Without her man to take care of her and an apartment in which to live, Paula says her mind just gave out; she could not tolerate this last abandonment and was hospitalized for a severe depression after a period of homelessness. She was totally unable to care for herself and sat for hours staring into space.

Since joining a project for homeless women and being assisted in finding an apartment of her own, Paula has recovered from homelessness but not from fear; she continues to be afraid of things that she cannot control, unnamed dangers and catastrophes. She also worries that she will be abandoned once again and that she will be unable to cope and to handle the requirements of her life on her own. In talking with Paula, one can sense her powerful identification with the role of victim. She feels incompetent, weak, and vulnerable, and, although she would like to be otherwise, she does not know how to transform herself from that girl of twelve to the adult woman that she now is.

Vague and pervasive fear is not uncommon among homeless women who have identified with the role of victim. While Paula's fear is focused primarily on the dread of being left alone, other women seem equally afraid of some kind of violence or abuse that may be waiting for them in the future. One woman interjects her conversation with the psychotic phrase, "Please do not let the gunman get me." When asked to explain her fear, she is unable to think rationally about what it is that troubles her. She only knows that she is terrified that some unknown person, either real or imagined, will hurt her, beat her, and take from her what little she has.

Another woman's fear focuses on anything that is of a dark color. She is afraid of people who are dark-skinned; she is afraid of food that has a dark color; she avoids clothing that is dark; and she will not take any pills that are coated with dark-colored material. She is unable to explain what this fear of darkness is about, and one can only speculate that perhaps something terrifying happened to her in the dark at one point in her young life, or perhaps someone of dark skin abused and used her at some point in the past. She is a woman who has been in multiple foster homes, abandoned by her natural parents at a young age and transferred from temporary home to temporary home, so it does not take a very vivid imagination to construct the scenario in which she was indeed victimized and hurt at the hands of someone or something that seemed to her to be dark and ominous.

For many of these women who seemed frightened and confused, the repair from homelessness and victimization is difficult indeed. They are often unable to articulate what it is that scares them, and perhaps it is the case that the whole world has come to seem an unsafe and dangerous place.

Laura's Story

In many ways Laura looks the very portrait of vulnerability. She is small, frail, and old. Yet most of her victimization, rather than coming from physical or sexual abuse, has been the result of social forces that have colluded to produce a set of debilitating life circumstances. Laura is part of the large underclass of poor Americans who are uneducated, unskilled, and without resources. Their opportunities are limited, and they are often afraid to even dream of new possibilities, knowing that the likelihood of a real change in their lives is slim.

When Laura was a young girl, she was forced to leave school because her family needed even her meager income to be able to subsist. Consequently, she was without a high-school diploma and was forever limited to unskilled jobs that paid little and presented her with few, if any, opportunities. When she was able to work, Laura usually found jobs as a waitress or as a maid, but even these were often short-lived. Without much skill or many street smarts, Laura was often the first to be laid off when cutbacks needed to be made. Laura's lack of education, in addition to limiting her real possibilities for employment, also left her feeling inadequate and deficient.

Because her whole family was poor, Laura was unable to receive help and assistance from anyone in her immediate network. No one had it much better than she. Consequently, no one was available to provide any instrumental help, nor were family members, themselves exhausted by poverty, available to just listen and hear her complaints.

Perhaps the greatest tragedy for Laura that resulted from her lack of education and her poverty was the very poor medical care she received at a time in her life when it was important for her to be properly attended. In her early twenties, Laura became pregnant and very much wanted to have a child; however, she did not have the funds for reasonable prenatal care or subsequently for good medical care. The circumstances of her pregnancy are vague because Laura is unable to recount exactly what happened except that labor was painful for her. She was unable to deliver a live child, and she was told by the doctor in attendance that she would never be able to have other children. Because she was uneducated and poor and felt unentitled, it did not occur to her to find out exactly what had happened. She did not know if she had had a hysterectomy; she did not know why she could not have children; and she never found out if her condition was reversible. Instead, she just passively accepted the verdict that was given to her. The loss for her was enormous. One of the only things that this woman allowed herself to hope for was a child. She wanted to be a mother and to nurture someone into the next generation. Despite the fact that she is now well into her sixties, she still recounts the time in her life when she was pregnant as her happiest time.

The lack of competent medical care not only affected Laura during the time of her pregnancy, but it subsequently affected many members of her immediate family who died young of illnesses that need not have been fatal if they had had the resources to have them treated. Her husband died at the age of forty-two leaving her frightened and alone and so panicked that she tried to jump into the grave with him.

Laura's marriage, although one to which she clung for twenty years and valued greatly, was hardly idyllic. Both she and her husband were young when they married and naïve about what was required to make a marriage work. He was jealous and alcoholic throughout their marriage although he did not abuse her physically. Instead, his jealousy caused him to restrict her access to other people, and he demanded that she remain locked in the house each day while he went out to work. She passively complied with this order for twenty years.

The world in which Laura grew up and the world in which she lived was one in which people felt a lack of personal power. She did not feel, nor did her immediate family members feel, that they had the capacity or the will to influence events. Instead, she was and still is a passive recipient of what life has to offer her.

Psychologists, attempting to understand various depressive syndromes, have used the phrase "learned helplessness" to describe the phenomenon in which individuals cease trying to intervene in the environment.[31] After repeated failures in attempting to change his or her circumstances, the individual eventually gives up and no longer tries, even in situations that might hold the promise of success. In experiments with animals, researchers have found that when dogs are administered unavoidable, inescapable electric shocks, they become passive, seeming to give up.[32] Even when they are given an opportunity to escape from a noxious situation, dogs who have learned to be helpless will do nothing. In human terms, they have come to believe that their actions are irrelevant.

Laura embodies this kind of learned helplessness. She is a woman who has never been able to influence her environment—not economically, not socially, not interpersonally. She has accepted passively the situations and the events that life has offered to her, and she continues to do so without any belief that her own desires or wishes can make a difference in her circumstances.

Physically, Laura looks as if positive life energy has been drained away from her. She looks older than her years, dried up, dessicated, as if those life juices that might have empowered and infused her at one time no longer flow. Her victimization, while perhaps not as dramatic and vivid as that of Paula and Trixie, is just as real. She is the victim of circumstance, the victim of being born poor and being uneducated in a land that is rich and ambitious.

Summary

Women have been victims since the beginning of time. Historically, mythologically, and in the reality of our city streets, women present their victimization for all to see. As long as we live in a world in which there are power differentials among people, in which there are some who are strong, some who are weak, some who are powerful, and some who are vulnerable, we will always have perpetrators and predators, and we will always have victims. As long as the role of victim remains undesirable, most of us will try to deny that we have the potential of ever being victims, and we will continue to project our vulnerability out onto others. Victimization, especially chronic victimization, makes most people uncomfortable. The prospect that one might be vulnerable indefinitely, subject to repeated abuse as were Trixie and Paula, is disquieting and frightening.

Chapter 7

The Exile

The process of psychological and physical differentiation, which marks one individual or group of individuals as separate and distinct from others, makes possible the emergence of the exile. In a state of symbiosis there is no "we/they" or "in/out" split, hence no possibility for banishment or estrangement. Only when individuals emerge as being distinct from others do they have the risk of being cast out.

So fundamental is the experience of exile to the development of men and women as psychological beings that one might argue that human history begins with an exile. When Adam and Eve became aware of themselves as unique individuals, they were expelled from Paradise, cast out, and forced to make their way in a cold and less-inviting world. Taken literally, this expulsion marks the alienation of men and women from God and from the paradise of the Garden.

So totally does the role of exile consume an individual that our language fails to distinguish between the process or state of exile and the person exiled. The same word denotes the state of banishment or wandering and the person who is outcast. The individual may well experience a sense of personal nonbeing when he or she becomes an exile, leaving behind treasured possessions, familiar surroundings, and established relationships. Without those external markers that structure one's uniqueness, an individual may become lost in the anonymity of exile and defined by its process.

The essential characteristics of what it means to be an exile are well defined by the Jewish philosopher Elie Wiesel. Wiesel himself has legitimate claim to the title of exile. As a member of the Jewish people he participates in a long history of shared wandering and exile; as a Holocaust survivor he joins a small group of individuals who were exiled in a most profound way from their homes and communities. Wiesel contends that the exile is someone who fundamentally does not fit, whose personal rhythm is out of synch with the rhythm of the society in which he or she must live.[1]

The individual who is in a state of alienation from the rest of society may "not fit" in one of several ways. The exile may feel that he or she is moving, but the rest of society is standing still; or the individual may feel stagnant and stationary while the body of society moves and evolves. The individual may believe that both he or she and society are moving, but they are moving in different directions. Hence the individual experiences a sense of disharmony or discordance between the movement of the self and the movement of the surrounding milieu.[2]

I remember a young schizophrenic woman who described her own sense of alienation and exile from other persons, resulting from her mental illness, in a similar way. She said that being schizophrenic was like marching in a band but never being able to march on the same beat as everyone else. Consequently, she always felt one or two steps off, never in synch, never going with the flow of those around her.

While the state of exile generally refers to an individual and his or her relationship to a separate group of other individuals, taking a psychological perspective allows us to apply the term exile to an individual's relationship to his or her own inner self. During psychological exile, the individual feels alienated from his or her own core self. For example, when individuals invest too much energy in the development of their external, public personalities, they may find themselves cut off from their own inner values and beliefs. In this instance, a state of internal alienation may occur in which the individual contains the exile within his or her own psyche.

The power of the concept of exile derives from the tripartite nature of its influence: on the individual, on the community from which the individual is exiled, and on the community to which the individual goes. Exile implies a dynamic tension between an individual and something outside that individual or, in the case of psychological exile, something that comes to be experienced as being outside the individual. It makes sense then to look at the impact of the role of exile on the individual, on the outcasting community, and on the receiving community.

The Individual

Being an exile is often the central organizing principle of a person's existence. Indeed, being cut off from his or her culture, country, or society has resulted, in some cases, in death, in madness, in disorientation, and also, paradoxically, in positive transformation. At times the experience of being cut off from his or her homeland is so powerful that the exile cannot survive in another environment. There are examples from primitive tribes of individuals who are cast out and within a short time die, not because they have been killed, not because they starve or freeze, but because the isolation and the disconnection from the human community is so disorganizing that they cannot survive.[3]

In the 1980s, Laotian exiles settling in the United States were reported to be dying mysteriously either of strange nightmares or of unanticipated heart problems. Some researchers conjectured that these deaths, rather than being brought on by some physical ailment, were in fact the product of a profound sense of exile and disorientation experienced by these individuals.[4] Cut off from their homeland, its customs and its values, these Laotian refugees were unable to survive.

Some exiles, able to survive physically, are unable to survive psychologically. The ancient story of Medea presents us with one such portrait. Medea is a woman who exiles herself from her homeland to go off with Jason her lover.[5] In leaving the land of her parents, she also helps Jason to kill her brother. Consequently, she is exiled not only from her country, but also from her family; and by virtue of her traitorous act, she is exiled from the human community. She is so estranged from communal values and standards that she eventually defies the most basic and instinctual norms, murdering her own children to spite her husband, an act which alienates her even further from normal human behavior. When Jason leaves her and she realizes her fundamental isolation, she laments: "Oh country I left in disgrace." She is a woman who has never recovered from the total disconnection she experienced when she left her homeland years before under heinous circumstances.

Perhaps less dramatic, but certainly more prevalent, is the estrangement many adults experience from the traditions and rituals of childhood. During childhood most individuals participate joyously and unselfconsciously in a host of familial, social, and religious ceremonies. As they become adults, many men and women find it increasingly difficult to maintain an active connection to this world of the personal and cultural past and its rich traditions.[6] Consequently, many individuals experience an estrangement from the secure, structured, and meaningful world of childhood ritual. This personal alienation from the past and from cultural traditions and roots has been identified as one cause of the sense of meaninglessness and emptiness that many modern individuals feel.[7]

While the experience of psychological or physical exile is disorienting and jarring for the individual, it does not automatically or necessarily lead to a negative outcome. There are examples of individuals who used the experience of exile to facilitate a positive personal transformation. For example, many of the religious hermits of the fourth century voluntarily chose a life of isolation and exile with the hope of experiencing a spiritual transformation and attaining salvation. Mary of Egypt was one such Christian hermit.[8] As a young woman she was blatantly libertine, a defiant and rebellious harlot. At first barred from entering a holy shrine, she experienced a miraculous conversion outside a church in Jerusalem and then willingly renounced her life of luxury and wantonness. As a result of her conversion, Mary banished herself to a life of isolation, abstinence, and prayer in the desert. After forty years of self-imposed exile, she was fully transformed into Saint Mary, a holy and religious woman.

The life of Saint Barbara provides another example of a young woman whose banishment facilitated her spiritual transformation. Barbara did not choose exile, however. Rather, she was banished to a tower by her father who wanted to protect her from the influence of Christianity. In her exile and estrangement from her past, she found a new direction for her life and made a commitment for which she was willing to die. In discussing Saint Barbara's life, writer Betsy Caprio suggests that the period of exile, whether it is voluntarily assumed or externally imposed, may be a time when an individual moves in a new and positive direction.[9] It is up to the individual as to how he or she will utilize the potential for change inherent in any experience of exile.

Regardless of how the individual interprets or exploits the time of personal alienation, what remains clear is that the individual cannot experience exile without being profoundly affected. Exile marks an abrupt and radical disconnection and thus demands that the individual forge a new relationship not only to the self, but also to the society of other men and women.

The Casting-Out Community

While less immediately obvious than the effects on the individual, the effects of an act of exile on the community that casts out the individual are far-reaching and substantial. Some of the early history of exiles indicates that the exile had an important and meaningful role in the life of the community.

The Old Testament Book of Leviticus, for example, provides detailed instructions for a ritual of exile.[10] On the day of Atonement, the High Priest is to prepare two goats for sacrifice. One is to be given to God, and the other is to be sent to Azazel, the evil spirit who resides in the desert. The goat designated for God is sacrificed as a sin offering for the community. This goat is killed, and its blood is sprinkled around the altar to atone for the sins of the people. Thus, the altar is made hallowed by the blood sacrifice, and this atonement lasts for one year, to be repeated in ritual fashion each year on the Hebrew day of Atonement. The other goat, who came to be known as the escape goat, is sent into the desert, carrying with it the sins of the community, which have been placed symbolically on its back. It was believed that this goat would wander solitarily in the wilderness, eventually die, and thus be given over to the evil spirit.

By taking the community's sins away, the escape goat served several functions. The goat symbolized the members' accumulated transgressions and collective evil; consequently, by casting out the ritual escape goat, the people also cast out their own evil and unwanted selves.[11] The goat's departure also served to purify the community so that its members were seen as being free of transgression and free of sin once the goat left to wander in the desert.

Anthropologists have gathered repeated evidence of similar ritual expulsions in which either an animal, an object, or a human is sent out of the community to purify it from sin.[12] Frequently, the individual is cast out with no hope of ever rejoining the group again. Moreover, to make explicit the community's disgust with the ritual sinner, its members often beat, hiss, or denigrate the outcast as he or she leaves town. Such hostility not only establishes the people's disapprobation for the departing member, but also reinforces the psychological distance believed to exist between the main body of the community and the exile who is carrying with him or her the sins of the group.

While in most cases the individual who functions as this symbolic escape goat does not return to the community, there are some examples in which the individual, having survived the ritual exile, is allowed to return. In some medieval European locales a man was chosen on the first day of Lent to be cast out of the community, carrying with him the sins of the group.[13] This individual was formally ostracized and was forbidden from entering the church or speaking to anyone during the time of Lent. On the day before Good Friday, if the man survived and was still within the physical boundaries of the community, he would be readmitted to the church, consecrated, and absolved of any residual sin. In his purified state, the individual was now called Adam and welcomed back into the group.

The man or woman who is exiled serves a function for the group as a whole as well as for individual members of the community. By attributing all sinfulness to one group member, the other members may exult in their collective innocence and be free of any responsibility for personal repentance or atonement. At an individual level, each member of the group may allow the exile to symbolize that part of the personal psyche that he or she disowns and denies. Thus by casting out the ritual sinner, each person participates in a metaphor for the projection of his or her unwanted psychological parts.

The Receiving Community

In discussing the life of an exile, it is not uncommon for writers to ignore the impact that that person has on the community that accepts him or her. Yet, it is the case that most individuals who are cast out go somewhere. Even if their rest is only temporary, they do wander to some new group or attempt to build a home in some new land.

Because the exile is often associated with wrongdoing, sin, or evil, new communities may be reluctant to receive such individuals with open arms. In fact, established groups are initially skeptical of newcomers who appear different, foreign, or alien. Sometimes that skepticism gives way to eventual acceptance, but often skepticism leads to paranoia, distancing, and a need to disown or destroy the interloper.

Although this fear may be irrational, community members often believe that a refugee—a newcomer from some distant place—will contaminate or endanger them. Such fears may stem from the symbolic connection between the exile and the evil undesirable parts of the human condition that he or she represents. When these fears are directed toward newcomers who do indeed have some contagious disease, however, mass hysteria may result.

The fear of the exile may be so great that communities will take drastic measures to keep the outcast out. A district in New York State considered seceding from the county and forming a township of its own just so that it would not have to receive homeless people within its boundaries.[14] The fear of the outsider was so powerful that this group was willing to go into voluntary exile to avoid contamination by these dreaded outsiders.

While this combination of exclusion, hostility, and paranoia is the most common reaction to the appearance of the exile, communities do occasionally welcome an outsider and are transformed or enriched by taking in this exiled individual. It is often easier, however, for us to accept aliens when they come singly rather than in groups. Our popular fiction romanticizes the single alien, the adorable E.T., who finds his way into a family and becomes accepted and valued by them. When outsiders attempt to cross our boundaries in greater numbers, we often experience them as being more threatening and thus are less able to take them in. Again, this may have implications for the pacing of psychological reintegration. Individuals are often better able to reintegrate split-off parts of themselves when those parts are presented gradually, one at a time, rather than when the individual is confronted en masse with many aspects of his or her disowned psyche.

It is paradoxical that while the exile embodies estrangement and isolation, he or she continues to exist in some relation to the larger society, even if that relationship is a tense and dysphoric one. A person can be defined as an outcast only in relation to some society or some group to which he or she originally belonged. Just as the concept of an outside implies the existence of an inside, the concept of exile requires a community or self from which parts are cast out. Exile is a relational concept, existing in the space between the society and the individual and implying a dynamic tension between that which belongs and that which does not belong.

To better understand the various embodiments of the exile and the different aspects of physical and psychological alienation, let us turn our attention to exiles that have gained ascendancy in history and in our political consciousness. We will also look to mythology and fiction and see the ways in which the role of the exile has been portrayed. Finally, in keeping with the central theme of this book, we will turn once again to the lives of real homeless women and understand the ways in which many of these women have been cast or have cast themselves into the role of exile.

The Historical Exile

The philosopher Elie Wiesel has described our planet as a place filled with refugees, with exiles, with wanderers, and with nomads.[15] Repeatedly, acts of relentless persecution have resulted in single individuals and groups of people being cast out from their native lands and forced to wander, searching for a new place to settle.

Some of these historic exiles are cast out from the countries of their birth because of political, philosophical, or religious beliefs that differ from those held by the majority of the populace. Other individuals leave their countries because they are propelled by some ideal, some vision of a better life elsewhere. While the flight of the exile may resemble that of the immigrant, the exile, in contrast to the immigrant, feels fundamentally disconnected from his or her homeland and unable to return. Regardless of whether exile has been chosen or is forced, those who leave their homeland often believe that they must rebuild their entire lives and begin all over.[16] It is as if what they bring with them, if they bring anything at all, is unusable or inappropriate in the new setting.

In examining the role of the exile historically, it is striking how many different nationalities have at one time or another been forced into exile. Exile is not peculiar to any race, any religion, or any geographic group. It seems to have affected almost all groups and all peoples. The Jewish people, for example, have often been identified as the quintessential exiles. The Diaspora forced Jews to wander all over the world for two thousand years. Recent times have seen exiles and refugees from Central America, Southeast Asia, Africa, and other parts of the world as well. It is ironic that the Jewish people, themselves the victims of exile and banishment for so many years, now house within their borders one of the twentieth century's most prominent exile groups, namely the Palestinians.

Those who were themselves exiles now contribute to the exile of others. It is as if within the human community, there must be some exiles. When a particular exile group ceases to be outcast and reintegrates into a larger community, the mantle of exile passes necessarily to some other group. The human community seems to be structured like the children's game of musical chairs. There is always one less chair than the number of players, and when the music stops, someone is left standing on the sideline, no longer part of the group. It is beyond the scope of this work to comment on all those groups and peoples who at some point in time have been exiled or outcast. Examining the stories of a few exile groups, however, will serve to illustrate and make more tangible some of the essential features of the nature of exile.

One of the most bizarre examples of exile occurred in fifteenth-century Europe when communities within Germany cast out mad or ill members of the society forcing them to wander outside the town.[17] These individuals were eventually picked up by river boatmen who put them on boats, floating from town to town never being able to dock in any one place. The image of boats full of insane people floating endlessly from town to town has an otherworldly quality to it. Yet these literal ships of fools did indeed exist.

In commenting on this practice, social philosopher Michel Foucault suggests that such a phenomenon must not be evaluated solely in terms of its social utility. That is, the practice of floating undesirable members of the community up and down the river was not put into practice because it was the most economic or wise way to rid the community of undesirable persons; rather, such an elaborate procedure must have had a ritual or symbolic significance. In fact, Foucault suggests that these insane people were sent on a ritual exile.[18] One can imagine these individuals floating forever on this fluid limbo, never being allowed to come to rest, going on for eternity, and becoming the objects of fantasy and fiction.

Because of the symbolic nature of this activity, Foucault maintains that the use of water as the means of transport was not at all coincidental.[19] Rather, it is often the case that water symbolism is associated with purification and spiritual renewal. These ill, disorganized, and crazy members of the society were sent off to be symbolically baptized or cleansed on the waters, thus not only ridding the larger community of them, but also ridding the exiles of badness and returning them to a more innocent state.

The case of the ship of fools is somewhat of an anomaly within the history of exiles. Not only were the circumstances of exile unusual, but it was an example of exile in which single individuals were brought together in an artificial kinship of banishment. Most instances of historic exiles involve large groups of people, ethnic, religious, or political minorities who are exiled en masse. Their departure from their homelands is generally precipitated by some rupture in the social or political life of the community. Despite the fact that dislocation from one geographic region to another has far-reaching consequences for those people involved, diverse exile groups historically have responded differently to the experience of their collective displacement.

For some Indian groups, exile from homelands has meant extinction. Indians, in addition to being geographically dislocated, have experienced a religious and spiritual exile that has been equally as debilitating. Vine Deloria, a political scientist and writer on Indian affairs, has commented that the devastation that many tribes experienced came as much from the disruption in their ceremonial and religious life as it did from the actual dislocation from one physical setting to another.[20] For many tribes, especially those in the Ohio Valley and in the South, ceremony and ritual were tied to particular locations. Certain places were deemed to be sacred and were imbued with magical and spiritual power. This power was not transferable from one location to another, so when groups were moved or cast out from their native areas, they lost not only their physical homes, but also their link with certain holy and ceremonial places. Deloria maintains that this separation from sacred places had a long-reaching and profound impact on Indians.[21]

With the erosion of ceremonial life, tribal identity became more difficult to maintain. Consequently, what began as a physical exile became, for many, a social and spiritual exile as well, with individuals being increasingly cut off from the rich and meaningful traditions and customs of their past. Without an identification with certain ceremonies and ritual activities, many Indians found it increasingly difficult to maintain their connection to a tribal identity. Moreover, without a sensible and cohesive alternative to the old traditions, many tribal groups found it increasingly difficult to maintain a stable society, and Deloria suggests that some of the erosion of fundamental values of the tribe may be traced to this state of exile.[22]

In a series of drawings entitled *The Trail of Tears,* artist Jerome Tiger depicts the migration of Indians.[23] What is telling in many of these drawings is the utter dejection and sorrow that fill the forms of the departing men and women. They appear beaten, battered by the wind, and battered by the changes that are going on around them. These individuals appear to be leaving behind more than their homes and fields and hunting grounds; they are leaving behind a way of life.

The response within Tibetan society to years of exile has been quite different. In 1959 the Dalai Lama of Tibet fled invading Chinese armies and established a government in exile.[24] The structure of the Tibetan government has been reproduced in exile with cabinet bodies, elected representatives, and numerous governmental agencies. What is more significant, however, is not that the Dalai Lama has established a government in exile, but that he and, to a lesser extent, the Tibetan people have actually embraced exile.

The Dalai Lama himself has thanked Mao Tse-tung and the Chinese armies for teaching him the realities of impermanence and suffering.[25] His exile has been a lesson in some of the harsher realities of life. Nevertheless, he felt that it was a lesson he needed to learn to more fully transcend the human condition.

Buddhist tradition, in contrast to other religions, embraces the role of exile.[26] The Buddha taught that it was a virtue for individuals to disencumber themselves from the trappings of everyday material life. Moreover, they should dispense with material possessions and concrete identities that hold them in the mundane rut of their lives. Perhaps the most profound example of unfettering oneself is to be without a country, to be without a homeland. In such a situation a person not only has no possessions, but literally does not have a place to rest his or her head.

Stories of his life reveal that the historic Buddha was a famous exile in several ways.[27] He was repeatedly cast out of his community for behaving in a way that was deemed to be too good to be true. His generosity and his charitableness were so extreme that he was cast out of the society because of them. Such an individual was a literal exile because he was banished, but he was also a spiritual exile because his own philosophy and his way of understanding the world were so out of synch with the others in the society that he seemed to be an alien.

Within the Buddhist and the Tibetan tradition, the most profound form of exile that can be experienced is an internal and psychological exile. Because of the strong focus on the development of an inner life, an individual might be less susceptible to physical, geographic, or political exile. As long as an individual remains integrated and whole and connected to his or her own inner development, then he or she cannot be an exile in a psychological sense. It is only when the connection to his or her inner self is lost that a person reared in such a tradition might indeed experience the alienation and disconnection of exile.

The story of the Falashas, the black Jews of Ethiopia, offers the promise of a return from exile. These individuals, exiled from their homeland, believed for centuries that they were the only surviving Jews, and consequently, they clung scrupulously to Jewish laws and observances.[28] Yet, they were always considered to be aliens or strangers in the land that they inhabited. Indeed, the very name Falasha means alien and is a term of abuse or derogation.[29]

What is remarkable is that these individuals managed to maintain a culture and a religious identity with almost no contact with the outside world or the larger Jewish community. They kept a close-knit society that not only preserved its traditions, but was bent on returning to its ancient homeland. For many years these individuals were not recognized as ethnic Jews, and indeed they were considered outsiders to the larger Jewish community. It was only in 1975 that the Chief Rabbi of Israel declared the Falashas to be remote descendants of one of the lost tribes of Israel.[30] In this way they were deemed to be ethnic Jews and allowed to emigrate to Israel.

The story of the Falashas does not end there, however. Other governments were involved, governments that did not want these individuals to return to Israel. Consequently, the airlifting of many Falashas to Israel had to be done in secret. Even when these individuals arrived in Israel, they could not be immediately assimilated into the culture. They needed to spend a year in an absorption center in which they could learn Hebrew and really be integrated into the twentieth century and into modern Israeli life. It is remarkable that this integration has in fact taken place. A people who have been exiled for almost fifteen hundred years have, at least in part, come home and been accepted and reintegrated into an existing society.

This example of return is important in many respects. First, the tenacity with which the Falashas held to their beliefs is impressive. These individuals maintained a culture in exile for hundreds of years. Also interesting is the difficulty that surrounded their reintegration into their homeland, difficulty not only from the country that they were leaving, but also on the part of the country to which they were going.

While the return of the prodigal son or the lost child is appealing as a myth or a metaphor, in practice it is often very difficult for us to bring back either individuals who have been exiled or lost or parts of our own consciousness that have been lost and cast out. The process whereby the Falashas have been integrated into Israeli society may serve as a model for the return of the exile.

At first we may be put off by the idea of an absorption camp in which individuals are placed for an extended period of time before they can be relocated within their homeland. When we consider the difficulty of assimilating any new information or any lost information about ourselves, however, the wisdom of such a slow process of integration becomes apparent. If we really believe that a person or that a part of a person's psyche has been exiled and cast out, then we need to take great care in readmitting that lost part of the society or that lost part of the self. We cannot be cavalier about the process of reintegration.

Anyone who has been through the process of psychotherapy knows that brutal confrontation or bombardment with new information rarely results in any kind of positive change. Rather, for the individual to take in new and foreign or difficult information, he or she does indeed need a process of absorption during which new ways and new thoughts are tried out and gradually assimilated. The Israeli process of reintegrating the black Jews of Ethiopia mirrors this process of psychological reintegration in which there is a period of assimilation; those who have been lost slowly return, and those who are already home get comfortable with accepting those who have been cast out.

While the existence of political and social exiles has historically had special meaning for those groups who have suffered exile, the mere existence of exile groups has implications for all of us. It is difficult for us to ignore the existence of outcasts when we hear about them on the nightly news, read about their dislocation in magazines and journals, and see some of them wandering on our city streets. Confronted with real exiles, we are forced to acknowledge the fact of exile as a human possibility and to contemplate that we, too, might face isolation and ostracism. At a psychological level we are forced to consider our own separateness and sense of personal alienation when we see individuals who wear their exile publicly.

Fictional or Mythological Exile

While the historical exile has often been a wanderer or an outcast from a particular geographic or political homeland, the fictional outcast is more often depicted as being isolated or alienated from a social community or, in a psychological sense, from some part of his or her own essential self. Themes of exile in fiction or mythology focus very much on the experience of the individual, either in relation to the larger society or in relation to him- or herself. It is the particular personal and emotional reactions to the state of exile that are of most concern to the writer of fiction or to the mythologist. Consequently, in looking at exiles in myth and fiction, we will turn our attention away from societal, political, and geographic movements and focus more on the psychological reality of the state of alienation and exclusion that confront the exile.

In her novel *Clan of the Cave Bear,* Jean Auel deals repeatedly with the theme of the exile.[31] The story is about a young woman, Ayla, who is estranged from her own people during a natural disaster and is found and cared for by a clan very different from her own. Even though she is a small child at the beginning of the story, clearly vulnerable and helpless, the clan members are reluctant to accept her because she is different from them. She looks different, and they are wary of including in their midst one who is not of their own kind. Throughout the story, the heroine must deal with her difference and her separateness from those around her and those close to her.

In addition to themes of estrangement and isolation, the author deals at one point explicitly with the idea of banishment. As she grows and develops physical prowess unusual for women of the clan, Ayla learns to do things that women are prohibited from doing. Specifically, she learns to hunt. When the clan members discover that she has engaged in this forbidden and tabooed behavior, they invoke an elaborate ceremony of ostracism. As punishment for breaking the rules of the tribe, Ayla is condemned to death. The clan does not define death as her being killed, however; rather, death is the equivalent to her being exiled. From the moment that she is declared dead, she no longer exists as a social or psychological entity for other members of the clan; people that she had known just moments before no longer see her. They do not respond when she speaks to them, and they engage in mourning, wailing, and lamenting her demise.

In front of her eyes her most valued possessions are burned, and she becomes aware that she has ceased to exist in any real way for the clan members. Moreover, clan custom dictates that to acknowledge her physical presence in any way will bring bad luck to the viewer, so this additional prohibition causes those who once loved her to turn from her as if she were a nonperson. This exclusion from the group is so total and so abrupt that clan members who have been condemned in the past have indeed died. Without family, without loved ones, and without a clan to acknowledge his or her existence, the individual often feels as if he or she has no reason to go on living, and it is not long before the person falls ill and dies.

In some orthodox Jewish sects, a similar procedure takes place when a group member marries someone not of the Jewish faith. The family conducts prayers and ceremonies for the dead, mourning the individual as if he or she no longer existed. Moreover, there is a prohibition within the family against acknowledging the person who has violated the rules of the clan in such a fundamental way. It is intriguing that in both of these examples the punishment for violating the rules or laws of the group is psychological death or exile. In reality, the threat of exile is so potent for individuals that it is sufficient to keep group members mindful of the rules and regulations and thus loyal to the clan.

Social commentators have remarked that each member of a society is engaged in both a literal and a symbolic ongoing conversation or dialogue with other members of the society.[32] When and if this interaction ceases, the individual will experience not only alienation, but a sense of nonbeing with respect to the culture. As long as there is dialogue, as long as there is interaction, even if that interaction is hostile or antagonistic, the person stays in connection or in relation to the rest of the community. It is only when the dialogue ceases that the individual is exiled and that there is no chance for a rapprochement or a connection. In both of the examples cited above, the orthodox Jewish community and the clan in Auel's novel, the individual is aware at the outset of the rules and regulations for inclusion and exclusion. The taboos are public, and the individual knows that if certain boundaries are crossed, he or she will no longer be a social or psychological member of the group. This does not mean that ostracism is any less painful when it actually occurs; however, the individual is forewarned, and the conditions for continuing the dialogue with other members of the human community are explicit. It is, I think, far more disturbing and psychologically brutalizing for individuals when the rules are not explicit, that is, when the dialogue with others ceases and the person does not know what offense has been committed. Under such circumstances, a person finds him- or herself in a Kafkaesque scenario: outside the human community yet not knowing what he or she has done to cause his or her exclusion.

This feeling of confusion and perplexity is often part of the subjective experience of many schizophrenic patients. They know that they are no longer in genuine communication with other people, but they do not understand why they cannot make themselves understood and cannot understand what other people are saying. For most mentally ill people it is difficult to accept as adequate the explanation that their brains are not functioning properly. Consequently, they often search for some element of personal behavior that might explain this abrupt and painful rift with other humans. Many schizophrenic men and women construct elaborate explanations, often self-punitive ones, to rationalize why they now feel outside the human community. The experience of being out of synch with other people, with family, and with friends, is in itself so painful that to have no explanation for this disconnection is more than any individual can bear. A self-blaming or a delusional explanation may be preferable to no explanation at all.

Many modern writers have chosen to address the psychological pain and confusion that accompany exile or banishment. Yukio Mishima, in his novel *Confessions of a Mask,* deals with the subjective experience of a young man who finds himself becoming an outsider in his community.[33] As he grows into adolescence, this young man realizes that he does not have the same sexual attractions for women that seem to occupy his friends. Rather, he is compelled by and drawn to young boys. His emerging homosexuality sets him apart from other young men in post-war Japan.

To survive in a society that does not condone or embrace such difference, the young man must appear to conform. Consequently, he feigns interest and attraction for young girls when talking with his friends. He even goes so far as to try to convince himself that he does feel the same things that his young friends feel; but this self-deception only furthers his alienation. In fact, it introduces a new dimension of alienation, for not only is this young man cut off from others, unable to share his secret desires and passions, but he also becomes, at least temporarily, cut off from himself, unclear as to what is real and what is a sham. At one point he muses to himself that his masquerade as normal may well have corroded whatever real normality he in fact possesses. In this statement, the young man alludes to one of the most painful dilemmas of the exile. If a person is exiled because he or she possesses certain feelings or beliefs that put him or her outside the mainstream, then he or she is confronted with two equally untenable choices. Either the individual conforms and adopts a persona or a public face that seems acceptable to the society and in so doing causes some damage to the inner or true self, or he or she refuses to conform, stays true to what he or she is or what he or she believes, and faces ostracism from the community. Thus, an individual whose desires or beliefs set him or her apart must be exiled, either exiled from the self or exiled from the community.

Edward Whitmont, the Jungian analyst, has observed that one of the ways in which we attain a sense of personal value is by identifying with collective rules.[34] If we are part of a community that accepts us and if we in turn value that community, then we participate in the community's power and prestige. If we experience feelings or urges that the society does not condone, however, then we must hide our own reality, our own subjective experience, to gain the communal acceptance that we need.

In addition to the young man's sense of internal turmoil, what stands out in Mishima's novel is the overwhelming sense of shame that the young man feels. Those urges that set him apart from his friends, his secret inner reality, is not something of which he is proud; rather, it causes him to feel tremendously ashamed. Regrettably, for many people to live with themselves and to be true to themselves is to be beset by feelings of shame and self-disgust.

The internal chaos of a man who knows that to be honest with himself is to be outcast from society is the subject of a theatrical production by David Hwang.[35] The production entitled *1000 Airplanes on the Roof* tells the story of a young man who encounters beings from outer space. These extraterrestrials capture him on several occasions, take him away from his home, and perform bizarre medical experiments on him. While he is with these aliens, they instruct him that it is better for him to forget what has happened to him, that it will be pointless for him to remember, and that if he attempts to tell people about his experiences, they will consider it heresy and he will be outcast. This particular refrain is repeated by the main character throughout the performance. This warning contains the essential dilemma of the exile. His choice is to lie to himself and to be alienated from his own true self, but in so doing to be acceptable to others, or to be honest with himself, to say what he knows to be true, and thus to be considered crazy by others and outcast within the human community.

It is chilling to realize that this particular dilemma faces many young children who are the survivors of incest or child abuse within their homes. We can only guess how many parents have said to their children that it is better for you to forget this, that it will be pointless for you to remember, and that no one will believe you if you tell what just went on. The child is faced with having to distort his or her own reality to fit in, or to tell what he or she knows and then be accused of lying and distorting the facts.

As with the hero in *Confessions of a Mask*, the young man in this theatrical performance also adopts a persona that will be acceptable to the rest of society. His persona, while not a very interesting one, is a safe disguise behind which he can hide and fit in with the rest of society. The impact of living a lie, of living alienated from his true self, is not insignificant, and the protagonist says at one point that he has worn the disguise for so long that it has started to seep into his skin. If a person pretends that things are true for long enough, after a while it will be difficult to know what is true, what is not true, what is lie, and what is reality. Clearly, this is the dilemma that faces so many individuals who seek psychotherapeutic treatment in an attempt to come to terms with some past abuse or trauma but who are no longer certain as to whether or not the abuse actually occurred or was invented by them much earlier.

In the last scene of the play, the young man, having been arrested by the authorities, is questioned by a psychiatrist. The psychiatrist proceeds to ask him whether or not certain events are true or false. These are events that depict his capture by the aliens, events that he has described while asleep. Realizing that if he acknowledges or owns the truth of his experience, he will be considered crazy by the psychiatrist, the young man methodically answers no to each of the psychiatrist's questions. In this way he denies the reality of his own experience, and he denies his own true self. The experience of lying repeatedly about what has happened to him has a bizarre effect on the young man. With each subsequent lie he finds himself losing his memories, so that his own personal connection to the truth and to his inner reality diminishes as he lies to the outside world.

I have heard patients in psychotherapy refer to their own true self as being small, dark, hidden, a little flame that seems to flicker almost imperceptibly. After years of having to deny repeatedly the reality of one's experience, the true self does indeed seem to recede into the background, existing only as a faint memory or a slight flicker.

The play ends with the main character being freed by the psychiatrist, but in a paradoxical and provocative twist, he is free only to lie. As soon as he begins to tell the truth, especially to others, he will no longer be free. Free in one sense, he is trapped in another. The person who must choose between being cut off from him or herself or cut off from others exists in a hellish nightmare that might well have been constructed by Dante as punishment for some unspeakable crime.

The untenable and no-win position of the psychological exile is the subject of Elie Wiesel's comments about another fictional exile, Odysseus.[36] Following the Trojan War, Odysseus was forced to wander the seas for nineteen years as an exile and nomad before he was allowed to return home. Wiesel comments that despite the return that concludes the epic, Odysseus can never return home in a psychological sense. Having experienced exile, he will forever be a stranger.

Upon his return, Odysseus is confronted with one of two options: either his world has changed, in which case he is a stranger to the land of his birth; or he returns to find that nothing has changed, but he is still a stranger because he has experienced nineteen years of exile so that he is not the same Odysseus who left as a young warrior to fight battles years ago. In either case, even if physical return is possible, psychological return does not exist as a real possibility. The world will never be the same; the individual will never be the same; consequently, any reunion must necessarily be a reunion of two different parties.

Certainly, parallels with homeless individuals are apparent. For many of them, the experience of being homeless marks them forever as different within the human community. Even when they have homes and come in off the streets, they often are unable to rid themselves of the subjective and psychological sense of being outside the human community. It is almost as if they feel they wear the mark of Cain and are forever noticeable as outsiders or aliens.

Living Exiles

Most of the women who were interviewed for this book experienced some form of exile or ostracism. Many were exiled from their families and had experiences of being repeatedly put out by family members and told not to come back. By virtue of living on the streets or living in shelters, all of them felt that they were in some way outside the human community. Indeed, as with the homeless women interviewed in the British study discussed in chapter 2, many of them referred to themselves as outcasts, wanderers, exiles from normal society.[37] A number of them had had the experience of literally drifting from place to place.[38] Whether their drifting consisted of modest movement from one shelter to another within the same community or more drastic movement across state lines to different parts of the country, each of them had experienced herself as someone on the run, on the move.

Some homeless women who live exclusively on the streets, who talk with no one, who refuse even to apply for entitlement benefits, are so outside the human community that their stories have been lost to us. Their exile and alienation is so complete that they are unable to come in from the cold long enough to share their experiences. Two such women were approached to be interviewed, and both refused. One woman lived underneath a plastic sheet that she had positioned outside one of the women's shelters. She would allow herself to be near other people, to watch them at a distance, but never to approach. A second woman began the interview process and even agreed to accept some help in finding permanent housing. At the point that an apartment was found for her and she was about to come in from the streets, she became disoriented, delusional, and hostile. She refused to acknowledge her own name, threw her social security check in the trash, and resumed residence on a city grate. She was unable or unwilling to participate in the society of other women and men.

Other women who experienced exile and alienation, yet who maintained some rudimentary involvement with others, were willing to share their stories. Their exile was less total than those who could not talk. These women differed, however, in the extent to which their identity as exile had seeped into their skin and become an integral part of their self-concept. One woman now labeled herself a professional panhandler; another referred to herself as a rambler. For both of these women the sense of themselves as being a rolling stone, someone who moves along, never connected, never really on the inside, had become an integral part of their self concept. For a few women, in particular, the position of being an outcast or exile continued to cause them great personal pain, and while they had become resigned to that position, it was clear that they continued to suffer because of their isolation. For all the women who agreed to tell their experiences, the story of exile is filtered through their own response to alienation. These stories are, in that sense, as much about how to cope with or understand exile as they are about exile itself.

Trixie's Story

Trixie's story of abuse and victimization was described in detail in the previous chapter. Yet, despite her position as a victim, Trixie identifies herself primarily as an outsider, someone who is cut off from the normal comforts of a family and a home. When she discovered the identity of her true mother, Trixie experienced a profound estrangement from the family that had reared her. The people she thought were her brothers and sisters were not really her brothers and sisters, and the woman she believed to be her mother was not really her mother. While she did discover the identity of her real mother, Trixie never learned who her father was. On several occasions, as an adult, she returned to her home-town for the funeral of some distant male relative. As the casket was being lowered into the ground, Trixie always had the same thought, "I wonder if that man was my father."

Trixie also experiences a sense of internal alienation. She feels as if she has been split into two separate people, the girl she was before age twelve, and the child-woman she became after learning the identity of her real mother. Trixie has never been able to reconcile these two different sets of life experiences and these two different senses of personal identity. Trixie often feels uncomfortable with herself, plagued by a feeling that she "does not fit in, does not belong."

Much of the pain that Trixie has felt as an outsider has focused on her gay life-style. At the age of fifteen, she decided that she was a lesbian after entering into a relationship with an older, more experienced woman. She herself speculates that she was looking for a mother in this relationship, but she believes that she found her own sexual identity with this woman. Coming from a small southern town, Trixie always felt that she needed to hide the truth about her sexuality; consequently, she engaged in relationships with men in order to conceal her homosexuality. Trixie thus experienced the characteristic dilemma of the exile: she had to be alienated from either her own inner self or from other people. When people within her town found out that she was gay, Trixie was run out of town, ridiculed, and abused. As she describes her departure from her hometown, it sounds like the departures of ritual exiles who were beaten and banished for some communal sin.

Throughout much of her life Trixie has hidden her sexuality to avoid being further alienated from other people. She has from time to time, however, used her status as an anomaly within the lesbian community to gain some affection for herself. She realized early on that black lesbians were somewhat rare, especially outside of large urban areas. When she was feeling especially lonely, she would go to some small town, a town where she was unknown, and find the neighborhood gay bar. She would position herself in a corner of the bar, setting herself up as a mysterious outsider. She would then watch and see if she attracted the curiosity of any of the other patrons. If any woman looked her way, Trixie would buy the woman a drink and invite the woman to join her. Trixie speculates that she may have been the only black patron ever in some of the bars and she knows she was viewed with a combination of curiosity and fear. Yet she used her status as an outsider, a conversation piece, to attract the attention of someone who might temporarily ease her loneliness and isolation. Trixie knew that these random encounters would never lead to a permanent relationship and that the other person was only approaching her out of curiosity, but she was willing nevertheless to accept any morsel of human companionship. It is tragic that Trixie felt compelled, even within the gay community, to set herself up as an outsider.

Tina's Story

Tina is a feisty, mischievous woman with a Cheshire-cat grin on her face. Her stance to the world is, "I'm homeless and proud of it." This bravado reveals much about Tina's relationship to her own status as an outsider. Circumstances may have made her an outsider, but she is now an outsider by choice. It is as if she recognized that life dealt her a particular hand and consciously decided to play that hand with as much enthusiasm as she could muster. Tina's nomadic existence began when she was a young child. She was the only daughter of military parents, and her family moved many times, not only to different cities within the United States, but in and out of the country on several occasions. Each time they moved she had to leave friends and schools and neighborhoods behind and developed a bravado that said, "I don't care about this. In fact, it's fun to always move. I can't imagine any child who wouldn't want to live like this."

In addition to the sense of being an outsider that Tina experienced from moving all the time, her family was also outside the mainstream of military life. As a black Army officer, her father did not have many peers, and the family was not included in some of the camaraderie that accompanies military life. In addition, even within her family, Tina had the experience of being extra baggage, unwanted and alienated. Neither of her parents seemed to have much time for her, and she was often passed around to other relatives. When she was staying with her parents, she remembers often being put out of the house, either for no reason or for a reason that seemed capricious. After she graduated from high school, her mother decided that Tina should be out of the house from 8:00 in the morning until 8:00 in the evening. Presumably this was to encourage her to find a job or do something constructive. Tina, however, experienced this routine as just one more time in which she was displaced, put out, sent away.

It is ironic that many of the women's shelters in which Tina eventually came to live have similar rules. Women are asked to be out of the shelter from early morning until dinner time in the evening. Again, while there are reasonable rationales for these rules, many women feel as if they are being evicted from their homes on a daily basis.

By deciding that she was choosing to be an outsider rather than being forced to be one, Tina at least imposed some control over her own experiences. She recalls thinking that it would be great fun to be an orphan, having to make it completely on her own, without a family, without anybody to care for her. While it is certainly conceivable that Tina may have felt like an orphan, belonging to a family that really did not want her, or that she feared being completely left alone, it is doubtful that any child would really embrace this as an option. Yet, in order to be strong in the face of circumstances, Tina imagined for herself the worst possible situation and then decided that she would embrace that possibility with all her heart.

Believing herself to be an outsider, Tina even adopted an objective, detached view toward her own life. She describes events in which she herself participated in much the way a clinical observer or a program analyst might. Her exile thus extends to include a sense of alienation from her own internal process and personal experiences. She approaches her life as if events are happening to some one else, and she, Tina, is an outside observer. Her detachment allows her to distance herself from the pain of her loneliness. She can describe how some unnamed homeless woman might feel in a particular situation without acknowledging those same feelings in herself. Ultimately, her defensive detachment only serves to deepen her alienation by cutting her off from herself. Moreover, her detachment prevents her from genuinely engaging with others. When she seems emotionally flat and uninvolved in the events of her life, she is unlikely to move a listener to empathy. It is hard for an observer to take seriously the pain of someone who sounds slightly bored with her own story. Again, her defense only further distances her from others and renders her estrangement all the more permanent.

When talking about the group of homeless mentally ill people who drift from place to place, the psychiatrist Richard Lamb mentions that for some of these individuals the constant movement is an attempt to deny attachment, to deny dependency.[39] Whenever a person feels too connected and consequently too vulnerable to being hurt, he or she moves on to the next place, each time proclaiming that it is liberating to be so free. Underneath the facade of autonomy, however, often lurk the terrible fear of being hurt or wounded and the desire to stay isolated so as to be insulated from any further pain.

In the lines of a poem that Tina wrote is perhaps the best glimpse of her relationship to her own isolation. The verse concludes with the line, "Lost sheep, beep, beep, it's the roadrunner." Tina, perhaps feeling like a lost sheep, isolated and exiled from the group, transforms herself into the rebellious and feisty roadrunner, the cartoon character who zips around and moves so fast that we never quite know where he is. While her transformation may primarily be defensive and self-protective, it is understandable why she would prefer to be the independent and free-spirited roadrunner, isolated and alone by choice, rather than the lost sheep, fearful and vulnerable, yet unable to get back home.

Mary's and Jody's Stories

For both Mary and Jody, two women who suffer from a serious mental illness, the option of distancing themselves from the pain of isolation and loneliness does not seem to be a possibility. For both of these women, their position as outsider is incorporated into their delusional systems. Mary, a young woman who was placed in foster care at the time of her birth, has never had a family. Indeed, she did not even have a name until she was taken in by a foster family who gave her their last name. Having been made part of a particular clan, she now gives that surname to anyone who comes to mean anything to her, thus constantly adding to her imaginary family. With enough honorary brothers and sisters, she will no longer experience herself as being so isolated and alone in the world.

When directly asked about her family, Mary responds in a psychotic manner, saying that she came into the world by magic, magic that she caused by herself. She "birthed herself and transformed herself." While this language sounds delusional and psychotic, it is understandable that a woman who has never had a family, never known a mother or a father, might come to believe that she indeed had been born of herself, and by herself, without the aid or assistance of anyone else.

Mary currently has two great desires, both of which seem connected to her need to lessen her sense of loneliness and isolation. First, she wants to learn to read and write. Partly because of her movement from one foster family to another and the subsequent disruption in her schooling, she has arrived at adulthood without some very basic and fundamental skills. Her inability to read signs, to write things down, and to make simple change all contribute to her feeling like an alien. It is almost as if she has been transported from a different planet, a different country, and some of the simple rules of communication are unknown and unavailable to her. Thus, in a very concrete way, Mary wants to gain some of the skills and information that would allow her to feel as if she belongs in the human community.

Her other wish, while also aimed at lessening her isolation, is somewhat more delusional. Believing that she must be of Indian descent, she wants to become part of a large Indian tribe. She extols Indians as a good and proud people, and she longs to be reunited with her lost clan. This wish, while psychotic in its content, is poignant and transparent in its intent. Mary is a woman who feels that she is outside any community, ostracized from any real family, and she consequently imagines that she must be part of some family somewhere, a family of which she can be proud. It is her fervent desire to be reunited with this imagined tribe.

Jody's delusions are not focused on her reunion with a lost clan, but rather on her attempt to understand why she is so alone and so isolated. When she describes her childhood or her time in school, all she can remember is that she has always been alone. Consequently, she has developed a theory that people around her are disappearing. As Jody looks around her and compares her life experience and her social group to those of other people, she cannot quite understand why there seem to be so few people in her life. Consequently, she has concluded that while she started with the same sized family, the same number of supports, and the same number of friends that other people have, those who belong to her are being magically taken away. In fact, when talking about all the things in her life, not just the people, Jody comments that everything that she owns seems to get lost, seems to disappear. Any books that matter to her or articles of clothing that she likes just seem to vanish. While most people might be distressed, even terrified, at the belief that relatives and friends were randomly disappearing, Jody finds this a more tolerable perception than the realization that her world is, and always has been, empty.

While Jody's belief about a conspiracy of magical disappearance does explain why there are so few people in her life, it also presents her with a view of the world as a transitory and unstable place. People are not to be trusted because they might disappear at any moment. She is never really sure of an experience or of a new relationship because evil forces, magical forces, seem to change the nature of things uncontrollably.

When Jody remembers relationships or connections with other people, she usually faces traumatic and unpleasant images. Most of the people with whom she has lived have rejected her for some reason, usually, she believes, because she did something objectionable. She frequently castigates herself for not being holy, righteous, or good enough.

Not surprisingly, with a belief in the haphazard disappearance of other people and a suspicion that there is something evil and unnatural about herself, Jody has been attracted to a number of unorthodox religious sects. She is convinced that people perform voodoo rites against her, and she frequently mumbles incantations to try to keep evil spirits and harm doers at bay. It is tragic that this woman has to choose between a world that is empty and barren and one that is evil and threatening.

The experience of being an outsider or an alien, a stranger in the community of other men and women, is a long-standing one for each of these women. Each woman, however, interprets her position as exile differently. Trixie is forever reminded of the difference between herself and other men and women. Tina embraces her status as exile, proclaiming that it is the only way to live. And both Mary and Jody build delusional explanations to help them contend with the reality of their lonely lives.

The experience of being an exile or an outcast predated the homelessness of each of these women. As young girls they felt disconnected or disaffiliated from the larger society. They often felt that they were outside their own families, as if they did not fit in or belong. For many, the pattern of drifting from place to place was also well-established before they became adults and actually became homeless. Yet, each of these women, once she experienced actual homelessness, also experienced an additional form of ostracism or exile from the larger community.

Homeless people clearly exist on the periphery of mainstream society. They are outsiders looking in, standing in lines, waiting to get in from the cold. Once homeless, individuals find additional reasons to keep running, to keep moving, and to impose a state of exile on themselves. It has been suggested that some of these individuals may even run in an attempt to outrun their problems, forever trying to find a new life or a new start in the next town or the next community.[40] Others keep moving, as was mentioned before, to avoid attachments that might be dangerous or hurtful. Some also drift because they do not develop the interpersonal comfort or the intrapsychic stability necessary to put down roots and establish a psychological as well as a physical home in any one place.

Beyond the personal function that exile serves for the women who wander the streets, the existence of exiles serves a function for the larger community as well. When we see people who so obviously do not fit in and so obviously seem to be out of step with the main rhythm of the society, we may reassure ourselves that we are indeed in step and comfortably accepted by the "in" crowd. The existence of a caste of obvious exiles also provides us with a ready pool of people onto whom we can project our own transgressions and sins. Like the escape goats of old, these modern outcasts can take our undesirable and unwanted parts away with them when they wander from place to place.

Chapter 8

The Predator

As a culture we are probably more ambivalent about our predatory selves than about any other aspect of our collective psyche. The predator is that part of the self that is capable of victimizing, destroying, or manipulating another solely for personal gain.[1] Put quite simply, predators kill. The killing may be physical or psychological; in either case, there is irreparable harm or damage. And while extreme violence and destruction may indeed be rare behaviors, they nevertheless exist on a continuum of more commonly occurring forms of predatory activity: assertiveness, aggressiveness, and competitiveness. The existence of predatory behavior among men and women is not at issue: people are capable of violent behavior. Individuals differ in the extent to which they manifest predatory behaviors and in the manner in which they react to such behaviors, observed either in themselves or in others.

It is in our reactions to acts of violence that we can discern the highly ambivalent relationship most of us have to our own evil and aggressive sides. We are proud of our aggressiveness, for example, when it is defined as strength and toughness; yet, when it slips into cruelty or sadism, we become ashamed and horrified. We revel in our assaultiveness as long as it is confined to the boundaries of a football field; yet, when it runs wild on our city streets, we lobby for more police protection, protection against that part of ourselves that has gotten out of control. Indeed, one of the primary ways in which we handle our own aggressive and predatory self is to contain it and confine it to certain well-defined arenas.

Perhaps the most obvious example of delimited aggression is the area of competitive sports; we allow ourselves to be rageful, vengeful, and even sadistic when it comes to the competition between hockey or football teams. Indeed, we allow ourselves to talk of crushing, destroying, or eliminating the enemy; and many of our athletic teams are identified with predatory totems. It is common to open a newspaper's sports section and find the Lions fighting the Bears or the Giants attacking the Tigers. This display of violent and aggressive behavior occurs within clear, limited boundaries: the game begins at a certain time, and it ends at a certain time. The activity is confined to periods or quarters that limit and control the behavior of the players. Moreover, there are clear rules and regulations, and, just in case the players are unable to follow these rules, these predatory games we establish for ourselves have built-in police officers, referees, or umpires who control the play of the competitors.

Similarly, with the sport of hunting we give ourselves permission to kill animals and birds only during specific seasons of the year. Regulatory boards decide when the killing can be done, how much killing can be done, and even who can do the killing. The boards license particular individuals and set quotas on the number of animals, fish, or birds a single hunter can bring in. In this way predatory behavior is allowed but its expression is strictly controlled, with sanctions for those who violate the established rules and regulations. Ironically, while we condone the frenzy that often accompanies competitive sports, we encourage our players to be good sportsmen and sportswomen, and we encourage our hunters to respect the sanctity of the wilderness.

Sam Keen in his book *The Faces of the Enemy* suggests that warfare, especially conventional warfare, allows men the periodic opportunity to realize their urge to be cruel and predatory.[2] War is sanctioned by the government, and individuals are praised and honored after the combat experience. We expend much financial and personal energy to train young men in the art of warfare. Such training in the techniques and lore of combat serves several functions beyond the most obvious one of preparing young men in the event of an actual conflict. It honors the warrior as a legitimate and noble model for identification among young men, while imparting the message that being a warrior is not a calling that comes naturally. Rather, one needs to be trained in order to perform predatory and aggressive behaviors. Such training once again imposes an element of control and discipline on what might otherwise become rampant violence.

Another way in which individuals channel their predatory inclinations is to redirect those instincts in the service of more esteemable and noble causes. Men are encouraged to be champions of industry, thus directing their aggressive and often predatory instincts toward the goal of making money. As Keen observes, the language of warfare is often used when talking about success in the corporate world.[3] A successful investor can boast of making a "killing" on Wall Street, and corporate innovators protect their ideas from industrial spies in the same way that countries protect military secrets. Indeed, corporate giants from Henry Ford to Donald Trump become not only the subject of biography and fiction, but also the object of admiration and envy for many young entrepreneurs. Similarly, we can justify being aggressive if it is in the service of eradicating some social ill.[4] As a country we are always declaring war on poverty, drugs, illiteracy, or some social problem that justifies our all out assertive and aggressive attack.

When we channel or contain our predatory instincts, we are at least acknowledging that we have those instincts, permitting them to have free reign only within certain limited arenas. It is far more dangerous for society when individuals deny that sadistic and violent impulses are part of our human nature; those affects are then projected, according to Sam Keen, onto the "face of the enemy."[5]

A complicated process occurs when we opt to project our own

evil and aggressiveness onto others. At the first stage, we merely project out the undesirable affect, seeing it as belonging exclusively to the other person. We are not dangerous and violent; it is the other person who has these capabilities. In stage two, however, we become frightened of the predator we ourselves have externalized. If the enemy is indeed as dangerous as we believe him or her to be, then we have cause to be worried or frightened for our own safety.

In stage three, in an attempt to defend ourselves from the evil that we now believe is securely lodged in other people, we begin to acquire some of the same aggressive and predatory behaviors that the predator possesses. These behaviors are in the service of defending ourselves and protecting our homes. Thus, we arm ourselves and become vigilant, perhaps even outwardly aggressive, not because we feel these emotions inside ourselves, but because we must assume these behaviors to defend ourselves from the enemy without. By stage four, we have become full-fledged predators, villains and perpetrators; however, we tell ourselves that this persona has not seeped into our skin. We wear it merely as a measure of self-defense and could cast it off easily, if only the enemy did not pose such a threat.

Given the complicated nature of this projection and the subsequent reintegration of aggressive behaviors, it is a wonder that it is ever possible for warring countries or warring individuals to lay down arms. A person would need to own his or her individual aggressiveness and violence, a process of self-awareness that, had it been present at the beginning, would have obviated the initial need for the projection.

Finally, we allow ourselves to participate vicariously in violent behavior. Despite warnings against the harmful impact of television and screen violence, commercial television continues to present viewers with over forty thousand murders a year.[6] Similarly, news tabloids depict everything from cannibalism to incest to serial murder and have no shortage of customers.

At a safe distance from our everyday lives, through the media of film or print, we can allow ourselves to participate in the world of violence. Some television depictions of violent crimes allow us additional protection from our own violent impulses by encouraging us to identify with law-enforcement officers and assist in bringing to justice the nation's most-wanted criminals. These dramas simulate violent crimes and invite viewers to ally with the "good guys" not only in fantasy but in fact. By phoning information anonymously to law-enforcement officials, viewers may assist in the apprehension of the criminals being portrayed. Thus, television spectators indulge their violent inclinations vicariously by watching the reenactments of real crimes while at the same time identifying with the protectors of law and order and believing themselves to be good citizens.

If acknowledging the inner predator is difficult for most men, it is a nearly impossible task for most women. Anne Jones, whose book *Women Who Kill* describes the lives and circumstances of women who actually commit murder, maintains that women have been socialized to think of themselves as nonviolent.[7] Aggressiveness, competitiveness and even assertiveness, are often discouraged in women, who, as little girls, are taught to be demure and mannerly. Consequently, most women find a confrontation with their internal aggressor to be an alarming and disorienting experience.

The image of female violence is so disconcerting for us that we must invent elaborate rationalizations to explain its occurrence. Not infrequently, these explanations invoke "necessity" as a partner in female violence. If we believe that women commit violent acts only because they are forced to do so, or because they must do so in order to survive, then we can acknowledge specific acts of violence while still maintaining our belief that women are essentially nonviolent.

In his discussion of the psychological meaning of specific Greek Gods, the mythologist James Hillman gives significant weight to the often-ignored Greek Goddess Ananke.[8] Ananke is the Goddess of Necessity, and she represents those things in this world which cannot "not be." Thus, despite free will and individual autonomy, there are certain elements of human existence that cannot be otherwise, that are given as part of human nature.

In describing the functions of Ananke, Hillman references the conclusion of Plato's *Republic*, in which each soul, after having been created, must pass beneath the throne of necessity.[9] In this final ritual, before a soul enters the world, the as-yet-unborn individual's future actions must be blessed or approved by necessity, that which must be.

Explanations of or attempts to understand female violence explicitly or implicitly suggest that some form of necessity, a modern-day Ananke, was involved in the violence. Thus, we assume that when a woman is violent, it is because she cannot be otherwise. The particular set of circumstances that necessitate her violence may vary widely. Often her violence is an act of self-defense; she is merely protecting herself from some egregious injury. Often she is transformed into a victim before her own destructiveness can be justified. As the victim of sexual, physical, or economic abuse, she has no choice but to strike out in an effort to free herself. In some instances, her violence merely reflects certain natural and universal rhythms over which she has no control. Regardless of the origin of the necessity that accompanies female violence, most depictions of feminine violence, occurring either in historical accounts or in the mythological and fictional literature, portray necessity as an accomplice to acts of violence committed by women.

In day-to-day life, necessity also plays a part in feminine violence. Many women who commit violent acts are themselves the victims of violence or sexual abuse. One warden of a women's prison in Pennsylvania reported that 30 percent of the women criminals were victims of incest or sexual abuse.[10] The tendency of victims to grow up and themselves become abusers has been noted often. Regrettably, young children are unable to contain the rage and disappointment they experience at being hurt or abused by a parent. They often feel the need to find some place to dump, and thus rid themselves of, this rage.[11] Such psychological unloading not only lessens the pain they feel at being wounded, but also allows them to gain some revenge without having to attack directly the powerful parent who committed the original offense. Victims thus find other victims with whom they can act out the prey/predator drama.

Psychiatrist James Grotstein comments that this tendency of abuse victims to reenact their violent dramas with another person now in the role of victim serves magically to ensure the safety of the original victim.[12] By identifying with the predator, a former victim feels safe from further abuse. If some victims of abuse feel compelled to commit violence, they may well be operating under the powerful sway of necessity. Having been victimized in childhood, some women may feel that they cannot do other than to victimize their own families or to brutalize others who are less strong than they.

Using a sociological filter rather than a psychological one, Jonathan Kozol also sees the inevitability of future violent behavior in the lives of some homeless children. Referring to one particular young child with whom he had spoken, Kozol comments "innocent tonight, she may be transformed into a tough and lean and predatory woman in two years."[13] Growing up in such impoverished conditions, a child often has only one of two choices: either she turns her anger upon herself and devalues herself, or she turns that anger outward and vents it upon society. A number of the children that Kozol interviewed had good reasons to feel intense hostility toward the larger society, and precious few reasons to accommodate themselves to the norms of a society that seemed intent on rejecting them.

Growing up in a shelter environment, some children do learn to struggle, connive, lie, and attack anyone who appears to be threatening. One homeless woman, in describing the circumstances of her own life and the limited options her children faced, said to Kozol, "My kids are not killers, but if they don't learn to kill, they know they are going to die."[14] One can hear the voice of necessity in such a statement. Children not only learn predatory behaviors, but they must utilize those behaviors if they are to survive in an aggressive and unkind world.

While we may not be surprised to recognize the necessity and the determinism that operates in the lives of real men and women, it is perhaps more surprising to see how many of the mythologies of violent women or violent goddesses contain an element of necessity as well. Many of the terrible mothers and death goddesses of transcultural mythologies are viewed as a necessary part of the normal cycle of birth, death, and rebirth that is natural to the universe. The violence of these goddesses is as normal and as necessary as the nurturing and life-giving side of the Great Mother. On a more individual level, many of the goddesses commit violent acts because they have been betrayed, abandoned, or injured. Even in the Pantheon of the Gods and Goddesses, necessity seems to be involved in acts of female violence.

In emphasizing the role that necessity plays in explanations of feminine violence, my intent is twofold: first, to depict the reality of feminine violence (many women do commit acts of violence because they feel they are powerless to do otherwise), and second, to acknowledge, once again, the difficulty most of us experience in accepting the true female predator. If we include necessity as an accomplice in acts of violence committed by women, then we can lessen the responsibility that individual violent women must bear. Explanations that appeal to necessity, over and above their veracity, allow us to temper our reaction to the female predator.

The stories of predators and our reactions to them, whether they are historical predators, mythological predators, or live predators, reflect the stories of our own ambivalent and conflictual relationship to our aggressive predatory side. Perhaps more than any other aspect of the shadow, violence and dangerousness make us uncomfortable and uneasy. Sometimes we deny our rage, at other times we try to contain it, and occasionally we enjoy it, but often we run from it. The stories that follow exist not only as stories in their own right, but also exist as examples of how our collective consciousness has tried to deal with the problem of the internal predator.

Historical Predators

Historically, one of the ways in which we have dealt with violence and aggressiveness is to assign those tendencies to single individuals. We contain our own violence and destructiveness by aggregating it and projecting it out onto one or two people who come to be known by name and to embody evil and destructiveness for the rest of us.

In contrast to the faceless and anonymous victim, the predator emerges as a distinct, identifiable individual. By so isolating and naming the predator, we can allow ourselves to believe that such reactions, such violent behaviors, constitute abnormal human events, occurring only on the part of a few named and unusual individuals. The tendency to identify and individualize the predator is so strong that we often do so even when we have no real name for someone who has committed a series of crimes. In some cases, famous criminals or famous murderers are known by the location in which their crimes were committed. Thus, the Boston Strangler was referred to by his location before detectives actually knew his unique name and biography. Similarly, the Zodiac Killer in California was identified by his method of operating when law-enforcement officials did not know the actual identity of the person committing the crimes.

When we particularize and name the criminal, the evil one among us, we can enjoy a sense of security. We can rest safe in the belief that dangerous, violent, and evil behavior is not the province of all humankind, but, rather, the specific deeds and acts of a few men and women. What is intriguing is that once named, many of these famous villains become the subject of folklore, rumor, and fictional accounts. By particularizing and individualizing criminal behavior, we gain some control over the predator, allowing us to get close enough to be fascinated by the nature of his or her crime.

Even after she has been named and identified, it has been difficult for us to understand the female villain or criminal. Because women who commit violent crimes frequently do so against their immediate families, against husbands, lovers, or children, we experience their crimes as shaking the very structure of our social and family life. To imagine a woman as the murderess of her own family is to challenge everything we believe about women. Indeed, for a woman to turn on those she is supposed to nurture and to do them harm seems an abberation of nature itself.[15]

In Hindu mythology there exists a story that illustrates the chilling paradox of the violent mother. The story begins with a devotee of Hinduism having a vision of the goddess Kali.[16] In his reverie he sees a beautiful young woman arising from the waters of the Ganges River. The woman is far advanced in pregnancy, and she emerges from the water glowing and radiant. As she stretches out on the side of the river, she proceeds to give birth to a charming and adorable baby. The visionary watches the woman as she nurtures and nurses her child. The vision is brutally interrupted, however, as the young woman undergoes a radical transformation. She is changed from a beautiful young mother into a cruel and frightening hag, a hag who turns on her own baby, seizes it, stuffs it into her mouth, tears its flesh, crushes it, and finally swallows it. Bloated now with her dead baby, as she was once bloated with new life, the goddess returns to the waters from whence she came.

This image is jarring and difficult to assimilate, not simply because of the horror of the act, but because the destruction is perpetrated by one who should be loving, nurturing, and caretaking. This juxtaposition of violence and lovingkindness in the same mother is almost impossible to comprehend. Because of this incompatibility and the psychological dissonance it creates, we have transformed many of the female villains of history in one way or another. These transformations allow us to comprehend the violent behavior of a woman, who is expected to be calm, demure, nurturing, and life affirming.

One way to comprehend the violence that a woman commits against those in her care is to decide that the person who commits the violence is not a real woman; she is a subspecies of human, different from other women and even from other humans, more animallike, more violent, and, thus, not really participating in the human community. Indeed, in describing some of the women who were accused of murder in the last century, Anne Jones comments that both the popular press and the legal system defined some of these women as subhuman.[17]

Bridget Durgan, a young woman who in the middle of the nineteenth century was hung for the murder of her employer, was described as being a combination of a wolf, a hyena, a hog, and a tiger.[18] Observers noted further that she had the eyes of a reptile, the cunning of a panther, and the mouth of a cat. In all likelihood, this uneducated young woman suffered from epilepsy, yet accounts of her behavior rarely mentioned any legitimate illness, and she was defined as being outside the human species.

As long as the female criminal is viewed as a hyena or a tiger, her behaviors have no relevance for other women or for men. Women do not have to fear that they might be similarly violent, and both men and women, who at one point in time were nurtured and cared for by women, do not have to worry that their mothers will turn into wild predators. Our mothers are women; murderesses like Bridget Durgan are animals.

In her discussion of anger, the Jungian analyst Marie Louise von Franz distinguishes between hot anger and cold anger.[19] Hot anger is burning, smoldering, impulsive affect that bursts forth in an emotional eruption. It is the anger that might induce a crime of passion, the anger that a young, impulsive woman like Bridget Durgan might have experienced. The anger that von Franz labels as cold anger is the scientific, highly intelligent, planful anger that guides such evil characters as the villainesses in James Bond spy stories. These are cool, mechanical exterminators. While some of the women who committed murder were dehumanized by being labelled as hot, out-of-control animals, others were transformed by being called ice matrons, ruthless fiends, vampires, creatures equally nonhuman but with a more cold and calculating style.

As an alternative to denying female violence by dehumanizing the woman who commits a criminal act, we refuse to recognize feminine rage and destructiveness by blinding ourselves to a woman's responsibility for a given crime. The infamous case of Lizzy Borden is an example of such mass denial.[20] Borden was the unmarried daughter of a wealthy businessman. She was quite literally the rich daughter of a patriarchal society. While Lizzy Borden was reputed to dislike and to quarrel frequently with her stepmother, public opinion, as well as the jurors in her murder trial, found it unthinkable that this young woman could actually commit the horrible crime that brought an end to both of her parents. Her parents were not murdered cleanly and genteelly with poison, but rather they were hacked to death with an ax.

The young woman was acquitted of her crime primarily because the jury and the judge could not believe that a woman of her social class would commit such a hideous crime. Her crime was not merely murder, but patricide, and as all of the people who judged Borden were themselves fathers, it was a crime whose very existence they refused to acknowledge.

Following her acquittal, Borden's behavior was somewhat unusual for a bereaved daughter. She not only spent her father's money lavishly to improve her life-style, but also flaunted her new independence. Moreover, her inappropriate behavior for an unmarried woman in mourning flouted societal norms and conventions. Yet, despite her unconventional behavior and clear physical evidence of her guilt, the legal system found Lizzy Borden innocent, because to consider her guilty would have been intolerable for her accusers.

Subsequently, Lizzy Borden's actions have been interpreted and fictionalized, supplying several different explanations for her crime. Some people have assumed that she must have had a lover, a man, who urged her to commit the crime. Others have assumed that she was epileptic and thus not responsible for her actions; recently, still others have labelled her as a prefeminist in revolt.[21] Regardless of current explanations, at the time of her trial society dealt with Lizzy Borden by denying her responsibility for her crime.

In the case of Lucrezia Borgia, the daughter of the infamous Borgia family of Rennaissance Italy, history has been split in its verdict as to her guilt or innocence. The Borgia family was implicated in a series of murders and political crimes. Murder by poisoning came to be associated with the infamous Borgia venom that eliminated many of their political rivals. Yet historians are particularly vague on what role, if any, the daughter Lucrezia played in these villainous machinations. She has been described as the most notorious woman in Rennaissance Italy: conniving, scheming, adulterous, and licentious.[22] She has been accused of having incestuous relationships with both her father and her brother. Such descriptions would cast her beyond the pale of normal behavior and relegate her to the ranks of those subhuman female predators.

Other reports, however, refer to her as the illustrious duchess and recount her patronage of the arts and her good deeds on behalf of impoverished young women. She has been described as a lovely and charitable woman who would undoubtedly rest in the "fragrant peace of her many good deeds".[23] Such an account identifies her as a woman who did no evil, because she was constitutionally incapable of doing evil. Historians have defined Lucrezia Borgia as either a subhuman monster or as a suprahuman saint incapable of any wrongdoing. In either case, there is a failure to see her as a real woman with a destructive and sinister side.

More recently we have come to understand many examples of female violence as acts of self-defense. Forty percent of the women who commit murder do so for this reason.[24] These are women who have been battered and beaten and who often kill to protect themselves and their children. Self-defense is recognized as a legal argument in the trials of men and women who commit violent crimes, and the legitimacy of self-defense as an explanation for murder is not at issue here. Many women, themselves the victims of abuse, have felt that they had no alternative but to commit homicide to save themselves. What is important for our current discussion is that self-defense is yet another explanation that allows us to deny the inherent violence and dangerousness in all of us. When we cast female violence as a reasonable and rational response to an intolerable circumstance, then we once again use the defense of necessity. An abusive set of circumstances made it impossible for a reasonable person to do anything but commit violence. We deny that violence is an inherent part of the human psyche and therefore a human possibility that all of us must confront.

We do not do justice to women who commit violence when we seek to find explanations for their actions that are primarily rationalizations. If we turn these women into animals so that we can distance ourselves from them or if we deny them responsibility so that we can maintain our notion that women are not violent, then we contribute to the real dehumanization of women. Women, just as men, contain within themselves all human possibilities, even violence and aggressiveness.

Indeed, Jones concludes in her book that it is not the exceptional woman who commits murder, but rather it is "every" woman who commits murder.[25] It is the average woman, perhaps in the unaverage situation, who becomes rageful and violent. She is not any different, any better, or any worse, than the rest of us. The violent woman has merely been pushed beyond her personal limits or has relinquished the social controls that allow most of us to contain and deny the potential villain that lives within each of us.

Mythological Predators

While there are numerous examples of female predators within classical mythology, most of these dangerous and destructive women fall outside the range of normal female behavior. Even when these women represent some aspect of the feminine goddess or the feminine principle, they are still portrayed as being so extreme and so grotesque as to set them and their actions apart from the behavior of most women.[26] While many instances of female violence exist, the women who commit the rageful acts are far from being ordinary women.

One of the most easily recognizable forms of the female predator is the woman warrior. She appears originally as the Amazon of classical Greek mythology, but she is just as discernible in the modern comic-book character "Wonder Woman." She is a powerful soldier, able to defeat many men at a single blow, preferring either to live alone or to be in the company of other women.

In Greek mythology, numerous references are made to the battling Amazons. While questions have been raised about the existence of such a society of combative women, their real existence is irrelevant for this or any purely psychological inquiry. What is relevant here is that such a figure existed and continues to exist in the imagination of both men and women.

The Amazon is a woman who enjoys bloodshed. She was born and reared to fight, and tribes of Amazon women were reputed to have conquered Greek city states and dominated the indigenous population. In addition to their prowess as fighters and the obvious pleasure which they took in competition and in bloodshed, these women developed an unusual social system in which traditional or conventional female behavior was avoided. The society's primary raison d'etre was warfare; anything that might conflict with that aim or with the continued dominance of women was quickly remedied. For example, it is reported that the Amazons routinely broke or crushed the arms and legs of any male children born to the tribe.[27] This brutal and unmotherly practice was designed to prevent male children from growing up to be strong and capable warriors who might overthrow the female leadership. Instead, the Amazons engineered the production of a society of crippled and defective men.

In a further attempt to deny men power within their community, Amazon women devised an ingenious plan for increasing their population. Each year women of childbearing age would retreat to the mountains for two months with a group of men, there engaging in frequent and anonymous sex.[28] The sex always took place in the dark, and the particular identity of a male partner was always masked. Consequently, it was impossible for a particular woman to know who had fathered her child, and it was also impossible for a particular man to know who his own offspring might be. Such a strategy was designed to maintain matrilineal descent. Each individual knew only the identity of his or her mother.

In both their behaviors and their values, the Amazons displayed a complex relationship to both masculine and feminine principles. They personally embraced traditionally masculine attributes of aggressiveness, assertiveness, and combativeness, but they only prized those masculine values in women. They preferred men to be docile, crippled, and anonymous. These mythological women cultivated the psychological man within themselves while devaluing and avoiding flesh-and-blood men.

Just as they denied the externalization of masculine values, the Amazons also denied the internalization of the feminine principle. They disallowed their nurturing, caretaking function with respect to their male children; they imposed strict prohibitions against any empathic bonding with a potential mate; and they denied themselves the opportunity to form a caring, loving relationship within a family unit. Their allegiance was only to the next battle and to the image of the warrior.

Perhaps the most brutal example of their denial of their own femininity was the mutilation that Amazons inflicted on their daughters. It has been reported that Amazon women burnt away the right breasts of their daughters.[29] This was ostensibly done to allow the girls greater ease in using their right arms for spear casting or archery. Yet this maiming also served the function of denying or reducing the feminine appearance and the feminine identification of the young woman. While Amazons are credited with being a nation of *women* warriors, it is paradoxical that they are predators and combatants by becoming de facto men. In this instance, the female predator is liberated only in a woman who denies her femininity and embraces a masculine way of life.

What is most intriguing about the stories of the Amazons is that they are mythological accounts and not historical reports. Thus the stories of a race of predatory women reflect the projected psychological content and the collective imaginations of men and women. One might speculate that these stories allow women to vent their repressed but secret desires and that the stories are all the more violent and extreme because they contain content that has been denied and sequestered. The stories may also reflect the secret fears of men, fears that if women are independent and strong, they will become violent and destructive.

The story of Penthesiliea, an Amazon queen who fought in the Trojan War, further illustrates the dynamic tension between masculine and feminine principles in the mythologies of predatory women. Penthesiliea was a headstrong, arrogant, and contemptuous young woman who believed that she could defeat anyone who came within the range of her sword.[30] She challenged the heroes, Achilles and Ajax, to battle, inspiring the demoralized Trojan armies to rally and fight. She was not satisfied with her victories alone, but wanted to humble Achilles, teaching him that women were indeed more powerful than men.

She prepared for her final battle, excited and pleased at the impending blood bath; she felt no squeamishness or hesitation as she headed off into combat. While she and her women were able to kill many of the advancing opponents, they were no match for Achilles and were eventually defeated, Penthesiliea herself being killed by Achilles.

The story does not end with the Amazon's death, however. Once Achilles slays Penthesiliea, he is himself slain by her, not in a physical sense, but psychologically and emotionally. He is overcome by her great beauty and falls into mourning and weeping, regretting that he has killed her and wishing he had taken her prisoner and made such a noble woman his wife. In the conclusion to the myth, we once again witness the tension between masculine and feminine principles in the female predator. The Amazon warrior feels she can only defeat the hero by becoming a better man than he is, fighting him more fiercely, more violently, than he has ever been fought before. In truth, the only way that she can, and does, defeat him is by being more of a woman not more of a man. It is as a woman that she brings down the great Achilles. As a beautiful and desirable woman, she weakens him; as a warrior, she is unable to defeat him.

While it was not the intention of the author of this story to suggest that women can be more deadly by being women than by trying to imitate men, this has been a common perception of the female predator. As a seductive, crafty, and sexual opponent, she is able to mesmerize, disarm, and at times destroy her male rival. By using her feminine attributes, she is more deadly than when she engages in hand-to-hand combat as was the way of the Amazons.

Unlike the Amazons, who were portrayed as fierce young maidens, most representations of the female predator are an embodiment of the Terrible Mother, the death-bringing and destructive half of the Great Mother goddess.[31] Most ancient civilizations contain evidence of a female figure who embodies the principles of the Great Mother. This goddess contains within herself the sum of human existence. She represents the ebb and flow, not only of the universe, but also of each individual's unique life. As the mother of all life, she is the creatress of the universe. Moreover, she nurtures new life, developing it and causing it to flourish. In a completion of the life cycle, however, she brings about death and destruction. Death is thus recognized as being as much a part of the human experience as life and birth. The universal life cycle, however, does not end with the death of a particular individual. There is new birth, new life, and new growth to continue the cycle.

In many civilizations these different aspects of the feminine principle, or the Great Mother goddess, were split and projected into separate goddess images.[32] The Good Mother was responsible for birth, nurturance, and the affirmation of life, and the Terrible Mother represented death and destruction. She was the devouring, consuming earth that at one time may have brought forth life, but eventually held the body of the dead in the form of the grave or the tomb.

Mythologically, many female villains, predators, and destroyers are a representation of this aspect of the Terrible Mother. Characteristically these female fiends take one of several forms: blatant and hedonistic murderesses who revel in the blood-bath that they cause; seductive sirens who use their sexual charms to destroy their victims; or cold captors who strangle the life energy of their prey, turning victims into nonhuman images.

As the bloodlusting goddess of death, the female predator delights in crushing her victims. She not only kills, but she enjoys the destruction, often bathing herself in blood and devouring the bodies of men, women, and children. When visualized, these goddesses of death are often seen as monsters. The Hindu goddess Kali, whose name means "black one," is described as being as dark as night.[33] She is frequently depicted as crouching or standing over the corpse of her latest victim. She haunts cremation grounds, surrounded by her consorts: jackals, snakes, and ghosts. In her many hands she carries the instruments and trophies of destruction, often holding a sword, a hangman's noose, a freshly severed head, or a trophy cup made from a human skull.

Kali is no ordinary woman; she is a monster who embodies death and destruction. Indeed, a temple dedicated to her in Calcutta, India, doubles as a slaughterhouse.[34] Believers come and have their offerings slaughtered at the temple; the head and blood belong to Kali and are left for the goddess, but the supplicant may take the body of the animal home to be used for food. Because Kali is so insatiable for blood, the extent of the slaughter is enormous, and visitors describe the temple as being a fetid slaughterhouse rather than a pure and holy place. It is, however, appropriate that Kali's temple should be frightening and brutal. Kali is not, after all, a clean and dainty goddess. She revels in blood, death, and destruction, and those who worship her must be prepared to confront the raw and physical nature of her power.

The Aztec goddess Coatlicue presents an equally horrifying visual image.[35] Instead of a woman's head, her head consists of the heads of two writhing snakes. Her hands and feet are clawed. Around her neck this female creature wears a necklace consisting of the hands and hearts of her human victims. Her warriorlike breastplate is made of a human skull, and her skirts consist of writhing serpents. This creature is hardly recognizable as a woman, yet she is a female goddess. She has been transformed, however, by her worshippers into an animallike creature who looks like the death and destruction that she brings. As with many of the death goddesses, it is hard to mistake her for a normal woman.

In contrast, the women who bring death and destruction by sexual seduction resemble beautiful, enchanting maidens. On his voyage back to Athens, for example, the Greek hero Odysseus encounters the beautiful Sirens.[36] These are the women who sing a song so lovely and so enchanting that any who hear it are bound to deviate from their course and go toward the Sirens. Of course, this seductive song is only an enticement; the Sirens destroy and devour their victims. Some unlucky sailors are shipwrecked on the rocks; others who reach the Sirens are turned into unwilling victims for these devouring witches.

Similarly, in the Biblical tale of Samson and Delilah, the seductive Delilah, whose name means "she who makes weak," charms the powerful Samson and tricks him into allowing her to rob him of his power and strength.[37] In the case of both the Sirens and Delilah, the female predator uses her feminine charms in the service of destruction. Part of the seductress's power comes from the fact that her victims find her irresistible and are duped into thinking her harmless as well.

More gruesome and more explicitly sexually destructive are those goddesses known as the vagina dentata. These goddesses, who are often pictured as having huge vaginas lined with sharp, protruding teeth, devour or rip their victims to shreds in the course of the sexual act.[38] The Navajo goddess Snapping Vagina, for example, squats beside her victims and engulfs them.[39] Her birth canal, once the passageway to life and to consciousness, now becomes the route to death and destruction. Thus the once life-affirming, nurturing mother becomes the devouring, hostile, destroyer of her own creation, her womb transformed into a tomb for her unwitting victims.

The combination of blood lust, sexual seductiveness, and the fertility cycle of birth, death, and rebirth can be seen clearly in the myth of the Celtic goddess Skadi. Known as the "queen of the shades," Skadi was an embodiment of the death-bringing goddess.[40] Each year a man was chosen to represent a god and to engage in a bizarre and lethal sexual dance with the goddess. A rope was tied to the genitals of the man with the other end of the rope being tied to a goat; the goat was then instructed to pull, ripping the flesh of the male victim. The goat pulled the sacrifice toward the goddess, and as his flesh gave way and his genitals were ripped from his body, he fell into the lap of the goddess, bathing her in his blood. Devotees of Skadi believed that if the goddess smiled, spring would return to the land and the crops would bloom forth once again. This violent sexual dance, ending in the death of the male partner, satisfies the blood lust of the Terrible Mother. Thus satisfied, she brings forth new life and new growth into the land.

Less passionate but equally destructive is the cold, vengeful anger of still another group of death-bringing women. Best exemplified by Medusa, the Gorgon whose hair is a mass of writhing snakes, these female predators kill by turning their victims into stone.[41] Their form of murder is not a bloody one; instead they sap the life force from their victims, turning them into inanimate figurines, a grim reminder of the life that used to be. These cold predators are so powerful that they do not even need to touch their victims. If the victim merely looks at the face of the monster, he or she will be destroyed. The Medusa's very essence is destructive, and any contact with her will petrify her victims.

While many female predators are gruesome in their deathbringing forms, they have themselves often been transformed from benign or even beautiful women into monsters. Medusa, for example, was once a beautiful young woman who offended the goddess Athena by desecrating her temple.[42] To punish her for this offense, Athena transformed Medusa into a deathgiving monster whose tongue protruded from her mouth, whose eyes glared like fireballs, and whose huge teeth hung from her mouth like fangs. She became a creature who only vaguely resembled the woman that she once was.

The depiction of the female predator as an extrahuman monster affords us the opportunity to speculate further on our relationship to the violent woman. Indeed, many people believe that when a woman becomes violent and rageful she does indeed cease to be fully human; she resembles an animal, a beast, a wild and out-of-control creature who is more monster than human. We can conjecture that extreme rage is inherently dehumanizing, contorting and distorting our features so that we look monstrous, not only to others but to ourselves as well.

It is also possible, however, to interpret the tendency to depict female predators as monsters in another light. It may be that only by distancing the female predator from normal women can we accept her existence. The need to gain distance from the woman of destruction is shared equally by men and women. For a man to imagine that he has a mother like the goddess Kali who might turn and devour him at any moment or a wife like the goddess Skadi who might rip his genitals from his body is terrifying. Similarly, for a woman to consider that there exists within her a raging beast who is as committed to death and destruction as to life and regeneration is a horrifying prospect. It may be the case that both men and women desire to see the female predator as something other than human; she is an extraordinary case existing off the continuum of normal human experience. As a result, we may look with horror and awe at her destructiveness but paradoxically remain safe in the belief that her destructiveness is not a human possibility.

Living Predators

Millie's Story

While Millie's story recounts her personal violence and aggressiveness, it also depicts the history of a violent family. Millie occupies the second generation in three generations of battered and violent women, a generational chain that ultimately produced a woman capable of murder.

Millie was reared by her father and stepmother and has early memories of watching her father beat her stepmother and rob her of any money she might have. He would use the money that he extorted from his wife to buy alcohol. Millie's stepmother, who was also her first female role model, was not an especially violent woman, and she passively accepted the abuse of her husband. Even as a young child, Millie could not tolerate watching her stepmother be hit, and even though she was only five or six years old, Millie would beat on her father while he was hitting her stepmother. Her punishment for her assertiveness was to receive beatings herself from her father. Being abused, however, did not stop her from challenging her father and meeting his violence and aggression with her own immature and reckless violence.

Once while her father was beating her, Millie bent her head down between his legs and took a bite out of his penis. He stopped the beating and began to scream; Millie took off down the street and remembers being triumphant at the obvious pain she had inflicted. Her punishment for this aggressiveness was to be sent away from her father's home and placed in the care of her paternal grandmother, who lived in the country.

At that point Millie's story begins to resemble that of Cinderella; she is beaten and abused by her grandmother, by her aunt, and by her cousin, who is the favored grandchild in the home. She is also made to do all the menial work around the house. Millie does not, however, behave like a passive Cinderella; she fights her grandmother, swearing, cursing, and hitting the old woman back. For several years, while living with her grandmother, Millie's life consisted of a series of attacks and counterattacks. When her grandmother died, Millie remembers doing a triumphant dance and singing "I'm glad you're dead, you old cow." This ritual sounds much like Dorothy's rejoicing at the death of the wicked witch in *The Wizard of Oz*.

Millie's experience with both her abusive grandmother and her father did not leave her unscarred. She learned how to be a street fighter, how to bite, claw, and attack in order to survive. Following the death of her grandmother, Millie's aunt assumed the role of arch-villain. By this time, however, Millie was fifteen years old and was not prepared to allow another tyrant to rule her life. One evening when Millie was at a dance enjoying herself, her aunt, who was also at the dance, ordered her to sit down and behave herself. Millie decided then and there that she had had enough of being ordered around by this woman, and she pulled a knife out of her boot and went after her aunt. She remembers cutting her aunt across the body and across the face several times. Each time she slashed her, she remembers saying to herself, "this is for the time you did this to me; this is for the time you did that to me." By her own account, her attack on her aunt was a violent act, full of vengeance and spitefulness.

When Millie was finally old enough to be on her own, she moved to Washington, D.C., searching for someone with whom to stay, but, in particular, searching for her natural mother from whom she had been separated as a small baby. Regrettably, Millie's story does not end with a happy reconciliation with her natural mother. Instead of finding the nurturing mother that she had lost, Millie found a man just like her father.

Millie's husband beat her, stole her money, and drank excessively. Millie, however, was not a woman like her stepmother, and she did not sit by passively while her husband abused her. Instead, she fought him frequently and violently. On several occasions they went after one another with knives and engaged in battles of cutting, slashing, and cursing. On one particular occasion Millie was injured so badly that she was hospitalized for several weeks, the story of her domestic violence being so extreme as to make headlines in local newspapers.

While she was in the hospital, her children were taken from her and put into foster care; however, the vision of their mother and father fighting to the death made a powerful impression on all of these children, especially on Millie's eldest daughter.

Several years later this daughter married a man like her father and her grandfather, who gambled, drank, beat her, and who took her money from her. Having watched the repeated abuse of her mother, Millie's daughter decided that she would not be a victim to years of violence. One day she called her mother over to her apartment and walked into the bedroom where her husband was sleeping. She carried with her a loaded gun and, pointing to her husband, said to her mother "I'm going to kill that man."

Millie was taken aback by the direct and flat way in which her daughter announced her intentions. The daughter went on to explain that she had watched someone abuse her mother and she was not going to allow herself to be the victim of years of abuse. Calmly, quietly, she took the gun and aimed at her husband's head. The young woman fired with every intention of killing her husband. With the deed completed, she sat down passively with no intention of hiding or running, prepared to accept whatever punishment might come her way. A neighbor eventually called an ambulance and the police. Millie's son-in-law survived, but her daughter was accused of attempted murder. One might speculate that Millie's daughter was acting not only for herself but also for her mother, her grandmother, and generations of other women who had been unable to act for themselves. Her invitation to include her mother as a witness to her violence suggests a desire to turn her personal vendetta into a ritual event.

While the story of violence within her family ends with her daughter's attempt at murder, Millie's personal story does not end there. She went from place to place, engaging in occasional scraps and unsuccessful relationships for quite some time. Eventually she settled into being a caretaker for an older man, a position that she occupied for close to five years until the time of his death. Following his death, she was without a residence and became homeless; she wandered the streets and shelters for almost three years.

In the subculture of homeless women, Millie was more often a predator than a victim. She used or abused other more vulnerable women, even intimidating some women and extorting their money.[43] Yet her years as a homeless person seemed to sap some of the fight out of Millie. Recently, after finally moving into an apartment of her own, Millie was hospitalized following an ambiguous suicide attempt. She apparently left the gas on in her apartment and had a seizure. It is unclear whether or not this was an intentional suicide act or an accident.

It may be that after years of directing her anger and fight out toward the world, Millie became tired and gave up. Some of the anger that had been inside of her for so long became directed inward and focused on Millie herself. No longer strong enough to fight the world, Millie found a more passive and, regrettably, a more willing object for her violence, namely herself.

Ruth's Story

Ruth's story is a classic tale of a victim turned predator. As a young girl Ruth was both physically and sexually abused by her father. He frequently fondled his young daughter and on one occasion actually raped her. In addition to his sexual abuse, he beat her and threatened to shoot her with a shotgun if she did not behave.

While the abuse by her father was clearly traumatic, Ruth was also damaged by her mother's failure to believe her when, at age thirteen, she accused her father of raping her. Her accusation resulted in her being examined medically and receiving psychological counseling; doctors and therapists confirmed that she had indeed been raped by her father. Despite this corroborating evidence, her mother continued to disbelieve Ruth's story, even telling Ruth that her own loyalty would always belong to her husband and that she would never allow herself to believe he was capable of such abuse. Following her mother's refusal to believe her story, Ruth stopped speaking, a behavior that lasted for almost four years. Eventually her inhibition became so severe that she was unable to speak and had to be sent for speech therapy and counseling.

Ruth's reaction to her father's abuse and her mother's betrayal did not end with her refusal to speak. She became a violent and dangerous young woman, she periodically ran away from home, she drank, she slept in abandoned cars, and she carried with her a two-by-four plank that she was prepared to use as a weapon against anyone who got in her way. She routinely and consistently got into fights, fights that resulted in physical violence both to her and to the other people involved.

Now in her fifties, Ruth's face bears the marks of repeated street brawls. She is scarred, swollen, and almost toothless. While many of her fights were impulsive, spur-of-the-moment affairs with Ruth engaging in combat with anyone who crossed her path, she occasionally set out after a particular person with the goal of repaying some former injury. On one occasion she went after her sister for a childhood grievance; she took a hot iron and held it down on her sister's hands, thinking to herself at the time that she was paying her sister back for past injustices.

During her street-roaming days, Ruth describes herself as a female Joe Louis, a real tiger on wheels willing to take on any and all comers. The image of a woman so filled with rage that she lives for the violent encounter resonates with the image of the ancient Canaanite goddess Anath. Anath, a goddess identified with war, was a savage and brutal woman who responded to any and all situations with tremendous violence and bloodshed.[44] When she was unable to find real victims to battle, she would turn on the objects of furniture in her home and fight in a wild frenzy, battling against tables and chairs, smashing them to bits. Anath embodies the woman who needs to fight, who creates battles for herself; when there are no real battles, she indulges in imaginary warfare. Such a woman seems plagued by inner turmoil and may feel as if there is a war going on inside her. In practice, she is engaged constantly in projecting her inner violence and anger outward and attacking enemies under every bush and rock.

One religious scholar has speculated that Anath may have represented the psychological projection into mythology of unreasoning, irrational rage, borne of frustration and despair.[45] Certainly Ruth was a frustrated and despairing young woman. The rage she felt at both her father for his abuse and at her mother for refusing to believe her story of violation was enormous; she became a walking tiger, fighting, growling, and snarling at everything and everyone that crossed her path.

When Ruth eventually married and started a family of her own, she vowed that she would make her home different from the home in which she grew up. Her children would come first, her husband would come second, and perhaps she would come third. While Ruth's husband occasionally beat her to get her money, she knew how to defend herself and would frequently fight back. For the first ten years of her marriage she managed to keep her anger within normal bounds and limits; however, when her daughter was nine years old and came to her one day to report that her father, Ruth's husband, had tried to rape her, Ruth flew into a rage. She became uncontrollable, rushing home from her job at a luncheonette and chasing her husband with an ax. In a frenzy she swung at him and cut off his penis. She then dragged his body, shoved his head up toward the chandelier, put a rope around his neck, and, as she says "watched him flap like a chicken with his wings cut."

This act is so brutal and so macabre that it must have been committed by a woman crazed. She was, when she attacked her husband, reliving her own experience as the young girl who was raped and not believed and was avenging not only her father's crime, but her mother's crime as well. She was the judge, jury, and executioner toward her bewildered husband.

Surprisingly, Ruth's husband survived the attack; Ruth, however, was taken to a psychiatric hospital and eventually lost custody of the children she so desperately wanted to protect. She recalls being taken away with chains around her wrists and ankles as if she were a wild beast that had just been subdued. Her behavior is reminiscent of a mother lioness whose young have been attacked and who fights back with all the fury and frenzy of one fighting for life.

In his book *On Aggression,* Konrad Lorenz cites the fury and violence of which all animals are capable when they fight to save their lives.[46] This aggressiveness is borne out of desperation, and we can assume that Ruth was fighting for her psychological life when she attacked and attempted to kill her husband. Once hospitalized, Ruth did not calm down. She remained a raging wild woman for quite a long time, attacking other patients, attacking hospital staff, and spending much time in isolation.

Since her discharge from the hospital, Ruth has spent most of her life on the streets. She is fiercely independent and, although she tries to control her violent and aggressive behavior, she is a street fighter, a woman willing to fight for her physical safety and to protect her turf against the invasion of others. She describes hiding in abandoned buildings with a small candle to see who might be entering her space and a trusty steel pole at her side prepared to take on any intruder.

Now that her daughter is a grown woman, Ruth has had a chance to talk with her about the incident involving her father. Rather than being pleased at her mother's violent behavior, Ruth's daughter remembers being terrified. Indeed, there were other times when the daughter subsequently experienced abuses and refrained from telling her mother, for fear that her mother would go berserk again. In truth, Ruth has no grey area when it comes to abuse; one is either guilty or innocent, and if one is guilty, then one deserves to die.

Despite her tough and hardened exterior, Ruth continues to experience inner pain as an adult woman. Her father has long since died, but her mother, now an invalid, continues to disappoint Ruth. Ruth helps her mother, cleaning her apartment, shopping for her, and visiting her frequently. She continues to hope that her mother will give her some sign that she, Ruth, is loved and valued, and she continues to seek an apology from her mother for the betrayal that occurred years ago. Yet Ruth waits in frustration for these signs of reassurance and support. Even as she herself nears sixty years of age, she wonders how she will survive when her mother is dead and there is no longer any chance for reconciliation.

Carla's Story

Carla can be an evil and destructive woman; yet she carries no weapons and bears no obvious scars. Indeed, she has never been involved in a physical fight and presents herself as a very cool and composed woman. Her violence, rather than being of the obvious physical sort, is of a more psychological nature. Because Carla's particular brand of violence is not of the kind that we usually encounter, it is useful to put her predatory style within a theoretical context.

In his book *The People of the Lie,* Scott Peck attempts to address the issue of personal evil and describes the kind of person who engages in violent and predatory behavior of a psychological and spiritual nature.[47] First and foremost, these individuals are committed to maintaining a particular view of themselves. This view is often idealized and certainly self-serving. Moreover, the individual clings tenaciously to this overly positive self-concept.

To maintain what Peck believes is an essentially deceptive sense of self, the individual is willing to sacrifice friends, family, or anyone who might present a conflicting view.[48] Unwilling to accept self scrutiny or self blame, such people, who Peck labels "people of the lie," repeatedly distort reality, constantly blaming others for their indiscretions.[49] Since experience rarely presents us with only idealized and positive views of ourselves, these people repeatedly distort and control their experience. In so doing, they also distort and control the experience of others. This is the nature of their particular brand of violence and destructiveness. They must control and ultimately destroy the contrary experience of anyone with whom they interact because their own fragile sense of self cannot tolerate any discrepant information.

Carla describes herself in glowing and idealized terms. She sees herself as an independent and unusual woman whose strong beliefs and incisive intelligence are difficult for others to appreciate. She blames any lack of recognition of her talents on the boorish and naïve nature of the world, which does not fully appreciate her.

Her description of her childhood is similarly idyllic. She defines herself as having been among the best and the brightest, precocious and lively. She defied social conventions within her neighborhood by choosing friends who were outside her social class, but, as she reasoned even then, friends who were more appropriate to her particular talents. Perhaps the most truthful thing that Carla reports about her childhood is that she engaged repeatedly in play acting: she constructed roles for herself and devised numerous scripts that she and her friends acted out. It is likely that to be able to maintain her idealized view of herself as a child, Carla did need to play a number of roles and to write and rewrite her experiences constantly.

As an adolescent and then as a young adult, Carla spent time experimenting with a number of possible careers. She reports that she was always successful and talented but frequently bored and unchallenged by the material. Consequently, she reasoned that any failure she experienced was not her fault, but rather the fault of the educational system, of teachers, or of classmates.

In her late twenties Carla decided that she would like to have a

child, and she went about having a baby in an unusual and me-
thodical way. She decided that she would choose someone who
had a good genetic makeup and allow this man to impregnate
her. She had no desire for a relationship or for the more conventional way of having a baby. Rather, she wanted to mix her own
biological heritage with that of an appropriate other person. She
comments somewhat proudly that she did indeed find an intelligent, good-looking, charming man as an appropriate mate. One
is reminded of ancient rituals in which a man is chosen to represent the god and to have sexual intercourse with a woman who
represents the goddess. This ritual mating is part of a yearly fertility
rite.

While Carla does not describe herself as a goddess, she certainly
does go about choosing someone who might be an appropriate
god to mate with her idealized image of herself. And indeed her
son, the product of this unusual union, is described by her as an
ideal child. Because he is such a perfect child and because Carla
feels a moral obligation to be what she terms a perfect mother,
she has set about to control and determine every aspect of her
child's life. She chooses his clothing, his interests, his friends, and
his schools. She is aware that she is unlike other mothers, but she
attributes her difference to the fact that she is better than other
mothers: she has higher values and higher standards than normal
mothers do. She is also aware that she uses manipulative techniques to get her son to conform to her wishes, but she justifies
these manipulations on the basis of her desire to protect her son
from any damage. Because he is so unique and so special, he
needs to be protected, and she justifies all of her behaviors on
that basis. What she seems to be totally unaware of is that her
attempts to control this child, who by now is a young man, dampen
and destroy any individuality or autonomy that he might have. His
need to make his own decisions or in any way to create his
own experience is denied by Carla. Control, manipulation, and
destructiveness have been redefined by her and are now called
"good mothering."

Carla has used her devotion to her son to explain all of the
failures that she has experienced in her own life. For example, her
failure to hold a steady job is explained by her need to be available
at home lest her son should need her in an emergency. The sorry

state of her personal finances, her failure to pay her rent, and her eventual eviction are explained by her as resulting from her decision to use all of her money to buy the very best for her son. She says that she was proud to be homeless because it meant that she was a mother who gave more of herself than the average mother. One can easily see how much Carla needs to maintain her domineering relationship with her son. By controlling him, she is able to enhance her positive identity as a good and devoted mother and she is also able to explain away any of her personal failures.

Following her eviction, Carla was homeless for almost a year, and during that time she lived in several of the women's shelters in the city. To preserve her view of herself as a superior and intelligent woman, Carla once again constructed an explanation of her tenure in the shelter that was somewhat unusual. She reasoned that she was something like a sociologist, different from and apart from the other women, doing a naturalistic observation of the lives and mores of homeless women. In a critical and analytical way, she observed interactions among other women in the shelter, always making sure to keep herself separate and distant from them. At the same time, she was described by shelter operators as hostile, critical, and condescending toward other residents. One assumes that she needed to maintain this posture to keep alive her fantasy that she was an intellectual researcher instead of a homeless woman down on her luck and dependent on others.

During the transition phase from shelter life, in which Carla moved from the shelter to a series of shared apartments before eventually obtaining an apartment of her own, Carla had three separate roommates. Each apartment situation deteriorated when the other woman was hospitalized for either a psychotic or a depressive episode. All three times Carla was implicated in the onset of the other woman's symptoms. She was hostile, critical, controlling, and demeaning toward her roommates. Often insightfully zeroing in on the other woman's vulnerability or low self-esteem, Carla would berate the other woman about her inadequacies. When confronted with her destructive behavior toward these other women, Carla commented that she was merely trying to be helpful and lamented being placed in the role of therapist toward these more impaired and disadvantaged women. She could in no way see that her controlling and contemptuous behavior was damaging to these other women, and she took no responsibility for the exacerbation of their psychiatric symptoms.

Ultimately, Carla moved out of the program into an apartment of her own and into a permanent employment situation. She seemed to have learned little from her experience as a homeless woman; instead, she felt confident and triumphant that she, in distinction to many of the other homeless women, was able to move on and become successful. She remained confident that she was a superior breed of woman.

For each of the women who lived as a predator, violence and aggressiveness (whether physical or psychological) played an important part in her everyday life. Perhaps because, as in the cases of Millie and Ruth, she herself had been the victim of abuse, or perhaps because, as in the case of Carla, she had to defend and buttress a fragile sense of self-esteem, each of these women indulged in destructive or dangerous behaviors. At times each felt proud of her power and her ability to intimidate others, and occasionally one could even detect a hint of pleasure in a particular description of physical or psychological triumph. What is striking in the lives of each of these women is how each came, however justifiably, to actualize the predator. The usual social and intrapsychic sanctions that restrict the predator in most women ceased to operate for Millie, Ruth, and Carla.

Because violence and evil are so frightening in others as well as in ourselves, we might be tempted to try to distance ourselves from women who lead violent lives and to say, as writers in the past have done, that they are less than human or different from ordinary women; yet, in meeting and interviewing these women, I was repeatedly reminded of how like "every" woman they were.

Chapter 9

The Rebel

Since it is the very essence of a rebel to defy, oppose, or resist some external force, one may be tempted to define a rebel by the nature of his or her opposition. Historically, rebels have opposed governmental, societal, and religious tyrannies.[1] To see rebellion purely as an act of opposition, however, would be to miss what the existentialist writer Albert Camus has labeled as the silent partner accompanying every overt renunciation in the act of rebellion.[2] That silent partner, rather than being a second opposition or a negation, is an affirmation. Camus maintained that when we say "no" to one set of values or principles, we say "yes" to another set.[3] Every genuine act of rebellion contains both a negation and a positive affirmation.

While the rebel may be affirming a set of external values, such as the liberty, equality, and fraternity championed by rebels of the French Revolution, he or she may also be motivated by a more personal level of affirmation. Frequently, the man or woman in revolt says "yes" to an essential part of the self that must be defended.[4] The individual feels that external demands, expectations, or forces are impinging on and violating his or her own authentic sense of self, and it is in defense of the true self that the individual revolts. While the individual's true self may be in danger of physical death, it is more often in danger of a psychological or spiritual death. Consequently, the rebel affirms the psychological life of the self and its right to an independent existence. In rebelling, the individual says "I have had enough; I will not tolerate, I cannot tolerate, any more of the existing conditions, and I will endure whatever psychological or physical pain may be forthcoming in order to put an end to this oppression."

In his book *Legends of Our Time,* Elie Wiesel, the Jewish writer and holocaust survivor, tells the story of a rabbi interred in the death camp at Auschwitz.[5] Watching the humiliation and destruction of the Jewish people and their apparent abandonment by their God, this rabbi declares that he has had enough, and he rebels against God. In explaining his reasoning to a young disciple, he says, "I have reached my limit; if He (God) knows what He is doing, then it is serious and it is not any less serious if He does not. Therefore, I have decided to tell Him, it is enough."[6] In this particular case his act of rebellion is primarily an act of affirmation. While he says "no" to God, he fundamentally says "yes" to himself, to that part of himself that cannot blithely and obediently accept intolerable conditions.

Considering the psychological development of the rebel, the writer Simone de Beauvoir comments that one must feel free and whole as an individual in order to rebel and that while an impaired or damaged person may be able to negate and oppose, it takes a self-aware individual to affirm positive values in the act of rebellion.[7] If one is not free to know the self and to know one's personal limits and principles, then one does not know when those principles or limits are being violated. Only when one perceives, however tentatively, the existence of an autonomous self, can one assume the position of a rebel.

While each act of rebellion may contain elements of affirmation and negation for the rebel him or herself, outside observers either approve or disapprove acts of rebellion depending on the nature of their outcomes. For example, if a rebellion results in expanded possibilities for a group of people, it is usually seen as being constructive, and when oppressed peoples riot, rebel, and overthrow a dictatorial government, historians are likely to praise their rebellion. On the other hand, some rebellious behavior is defined as being primarily destructive. When prisoners riot, rebel, kill their guards, and demand control of their own lives, journalists and political observers are likely to look with disapproval on such an uprising.

We need look no further than the classical Greek and biblical mythologies to discover two outstanding examples of rebellions that follow similar patterns but have been judged differently. Prometheus, brother of Zeus and one of the Titans, rebelled against Zeus in order to give fire to men and women. His act of rebellion was creative and life affirming in that he sought to benefit humankind by his actions.[8] By both defying and duping the Lord of the Gods, Prometheus not only rebelled against the established order, but he asserted his own right to be an independent and creative person. He was the son of a noble race, the Titans, and he would not be told what he could and could not do.

Similar motives empowered the biblical rebel Satan; however, his revolt against God, rather than being seen as courageous and creative, has been perceived as basically destructive and willful.[9] Satan, like Prometheus, wanted to be a creator; moreover, he wanted to be his own creator. Yet, in asserting his creativity, he was primarily destructive; he did not offer his defiance in the service of others, but it was instead selfishly motivated.

Scott Peck in his book *People of the Lie* describes a kind of evil rebellion in which the individual makes a destructive or violent choice simply to exercise his or her free will.[10] The individual knows that his or her behavior is rebellious, antagonistic, and oppositional, and, moreover, that its likely outcome will be destructive; yet, he or she proceeds solely to affirm his or her independent self. While such an act would qualify, under Camus's definition, as an act of rebellion, it is clearly a rebellion with an undesirable outcome.

Ironically, while rebellious behavior may be driven by the individual's relationship to his or her self, it is evaluated by others for its impact on the external environment. When the individual's rebellion results in needless death and destruction to others, even though the rebel may feel personally affirmed, society will likely condemn his or her actions because of the cost to innocent victims, putting more emphasis on the common good than on the individual's struggle for autonomy.

Generally, when we think of the heroic rebel, we are likely to picture a brave young man in that role. This affiliation of the positive rebel with the masculine gender follows from society's attitudes toward men and women rather than from the definition of the rebel itself. In reality, the majority of visible and romanticized rebels have been men. Women are often socialized to be conforming, passive, and respectful of authority. Such values make it difficult for women to allow the development of their autonomous, separate selves, much less to legitimize acts of overt rebellion toward the existing hierarchy. Many of our folklore and fairy tales depict heroines in passive and dependent positions. Young women are often found waiting, either awake or asleep, for a handsome prince to liberate them from oppressive conditions.[11]

I remember working in psychotherapy with a very dependent young woman whose favorite fairy tale was the story of "Snow White." In the story the young princess bites a poisoned apple and is confined to a glass coffin where she lays in a deathlike sleep, waiting for a prince to come, kiss her, and awaken her from her entrapment. I asked my young patient if she could rewrite the story, giving Snow White more power to act on her own behalf. The young woman was dumbfounded; she could not imagine an active heroine. While the story might easily have been rewritten without including any act of rebellion or defiance, an altered ending might require some assertiveness or autonomy on the part of Snow White. The patient in question was absolutely unable to construct or even envision such an ending.

The socialization that most women receive limits the number of women who feel comfortable actualizing the rebel in themselves. The few who do rebel must confront society's negative and critical response toward their rebellious behavior. While males who rebel may be labeled as creative and pioneering, women who rebel are often judged neurotic.[12] A woman's rebellion, rather than reflecting the assertion of her independent self, is often seen as stemming from the assertion of her neurotic and unhealthy self,

with true individuation for women lying along the path of conformity.

So uncomfortable are we with the positive female rebel that it
is common for us to define women who rebel as masculine.[13] If
we see the rebellion arising from the assertion of a woman's
essentially masculine self, then it is easier for us to accept the
woman who rebels. That one's *feminine* self might be the author
of defiant or rebellious behavior is more difficult for us to integrate
with our standard notions of femininity. Such notions do not
include the image of a woman in revolt.

More than just being alien to our experience, however, the
woman rebel is viewed with trepidation and misgivings. It is as if
many members of society feel challenged by the woman rebel,
believing her defiance and resistance to cultural norms and expectations to be a threat to the fabric and foundation of society. In
fact, many anti-ERA activists have made this argument: if women
are allowed to rebel, to challenge traditional expectations, and
to defy patriarchal hierarchies, they will eventually destroy the
substance and strength of family and communal life. Because of
the perceived threat from the rebellious woman, society has taken
pains to discourage and actively squelch her rebellious behavior.

In a Sunday sermon, a nineteenth-century clergyman admon-
ished the women in his congregation with the following warning:
"Stay within your proper confines and you will be worshipped.
Step outside and you will cease to exist."[14] As long as women are
obedient and respectful, they will be well taken care of and even
idolized; when they are defiant or rebellious, the established order
will have no choice but to ostracize them. This was certainly the
case with the Mormon feminist Sonia Johnson (whose story will
be discussed in greater detail below), who found herself excommunicated from the Mormon church when she chose to defy the
established hierarchy. One cannot defy and continue to exist.
Defiance is thus equated with annihilation.

Society's different attitudes toward male and female rebels can
be discerned by examining how we view the homeless population.
While it would be unjustifiable to define all people who are homeless as rebelling against social norms, it is possible to identify a
subgroup of homeless people who are in active defiance against
familial and cultural expectations. Specifically, researchers have

identified a subgroup among the homeless mentally ill who fit the sterotype of the rebel.[15] These individuals not only value their independence, but also prize their uniqueness and differentness from others. In their actions, and often in their words as well, they say to the world, "I will have a life on my own terms even if I have to live it on the streets."

The personal histories of these street rebels frequently reveal an unwillingness to conform to social conventions and communal rules. They often first become homeless when they are evicted from homes or apartments for not following the rules expected of tenants. These individuals tolerate the streets as an acceptable abode because only on the streets do they feel they can be themselves, free of other people's rules and expectations.[16]

Observers of the New York City shelter system have commented on the contrast between the shelters for men and those for women.[17] The rules and structure of most men's shelters reflect an appreciation of and a respect for individual autonomy and independence. The male homeless rebel is allowed to maintain his position of nonconformity, and residential staff in shelters for men often look the other way as residents develop a natural peer hierarchy within the shelter, resembling a "survival of the fittest" street culture.

The women's shelters present a marked contrast. Rules within these shelters are often overly rigid, and shelter staff adhere, often vehemently, to a hierarchical internal structure.[18] Rules and expectations begin before a woman even enters the shelter system as most shelters for women have a series of admission criteria designed to exclude those who do not conform to certain minimal standards. Once in the shelter, women must be in bed by 10:00 o'clock; they must sign in for all of their meals; and they must perform certain housekeeping chores and duties. Furthermore, they are prohibited from lying on their beds during the day.

While one might argue that these rules and regulations create a more livable shelter environment for women than the somewhat anarchist milieu of the shelters for men, these rules also might be seen as controlling or containing the female rebel. By requiring women to be present at meals, to perform housekeeping duties, and to go to bed early, shelter providers are inadvertently demanding that these women conform to standard expectations of acceptable female behavior. Ironically, these expectations are foisted on many women who have walked, if not run, away from traditional expectations. They are not homemakers, they may have abandoned husbands and children, and they live unconnected and often lonely lives, denying any need for affiliation and dependency. If a system were purposely desiged with the goal of containing or breaking the rebellious spirit of women, the design might not be dissimilar to the one that exists for women in New York City.

Without overdramatizing the difference between the shelter systems for men and women, one might at least see how these different approaches reflect differential attitudes toward the male and female members of society who are rebellious and nonconformist. We are, in general, better able to tolerate, and even to value, defiant behavior in men. We are more ambivalent about rebelliousness in women, we often deny its existence, we sometimes actively try to control or dampen it, and we are frequently frightened by it. These largely negative attitudes toward the female rebel are evident as we look at the lives of historical, mythological, and living rebels.

The Historical Rebel

Historically, women have rebelled as much with their lives as with their ideas.[19] By actively living lives that press against the normative boundaries of society, women have defined themselves as rebels. They have become outlaws by breaking societal bonds and expectations. It is not uncommon for a woman who is identified as a rebel to have a child out of wedlock, or to be involved in an unconventional romantic relationship.[20] By failing to lead traditional lives, these women say, in effect, that they refuse to live the lives that have been expected of them.

In her discussion of the lives of many early feminists, Alice Rossi maintains that while some of these women were able to rebel against the larger society from within the confines of a supportive, liberal family, others had to rebel not only against societal norms, but against the values of their immediate families as well.[21] Elizabeth Cady Stanton, the suffragist and friend of Susan B. Anthony, was disinherited by her father because she chose to lecture on behalf of women's rights.[22] To friends, she described herself as a woman at the boiling point, a woman in revolt, but she did not have the support of her husband, an active abolitionist who was not also a proponent of women's rights.[23]

Even within the feminist movement Elizabeth Stanton was a rebel. She chose to fight not only for a woman's right to vote, but also to challenge one of the foundations of patriarchal society, the Christian bible. Stanton wrote what might have been the first feminist version of the bible, changing some exclusively masculine language to include a role for women. Because her feminist colleagues realized that debunking the religion of the patriarchy might compromise their fight to win the vote, they tried to discourage Stanton from pressing her cause. Being a true rebel, she had a vision of a better way of life, not only for herself, but for others as well, and she would not be dissuaded, even when her closest companions attempted to turn her from a course of action. It is not uncommon for a rebel to act not only on his or her own behalf, but on the behalf of others as well.[24] The true social rebel is as uncomfortable with the oppression of others as he or she is with the oppression of the self.

Another early feminist who embodied the spirit of the rebel was Margaret Sanger. She led the fight for birth control and for each woman's right to control her own body. Sanger was an adamant and passionate campaigner and even published a magazine entitled *The Woman Rebel*. She strongly believed that women must say "no" to the exploitation of their bodies, for without control over the decision to conceive a child, women would never be truly liberated.

Margaret Sanger attributes her own awakening and the beginning of her revolt to a time when she was asked to help a young woman who had unsuccessfully tried to abort an unwanted pregnancy.[25] While Sanger was able to save the young woman the first time she was called to her home, she was unable to save her on a subsequent occasion when once again, pregnant by her husband but unable to rear another child, she attempted to abort the fetus. The death of this young woman and the pleas of so many other women who desperately begged Sanger to help them find a way to control their own bodies convinced her to embark on a campaign that would culminate in 1916 with the opening of the first birth-control clinic in the United States.[26] By her actions, in her writings, and in her passionate commitment to change,

Margaret Sanger was saying, "No, I've had enough," not only for herself but for the thousands of women with whom she identified, women who might not be able to speak with the same self-assured and confident voice, but whose impassioned pleas caused Margaret Sanger to say for them, "We have had enough."

More recently, Sonia Johnson, the author of *From Housewife to Heretic,* shared the story of her evolution from a dominated and perfectly conditioned Mormon housewife to a liberated woman.[27] The title of her book tells her story. She was a devoted wife and mother and, in the Mormon tradition, a woman who saw her place as being not only at the side of her husband, but slightly beneath her husband as well. Over the course of several years, during which time she became awakened to the women's rights movement, she broke away from not only the oppression within her family but, more specifically, from the oppression within the Mormon Church, committing actions for which she was eventually labeled a heretic and was excommunicated by the church.

Like many women rebels, Sonia Johnson remembers her first rebellious act. She recalls going, when she was fifteen years old, to a ceremony within the Mormon Church known as chastity night.[28] During the ceremony a respected woman within the church engaged in a ritual designed to symbolize the defilement of the female body that was likely to occur if any of the young girls assembled in the audience surrendered to sexual temptation. The speaker began her lecture by plucking and crumpling the petals of a beautiful white rose. As each rose petal fell to the table she commented that the fallen petal was similar to a young woman's fallen honor should she allow herself to be sexually available. Just as one could not put back together the beautiful rose from the crumpled and tarnished petals, one could also not regain one's chastity if one relinquished it.

Johnson recalls being horrified while listening to this church wisdom. She knew in her heart that there was another truth (that the God in whom she believed was a forgiving God and allowed the possibility of repentance, reparation, and renewal), and, she subsequently spoke out against the message that her elders had attempted to teach. While she did not receive much communal approval for her outspokenness, she knew that there was a voice within her that spoke of a reality different from the reality reflected by the external hierarchy, and she knew that that voice would need to be respected and honored.

As an adult woman, her rebellious self was nourished by feminist literature she read. She decided to embark on a committed struggle for equal rights for women within the Mormon Church. As an ardent supporter of the Equal Rights Amendment, she spoke and lectured around the country. Johnson describes hearing the sound of her own inner voice telling her that the patriarchal religion of her past was a sham and, moreover, that she must respect and honor her own authority and experience.[29]

The negation in her rebellion involved saying "no" not only to the Mormon Church, but to the patriarchal God whom she had been taught to revere and love. This negation was accompanied by a companion affirmation, an affirmation not only of her own internal voice, but also of a religious world in which both the father and mother in heaven might be honored. This religious world was not only closer to Johnson's own experience, but was also one in which she as a woman might feel affirmed and valued.

In Sonia Johnson's story, as in the story of other women rebels, we see a woman who was made to choose between honoring and affirming her own self, her own inner voice, and the voice of the external society. While she did ultimately choose to honor her own internal reality, her choice was not made easily. Indeed, much struggling, pain, and doubt went into the ultimate decision to follow an independent course of action.

For most women rebels, the denial or disowning of past values and a past way of life involves a loss. Often these values, rather than being felt as external, are an integral part of one's personal value system. Consequently, in the early stages of a rebellion one must distinguish among those inner values that belong to the true self and those other inner values that are solely internalizations of societal expectations.

For the artist Georgia O'Keeffe no such inner dialogue seems to have been necessary. She never doubted that she was unique and different from other people, possessing an independent self that deserved to be actualized.[30] With her life, with her art, and with her conscious definition of herself, Georgia O'Keeffe said, "I will be different; I will be unique."

She remembers that as a young woman she had a conscious

desire to avoid being confined by the limits that society placed on her gender.[31] Even as a child, O'Keeffe knew that she would not lead the traditional life of a wife and mother. She made her decision not to conform as a young girl and was known as the "black sheep" of her family for her crazy and different ideas. Her family's disapproval did not daunt her; in fact, it may have encouraged her for she continued purposefully to do things contrary to what others expected. She would sometimes dress differently or wear her hair differently from other girls just to be distinct and separate.

O'Keeffe recalls being asked when she was twelve years old what she wanted to do with her life and saying with absolute certainty, a certainty that surprised even her, that she wanted to be an artist.[32] She also shocked herself and her peers by declaring that she was certain God was a woman. Her unconventional and individualistic beliefs clearly set her apart from others, but they also helped to define her as a young woman who was confident in her position and in her power.

In her personal life, O'Keeffe defied convention. As a young woman, she lived with Alfred Stieglitz, a successful photographer, many years her senior, and married at the time that they began living together. Yet, knowing that she loved him, O'Keeffe let her own feelings define what was right for her and refused even to consider anything other than what was true to her own internal self. When she eventually married Stieglitz, she chose to keep her maiden name, a decision unique for a woman in the early 1900s. She chose to remain Georgia O'Keeffe because she wanted to make sure that whatever successes she accomplished, she got on her own.[33] In reading about her life, one gets the sense of her as a woman who repeatedly and actively willed herself to be unique and autonomous.

Despite the fact that she loved and was devoted to her husband, O'Keeffe left her husband every year to return to the Southwest to paint. When people criticized her for her abandonment of her husband, behavior not expected of a dutiful and devoted wife, she commented that she could not be a painter if she stayed home and held her husband's hand.[34] In this statement one hears the voice of a woman who says "I will be who I am, not who you want me to be."

As an older woman, O'Keeffe again defied convention by taking as an apprentice a young man who eventually became her heir and, as many speculated, her lover. While it was common for older male artists to take their female models or apprentices as mistresses or companions, female artists were sanctioned for similar behavior. Yet, Georgia O'Keeffe defined herself as an artist, not as a woman artist; consequently, whatever rules and mores applied to artists applied to her as well.

In her artwork, O'Keeffe often broke the rules of conventional painting. With color, size, and shape she ventured in new directions. She was committed to surviving as an artist at the turn of the century, a time when women painters did not support themselves with their art.

O'Keeffe was aware throughout her life that she said "no" to what people expected of her and what they wanted her to do. For her to be an artist was to say "yes" to her own self. She believed that in her art she could be free to be as she wanted to be and to do as she wished to do; when she was alone with a canvas, who she was and what she did was no one's business but her own.[35]

Throughout her life, O'Keeffe was surrounded by rumors about her personal life and about her psychological health. Toward the end of her life, she commented that she actually enjoyed those rumors and perhaps even encouraged them from time to time, believing that the more elaborate the rumors, the more distant they might be from her true self.[36] She could hide behind these rumors and stories and thus protect and maintain her own private and independent self.

Georgia O'Keeffe defined herself in opposition to certain expectations, certain rules, and certain boundaries within her social group and within the artistic community. She affirmed her own unique individuality throughout her life, believing that it was the courage to take risks as well as her own passionate commitment to her independent self that distinguished her as a genius.

In reviewing the lives of public women rebels, one is impressed by their uniqueness and by the force with which they defined themselves and upheld their personal convictions. One is also impressed with how few women rebels there are. Despite the fact that the few women rebels we know about are honored and admired, often after their lifetimes, they are not emulated in great numbers. Sonia Johnson's rebellion against the Mormon Church did not result in large numbers of Mormon or Christian women following in her footsteps. Nor did Georgia O'Keeffe's rebellion within the art world result in many other women deciding to take the same personal and professional risks that she took.

It may be that only a few personal rebellions attain the status of public events. The actions of Johnson and O'Keeffe may be in the category of "big rebellions," rebellions that take on a collective aura. While both of these women were engaged in a personal and individual rebellion, their activities touched the lives of many women who may have been able, in small ways, to assert their own unique individuality or their own commitment to a personal, creative self. These smaller rebellions, while not sufficient to shake up the Morman Church or to send shock waves through the art world, may have an equally important significance for the particular individual, who experiences her own rebellion just as powerfully as the larger society experiences the rebellion of those few who act in a daring and big way.

It may also be that society is only willing to tolerate the female rebel in small doses. We may admire a Georgia O'Keeffe or applaud a Sonia Johnson only as long as we are able to know them by name, as long as they are indeed unique and relatively rare. Society may give the message in covert ways that one is enough; one will be allowed, but no more than one.

Mythological Rebels

Mythological and fictional accounts of the lives of women rebels reveal the ambivalent relationship most societies have had toward the defiant female. Stories often begin with the rebellious woman portrayed in a favorable, even a heroic light. As the play or myth proceeds, however, the woman in question meets a disastrous and horrible end; she is burned, banished, hung, or tormented. In fiction, we are able to glorify or honor the female rebel only if we simultaneously punish her.

This dynamic is clear in the story of Lilith, the first female rebel. According to the biblical books of Adam and Eve, Lilith was the first wife of Adam.[37] She was created at the same time as Adam and believed herself to be his equal. Consequently, Lilith refused to be subservient to her husband in the sexual act. She demonstrated her displeasure at his request by cursing God, her creator, and leaving the Garden of Eden forever. In her rash departure from Paradise, Lilith was asserting her equality with her husband and refusing to submit to behaviors alien to her autonomous nature. Her moment of triumph was brief, however. Lilith was condemned to survive for eternity as a she-devil, obsessed by sexual desire and sexual assertiveness. She spent her time consorting with devils and demons and was the nemesis of men who slept alone, attacking their bodies in lascivious ways.

The Old Testament condemnation of Lilith and her rebellious behavior is also apparent in the creation of a second wife for Adam. In bringing forth Eve, the Creator is careful not to make the same mistakes made in the creation of Lilith. Eve has no ideas or aspirations toward autonomy and equality. She was taken from the rib of Adam, clearly subservient, an appendage of her husband, and Adam referred to her as "bone of my bone, flesh of my flesh".[38] This was not a woman who was going to rebel or demand equality from her husband.

Jungian analyst Barbara Koltuv suggests that Lilith was an embodiment of the feminine shadow representing the assertive and rebellious woman.[39] If Koltuv is correct in assuming that Lilith symbolizes feminine rebellion, then it is instructive for us to follow the story of Lilith, for in that story we may find clues to help us understand ancient as well as more modern attitudes toward the female rebel.

One of the most telling aspects of Lilith's story is that following her rebellion, she is made an exile. She is banished from the Garden, but more important, she is cast out of the human community, free to consort with only demons and devils. The life of a normal woman, such as rearing and being part of a family, is denied to Lilith; she is unable to bear human offspring and brings forth only monsters.

It has been the fate of many female rebels to suffer ostracism, excommunication, or some form of banishment because of their assertive and defiant behavior. In ancient Babylonia, women who broke their marriage vows were likened to the rebellious Lilith and exiled from the community. Apparently, to challenge one's marriage vows was an intolerable act of defiance in that premodern civilization. The priestly injunction that sent a divorced woman from her home read as follows: "Thou Lilith of the desert. Thou hag, thou ghoul. Naked art thou sent forth unclad with hair disheveled and streaming down your back."[40] The venom with which the patriarchal hierarchy condemned a woman who transgressed the marital relationship is telling. Not only is she likened to the rebellious exile Lilith, but she is stripped of her possessions, humiliated, and consigned to a life of wandering and restlessness. Clearly the society could not tolerate women who were unwilling or unable to perform their wifely duties.

The labeling of Lilith as an outcast is not the only judgment that biblical scholars have placed on the rebellious woman. In addition to being exiled for her assertiveness, Lilith loses all control over her desires and appetites. Her sexual assertiveness, once the symbol of her rebellion, burgeons into a wanton nymphomania. Lilith cannot control her desires, and she consorts in a wild and animallike manner with subhuman monsters. Not only in the area of sexuality, but in other ways as well, Lilith is out of control, sometimes even being depicted as a mad woman who screeches like an owl and mates with hyenas.[41] Her defiance and her exile have turned her into a wild-eyed, wild-haired woman who kidnaps and murders small babies.

This image of a woman so out of control may well reflect the fantasies and fears that both men and women have of the female rebel. Once a woman challenges traditions and social expectations and steps outside the bounds of normative feminine behavior, she may be unstoppable. Her rebellion may go beyond mere self-assertion, and she may commence to break all the rules and boundaries of civilized conduct. If rebellious women become raging she-devils, then it is no wonder society has tightly controlled a woman's options for actualizing her autonomous, "no-saying" self.

One way we have minimized the impact of the female rebel is to cast her mythology in an undesirable light. When the character of Lilith is mentioned at all in biblical history, she is presented as a crazed demon. Even if one applauds her assertiveness, one can hardly desire to suffer her exile or emulate her mad destructiveness. It is only recently that feminist writers have championed the cause of Lilith and have proclaimed her to be the first liberated woman, a woman who was unwilling to accept a position of submission and subservience to her husband. That positive interpretation has been long in coming, however, and earlier and more prevalent depictions of Lilith remain almost wholly negative.

The myth of the Danaids, fifty sisters who were ordered to marry against their will, offers more possibility for a charitable interpretation of the female rebel.[42] Despite their commitment to a life of chastity, their horror and disgust at having to perform marital obligations, and their repeated pleas to their father for a reprieve, the sisters were forced to marry. In defiance of the order, they devised a plan for preserving their much-cherished virginity. On the wedding night, each sister was to plunge a sharp sword into the throat of her sleeping husband and thus kill him. Forty-nine of the sisters did as they had agreed and killed their new husbands. One sister had a change of heart at the last minute and warned her husband so that he might run away and be saved. According to later additions to the myth, this one sister became the mother of a great nation and a heroine for having the kindness and gentility to spare her husband. The other forty-nine sisters were condemned to Hades where they had to fetch water forever in jars that leaked like sieves.

This myth has been subject to various interpretations that cast these female rebels in differing lights. One author, at the turn of the nineteenth century, praised these young women as rebels who resisted rape by marriage, believing the Danaids to be the first rebels against the practice of loveless and arranged marriages.[43] One can see how these women said both "no" and "yes" simultaneously. They said "no" to what they believed to be an unjust and inhumane request to marry men for whom they had no affection and to sacrifice their virginity. They also said "yes" to their own chastity, independence, and separateness from the world of men.

While some interpretations defend the courageous behavior of the Danaids, others condemn these women for their impulsive and murderous actions. They have been called monsters, lionesses, and defiant women who refuse to honor the noble marriage vows.[44] Some commentators have found their punishment especially apt; since the Danaids feared being pierced, penetrated, and violated, they must forever carry vessels that have been pierced and violated, a reminder for all eternity that they cannot hold the vessel (womb) inviolate; it must be pierced.[45]

A final interpretation of the myth denies that the sisters acted

from their own autonomous and rebellious spirit; rather, this interpretation attributes their violent behavior to their father, who supported their plans, encouraged them, and perhaps even initiated
the plot to murder the suitors.[46] In this interpretation, the reader
does not have to accept that these women were in fact rebellious,
that they devised a treacherous plan on their own, or that they
were courageous enough to carry out such an action without the
support of a powerful and authoritarian male. The sisters, in this
view of the myth, were not true rebels; they were women torn
between allegiance to father and allegiance to husband.[47] In either
case they were subservient. It was solely a matter of which master
they chose to serve.

The author of this interpretation must have believed that readers
might be more comfortable with a mass revolt on the part of
women if it were inspired by a man. It may be more anxiety
provoking to believe that a group of women could, of their own
accord, decide to transgress what has been called the "marital
destiny of womankind."[48] If these women could revolt on their
own, then others might follow suit, an idea clearly uncomfortable
to patriarchal society.

In the story of Antigone, we find a somewhat less ambivalent
view of the female rebel. Antigone was a daughter of the tragic
house of Oedipus, in ancient Greece.[49] Her self-assertive and
rebellious act takes place after one of her brothers has been slain
in the city of Thebes. As he dies, her brother asks her to ensure
that he receive proper burial. Creon, the ruler of Thebes, declares
that her brother is an enemy of the city and orders that his body
be left for birds and beasts to devour. Creon proclaims further that
any citizen who disobeys his order will face death by stoning.

For Antigone, her duty is clear. She knows that she has an
obligation to honor the body of her brother and also to honor the
rituals of the gods whose authority she holds dearer than the
command of the earthly ruler Creon. She proclaims, "What right
has Creon to tell me what to do; I know my duty."[50] Antigone is a
woman who responds to a voice within herself, a voice that tells
her what she must do. As she performs the burial rites, she does
so with a calm and purposeful air.

In planning her actions, Antigone discusses her intentions with
her sister. Her sister, unlike Antigone, is fearful of offending the

ruler, saying, "Remember we are women and we must obey."[51] This sister speaks for the conforming, subservient woman who knows her place in the hierarchy and knows that she must not act outside of prescribed limits. For Antigone, these limits do not apply. She will honor what she knows and believes to be right.

When the king discovers that someone has disobeyed his command and that the brother of Antigone has been buried, he flies into a rage and refuses to listen to the advice of counselors who warn him that to punish the young woman would be a mistake. Instead of the original sentence of stoning, Creon decides to place Antigone in a tomb with a minimal amount of food so that eventually she will starve to death. Again Antigone decides that she will be the creator of her own destiny; rather than waiting to be overcome by starvation, she hangs herself in the tomb to which she has been condemned.

The story of Antigone and Creon does not end there. Sophocles gives us a clear moral lesson and an interpretation of the play as we read the events that befall Creon after Antigone's death. Creon's son, who was engaged to Antigone, kills himself in both anguish and defiance toward his father. Creon's wife, on hearing of the death of her son, also takes her own life. Creon's opposition to the revolt and the independent action of Antigone results in tragedy for him and his family.

While it seems clear that the actions of this young woman are autonomous and self-generated, it has been difficult for subsequent interpretations to cast Antigone in a consistently positive light. It has been argued, for example, that rather than responding to her own inner voice, Antigone merely responds to the commands of the gods; consequently, she is adhering to a tradition and to an authority that transcends her own will.[52] She chooses to honor a heavenly authority rather than an earthly king. This interpretation suggests how difficult it is for us to accept true autonomy and rebellion in a female. We are so accustomed to women who operate in accordance with external, traditional standards that we seek to find those external guidelines as explanations for seemingly courageous and freethinking behavior in women.

This view of Antigone as an adherent to traditional authority contrasts with the more feminist perspective of her as an authentic and independent woman who took risks in order to be true to her own beliefs.[53] She took these risks knowing that they would lead to her death, and she accepted her death as a consequence of her independent action. While she is vindicated at the end of the play, the reader cannot ignore the fact that the play ends with her death. Part of the price she pays for defiance is her own destruction.

In his fictional account of the life of Saint Joan, George Bernard Shaw gives us yet another portrait of a rebellious young woman whose autonomous actions are inspired by God.[54] Her inspiration comes from her very personal relationship to an inner voice rather than from her adherence to the rules and rituals of any religious order. Shaw portrays the maid, as she was called, as a determined and defiant young woman. She had faith in her convictions and was fiercely loyal to France and protective of her special relationship with God and the saints who spoke to her.

One of the outstanding characteristics of Joan was her refusal to accept the lot of women during the time in which she lived. She dressed, fought, and lived as a man might live. At one point in the play she declares, "I'm a soldier. I do not want to be thought of as a woman. I will not dress as a woman. I do not care for the things women care for. They dream of lovers and of money. I dream of leading a charge and of placing the big guns."[55] In this affirmative statement, the young woman makes no mention of God or the saints; rather, she affirms those desires and interests that are dear to her own heart. She rebels against the expectations of her society and of her class and honors and respects what she knows to be right for her.

Shaw contends that Joan was a brilliant military strategist and that she knew she could see beyond the limited vision of those who were leading the French troops.[56] When Joan speaks during the play, she speaks with clarity and a sense of self-assuredness. She knows at each point what she wants and is clear and forthright in her demands. Yet, the image of a young woman speaking clearly and decisively is so out of character for a woman of her time that the men in the play initially respond to her as if she were mad. A woman who does not defer to the men around her and who knows and speaks her own mind is surely an anomaly.

In keeping with the dominant theme in the play, that Joan was inspired by God, those who meet her assume that her sense of inner security must come from the intervention of an other-worldly, divine father. Equally plausible is the explanation that Joan's aura of strength and calm derives from the fact that she is a woman who knows her own mind, a woman in tune with her own inner true self.

Shaw faults Joan for speaking her mind regardless of the impact her words have on those assembled, and he suggests in his prologue that she might have been more successful or survived longer if she had been more Machiavellian and politically shrewd.[57] One can speculate, however, that for all true rebels the inner voice speaks so strongly that the individual has neither the time nor the inclination to monitor his or her actions and words to make them pleasing to others.

At the conclusion of the play, Joan is given the opportunity to stay alive, albeit in prison, if she will recant her statements about her special relationship to God. Initially she does recant, believing she will be granted her freedom for doing so. When she learns that her reprieve will be severely limited and that she will remain in prison, she once again defends her own reality and chooses death over a life that has no personal meaning or relevance. She declares that a life without the things that matter to her—the wind, the sunshine, and the church bells—would not be a life worth living.[58] While Joan is speaking of life in a literal prison, one could argue that the rebel chooses to break out of a psychological prison and to abandon security and mere physical life for the chance to have an authentic life, a life that is true to one's inner values and desires. For the rebellious spirit, a life that violates or transgresses one's own inner voice is not a life worth living.

During her lifetime, Joan was condemned as a witch and a harlot and was finally burned at the stake. She was told that she must stand alone, outside the community, because of her insistence that her private judgment was more relevant than the judgment of her spiritual directors and guides. One of her con-demners in the play declares that she is infected with the leprosy of heresy and as a leper deserves to be placed outside the commu-nity of men and women.[59] She is excommunicated and con-demned to death.

Joan, knowing that she has acted from her own inner reserves, declares that she owes everything to the spirit of God that was within her.[60] While such a statement is obviously in keeping with her saintliness and Christian beliefs, one could, in a psychological sense, reinterpret Joan's statement to mean that she owes everything to the spirit of personal power and authority that was within her. In fact, when the voice of the true self begins to awaken and make itself heard, it must sound like the voice of God to many women who have been accustomed to listening only to those voices that emanate from outside.

Living Rebels

The acts of rebellion of many of the homeless women whose stories appear in this book had a more negative than positive quality. They were often clear about saying "no" to the expectations that society and family members had of them: "no" to their responsibilities to be faithful and devoted wives, "no" to their responsibilities to be nurturing and responsive mothers, and "no" to their responsibilities to be rule-following and law-abiding citizens. Yet they were unclear as to what they were affirming. Frequently they could articulate only a vague sense of wanting to be their own person, wanting to take an independent course of action, or wanting to be free of the demands others placed on them. Without being willing to say "yes" to some affirmative action as part of their rebellion, many homeless women found themselves to be angry rebels without a cause. They brought themselves to the point of being able to say "no"; yet, without the ability to craft a creative direction for themselves, they frequently felt frustrated and lost.

The Story of Kitty

Kitty is a wise and knowledgeable woman who has lived and worked in many cities around the country. She describes her life, with no regrets, as one in which "I did what I wanted to do, come hell or high water."

Early in her travels Kitty had a child out of wedlock. She tried to care for her daughter, but decided when the child was only five months old to give her to some friends to rear. Kitty felt that the responsibilities of motherhood did not suit her, and she moved to a new town, failing to have any contact with her daughter for over thirty years.

After considerable roaming from place to place, Kitty did settle down and get married. Her marriage was stormy and tempestuous because of her insistence on having her own way. Her independent actions often took the form of having multiple lovers. Frequently she would get up in the middle of the night, get dressed, and go out and meet a male friend at some appointed place. When confronted by her husband, she recalls telling him that she had lost control and was just unable to stop herself, but she knew that this explanation was false for she was in control of herself and knew exactly what she was doing.

After eighteen years of a stormy marriage, Kitty was once again on her own. She moved frequently, taking faculty positions at several small colleges where she would teach for a while, then become restless and move on. At one point she reunited with her daughter, the child she had abandoned thirty years previously. Her daughter had expectations that Kitty would now make up for lost time and become a good mother and grandmother. For a short time Kitty did attempt to comply with this expectation and helped her daughter with babysitting, cooking, and homemaking, but after a period of time she felt that she had had enough and she just left one day. This impulsive behavior was not uncharacteristic of Kitty, and she reports that she often just did what she felt like doing without planning or foresight.

We might speculate that once Kitty saw that her daughter's hospitality came with certain strings attached, she needed to flee. Her daughter's expectation and wish that Kitty respond like a traditional mother and grandmother caused Kitty to feel confined, trapped, and smothered, forcing her to reassert her independence impulsively once again. Apparently, once she felt thwarted in getting her way, Kitty moved quickly, without any plans or thought for the consequences of her behavior.

Kitty first became homeless because she left her daughter's home without any money or any place to stay. She arrived back in Washington, D.C., without resources and needing to seek shelter in one of the women's residences. Once in the shelter, however, Kitty refused to conform to the rules and expectations of the shelter providers. She was put out on several occasions because she broke rules concerning smoking and curfew. From the shelter she was transferred to a transitional residence where once again she broke the rules. She refused to contribute to the upkeep of the household and to do chores and communal duties. Once again, when asked to behave in typically female ways, Kitty said "no."

Kitty is quite clear that no one will make her do what she does not want to do. Routinely she will break a rule or defy an expectation just to assert that she is her own master and her own person. Once she acts, she is quite willing to accept the consequences of her autonomous behavior. When she was asked to leave the shelter or was sanctioned within the transitional residence, she did not object or complain. If these consequences follow from her independent action, she is willing to accept them. She is not willing, however, to curb her acting out. She declares, "I'm a self-made woman and no one is going to treat me like a child."

Kitty's desire to have her own way and to be free to be herself in all her relationships applies not only to her relationships to men and women, but to her relationship to God as well. Kitty maintains that her own voice is the voice of God and that her interpretation of the Bible is just as important as the minister's interpretation. She refuses to be limited by external authority, whether it be the external authority of a husband, of a societal norm, or of a church father.

In defending her right to her privacy, Kitty maintains adamantly, "I want my own life." She describes spending hours communing with her own reflection in the mirror. Kitty asserts that she shares her most private secrets about herself only with her own reflection. In this way she can hold on to that which is most precious and private and not reveal to anyone, other than to her own mirrored image, the secrets that are deepest in her heart.

Kitty's life has been devoted to making sure that she is not hemmed in, limited, or controlled in any way. While onlookers might lament that she has been unable to have more stability or consistency in her life, Kitty has no regrets. She has protected her independence and her right and ability to make her own decisions at all times, and in that way she has been true to her own, inner voice.

The Story of Bonnie

Bonnie is a young woman whose life story fits the profile of the rebel without a cause. She is a single mother who wanders up and down the East Coast, never quite fitting in wherever she is. Although she maintains that it is her fervent desire to find stability and a home for herself and her son, she always manages to do something to require that she move on from her current residence. She has lived on the streets, in shelters, and with friends, never quite able to fit in or to find a stable place for herself.

Her history reads like a textbook case of the acting-out teenager: she frequently skipped school, she was a disciplinary problem, she routinely fought with her mother, and she recalls deliberately doing small, rebellious behaviors just to get her mother's attention and to make her mother angry. Whenever she found herself in a situation where there were expectations of her that she did not like, she invariably would act out and run away. She has been trained for and left jobs in the middle of her apprenticeship because she did not like something that the instructor said or some requirement that was placed upon her.

At first glance, one is hard put to find any purpose to Bonnie's wandering and to her seemingly random acts of rebellion. Yet when one talks to her in more depth, one discovers that she has consciously adopted the persona of the bad girl to protect whatever true independent self she might possess. She desperately wants to avoid a life of poverty and despair, a life she sees all around her and a life she has been programmed to assume. Yet her attempts to say "no," to resist, and to defy society's negative expectations of her are misguided and ultimately self-destructive. Each time she attempts to free herself, by running from unpleasant circumstances, she merely tightens the grip that poverty and hopelessness have on her life. Bonnie does not have the emotional strength or the intellectual skills to devise a healthy strategy for surviving independently in the world.

When she was a young child, Bonnie's mother and father separated, and Bonnie went to live with her mother. She remembers, however, being much closer to her father and experiencing her separation from him as a major loss. She and her mother quarreled and antagonized one another often, with many of the fights focusing on the stream of male visitors and boyfriends her mother brought home. Bonnie felt unwanted by her mother, as if she was always in her mother's way.

During her school years, Bonnie purposely acted out in the regular classrooms so that she might be transferred to a program for mentally disturbed children, a program that she had heard gave children special attention. So desperate was she for attention that Bonnie was willing to feign illness in order to be transferred to a classroom in which she might receive the nurturance she craved. Her strategy for being "special," however, was ultimately self-destructive. Once identified as a child with mental and emotional problems, she was both stigmatized and limited in her high-school career.

When Bonnie was a teenager her mother moved to Florida with a new husband and told Bonnie that she was not welcome to join them. Desperate for a home, Bonnie sought a place with her father and his new family, but she was not welcomed in a household that now contained sisters and brothers whom she did not know. In an attempt to make herself independent, she enrolled in the Job Corps but became defiant and angry toward instructors who she felt were merely preparing her for a marginal job. Her anger at her station in life once again resulted in destructive consequences for Bonnie. By leaving the training program, she only further insured that she would have no means of supporting herself. Bonnie eventually became pregnant by a drug addict who left her before her son was born.

Following the birth of her son, her life has consisted of a series of welfare checks, evictions, lost jobs, and homelessness. The life that now faces Bonnie is one of deprivation and despair, the very conditions against which she rebelled. While one might argue that Bonnie's rebellious acts of self-assertion have served only to speed the downhill course of her experience, her behavior may also be viewed as her desperate attempt to rebel against what felt to her to be intolerable circumstances and to say, "I've had enough of impoverishment and deprivation, and I want something better for myself." Unfortunately, however, Bonnie grew up in a system that did not equip her to take the next positive step in her rebellion. She has been unable to affirm a positive and creative life-style for herself and her son. Consequently, she continues her attempts at authenticity by continuing to say "no" to those conditions and expectations that oppress and stifle her.

Belle's Story

Of all the women interviewed, Belle presented the only case of a rebellion with positive consequences. Not surprisingly, her attempts at autonomy were also less self-destructive than the other women's, and she was able to combine her rebellious, defiant behavior with a positive and creative thrust.

As a young child, her way of rebelling and asserting herself was to play the mischievous trickster, darting into a situation, playing some outrageous prank, and before anyone noticed, darting away laughing. She remembers constantly testing and challenging the limits that people put on her, and she often pushed those limits until they eventually broke. She recalls, for example, wanting to go her own way in school, doing what interested her, and even designing her own assignments. Once she had an idea she wanted to pursue, she would not be stopped. In science class one day, she was inspired to do her own experiment. As a result, she returned to school after dismissal and began mixing chemicals. Unfortunately, her dreams exceeded her scientific ability, and she almost blew herself and the classroom to bits.

At home, she was equally determined to have her own way. At one point she decided to repaint her parents' house and threw a paint party in the living room one evening when they were away. While her experiment in creative redecorating met with disapproval from her parents, Belle accepted their censure with good humor, glad, at least, that she had followed her own instincts to create something new and different. Perhaps because her rebellion was often tinged with playfulness and a good-natured ability to laugh at herself, and because Belle herself has an air of "don't worry, be happy" about her, she has never been severely hampered or punished for her independent actions.

Only when we hear of her relationships with her seven children do we begin to see the negative consequences of Belle's self-serving assertiveness. Before she began having children, Belle could do what she pleased, when she pleased, as long as she was willing to be personally responsible for the outcome. Once she became a mother, however, her behavior had a direct impact on the lives of others. As she put it, she "just did not have the hands for providing tender loving care to babies"; consequently, she left her children one after another with friends and relatives. While she maintained that the abandonment of her children was for their own good since she was not able to nurture them well, one senses, in listening to Belle, that mothering did not fit with the image she had of herself as a creative, free spirit and that Belle did not do anything for very long that did not suit her.

While she did not know any of her children very well, Belle probably gives the best description of herself when describing her children; she says "they fight for life, they push for life, they push to be somebody, and when they cannot do something, they feel depressed and angry about it." This statement, ostensibly applied to her children, is an accurate account of Belle's own struggle. She is indeed a woman who fights and pushes to make her life the best that it can be; and she is determined to make something of herself, something independent, free, and unique.

When Belle becomes thwarted or frustrated, her psychiatric symptoms are anger and depression, the same as those she attributes to her children. At several times in her life, Belle has been hampered in her attempts to be her own person. She has had to conform to external expectations or obey outside rules. On some of these occasions Belle has felt trapped and become rageful. She can be violent and intimidating at these times. On other occasions, she has reacted to disappointment with despair and depression, feeling hopeless, overwhelmed, and even suicidal. At these times Belle has benefited from psychotherapy, especially those clinical interventions that allow her to express her frustrations and that affirm her creative will.

Currently, Belle is pursuing training as an electrician. While this is an unlikely career for a woman, it is something that Belle has always wanted to do. She likes knowing how things work and feeling in control of problems that baffle most others, women in particular. She has already built a radio and is working on a few inventions of her own. Ignoring comments from friends that she has chosen an unfeminine trade and that she looks unattractive in her uniform, Belle has decided that this is something she wants to do, and she is undeterred in her course.

More than in any other arena, Belle's assertiveness and creativity appear in her artwork. She has painted and drawn since she was a young child and continues to express herself in this medium. When discussing her art, she comments specifically, "I like symphony music when I am painting because it puts my mind in another world. Then my mind drifts off to another country, another world, somewhere up on the moon, somewhere far away. I like to paint then because I am in a different place and I do not have any problems. I am away from everyone who bugs me, and I know I am going to have a good time with the canvas."

Her sense of losing herself in her creative work, of being alone and free when she is painting, is similar to the descriptions Georgia O'Keeffe gave of her own experience as an artist. When the O'Keeffe exhibit came to Washington, D.C., Belle went and saw the exhibit twice. She felt an affinity for O'Keeffe, the painter, a country girl like herself, who pushed herself to be the best that she could be. What Belle liked best about O'Keeffe besides her artwork was that O'Keeffe was a woman who said what she wanted to say whether other people liked it or not. The artist's thrust to be true to her own definition of herself despite external consequences resonated with Belle's most deeply held beliefs.

Of all the women whose stories were collected, only Belle requested to write her own story in her own hand. After being involved in a several hour taping session, she proceeded to write out her story longhand so that I would have a version that was uniquely and totally hers. Belle is a woman very concerned with creating herself, with affirming what is special and individual about herself. Fortunately for her, her rebellion against society's expectations and demands has been within the bounds that the world has been able to accept; consequently, she has not been punished too greatly, either overtly or covertly, for her decision not to conform to standard expectations.

In exploring the image of the rebel we find an aspect of the feminine self that has lived underground for quite some time. Women have been uncomfortable with their rebellious and autonomous selves; both men and women have viewed the female rebel with ambivalence. Often her actions confuse and disorient us, and we want to define her as a single aberration, an exception to her sex. Occasionally her actions have been denied, sometimes ridiculed, often condemned. Despite the increased independence and autonomy that many women now experience, both men and women have still not reached a point in our collective development where we can feel truly comfortable with the openly assertive and rebellious woman.

Summary

The four faces of the feminine shadow, the victim, the exile, the predator, and the rebel form a composite portrait of the unacknowledged self of most women. Each of these figures stands in her own right as an embodiment of disavowed and devalued feminine possibility. Yet the four aspects of the shadow do not exist in a mutually exclusive or necessarily antagonistic relationship to one another. Some rebels have been exiled for their defiant actions, some victims have exploded into dangerous predators, and some exiles have become victims as they wander alone from place to place. It seems that when one lives in the world of shadows and ghosts, one figment of denied reality easily blends into another.

We must remember that each of us contains elements of the victim, the exile, the predator, and the rebel as part of our essential self. At different times in our lives we may choose to publicly identify with one of these usually hidden parts of the self. When we do so, we bring that part of the self out of the shadows and into the light of conscious expression. Particular women, because of their personal characteristics and special vulnerabilities, become susceptible to absorb shadow projections when these images are cast out. Again, we must remember that individual homeless women identify only with projections that make personal sense in terms of their own lives and vulnerabilities. The special situation in which living women come to embody collective projections occurs only when shadow content and personal psychology match. Such a diabolical match occurred hundreds of years ago when millions of European and American women were executed as witches; and it is occurring now between the current content of the feminine shadow and thousands of homeless women.

Part Three

Repair

Repair for both homeless and nonhomeless women must begin with consciousness. Before we can begin to demythologize homeless women and help them to break the identification that many have made with aspects of the feminine shadow, we must become aware that a collective projection of intrapsychic content has occurred. Invariably, when individuals project out psychological content, they are inclined to believe that what has been disowned not only does not belong to them in the present, but has never belonged to them in the past. Moreover, they see the content as existing exclusively in the being of another person. Reciprocally, those who identify with a psychological projection and experience its debilitating impact come to believe that the projected content is, and always has been, part of their true selves. Jonathan Kozol has suggested that because homeless people have been so despised by the rest of the society, many of them have now come to see themselves as despicable.[1] These people have identified with a hated part of the collective self and have come to believe that they are that hated self.

Because projected content goes unrecognized and seeps into the identity of the person who receives it, the process of bringing that content into awareness is a difficult one. Homeless women must gradually emerge from the anonymity that shrouds them as embodiments of collective projections, and all women must be willing to acknowledge and to reclaim their own psychological shadows.

Imagine, for example, a woman who puts on a particular costume to perform a part in a play. She applies elaborate makeup, perhaps even having her features transformed to approximate the description of the character, and layers herself with clothing and finery in accord with the style of the character she is about to play. Unlike the usual performer, however, this particular player does not disrobe at the end of the performance, but continues to wear her costume indefinitely. After a while, the elements of the costume come to be intimately associated with this individual; she is no longer sure whether the makeup on her face and the putty around her mouth are hers permanently or whether they are part of the costume she acquired for the performance. Similarly, the robes she wears have become so familiar and so comfortable that she is no longer certain whether they are part of the costume or whether they are part of her personal wardrobe. Others who have become accustomed to seeing her in this costume feel the same. They recognize her only as the bedecked character she has come to play, and they forget that they once contributed some of the clothing that now constitutes her costume.

For a character who has lost sight of her own identity amidst layers of external garments to rediscover her own face and her own form, she must remove slowly all the pieces of clothing. In the process of disrobing, she may try to remove something that cannot be removed, something that is in fact part of her own person. Only in this way will she discover what is really a part of her own physiognomy and not part of her costume. Once disrobed and cleansed of her makeup, this woman will be able to look at her own face and to see, perhaps for the first time in a long time, what belongs to her and is intrinsic to her true self.

Taking this image and transferring it to the psychological realm, we may conjecture that an analogous process of psychological disrobing must occur for homeless women to discover who they are and what they look like. When they are free of excess psychological baggage, others will be able to see them as distinct individuals, not merely as actors in a psychological drama. Moreover, when psychological projections are acknowledged and returned to those who have sent them, the original owners may have no choice but to reclaim, and perhaps lovingly repair, those aspects of themselves that they have discarded and devalued.

I am reminded of a performance piece in which a young artist attempted to depict the tension between the inner and the outer self. She began the performance standing before the audience in just a body suit. Slowly she added layers of clothing. At the end of the first half of her performance, she was unrecognizable as the slim woman who began the piece. She was transformed into a bulky, shapeless, and somewhat grotesque figure, her own unique form now being concealed, hidden, and disguised by the successive layers of costume she had donned.

In the second half of her performance the woman began to disrobe. Piece by piece she removed the layers of clothing, taking off all the elements of the costume she had put on previously. With the removal of each successive piece, her own form began to emerge more clearly. At the end of the performance she was restored to her original self. Over the course of the performance piece the viewer witnessed the dialectical relationship between what is inside and what is outside, what genuinely belongs to one's self and what is merely illusion created by adding layers of external adornment.

Only when we realize that homeless women have become distorted, both personally and in the eyes of others, because of the many layers of projection they wear will we be able to begin the process of psychological disrobing, a process of removing the many distorting projections with which they have *been identified. When homeless women become so identified with the projections of our unwanted shadows that they forget, and we aid them in forgetting, that they were ever other than the carriers of those projections, it becomes difficult, if not impossible, for them to remove the cumbersome external layers. Only when we become aware that shadow projections have taken place will we be able to begin removing those projections, to see the real women who live beneath the layers of projection, and to reclaim our own unwanted psychological selves.*

Chapter 10

Repair for Homeless Women

Repair for homeless women is a process with economic, social, and moral dimensions. How we view homelessness and understand its causes will determine how we propose to repair it. We must be mindful to match solutions to specific problems. Psychotherapy will not feed a hungry woman; rental subsidies will not address the rage and fear of an incest survivor.

Affordable or subsidized housing helped every one of the women with whom I spoke move off the streets or out of the shelters. Economic solutions, however, did not help her cast off dysfunctional projections and begin to value herself; shelter alone did not help her heal the pain of repeated abuses and rejections; and financial subsidies did not repair the profound sense of disconnection she experienced between herself and other men and women. Because this book has been about the oppressive and ultimately dehumanizing weight that homeless women carry when they wear the unwanted projections of other women, this discussion of repair will focus on the process whereby homeless women can begin to shed those layers of projecton.

While it must begin with our awareness that homeless women are the carriers of shadow projections, the archetypal repair for these women is a many-staged process. Both homeless women and nonhomeless women must participate in the reaffiliation of those who have been exiled and disenfranchised. Together we must collaborate in building interpersonal and psychological bridges that facilitate the return of homeless women who have become so identified with our unwanted shadows that they have become isolated from the mainstream of society. Repair for homeless women from the distortions of the shadow also requires that nonhomeless women look beyond external appearances and see the real woman who exists underneath our own projected reality. At the same time, homeless women themselves must be active in casting off projections that have become familiar, perhaps even comfortable, albeit debilitating. The final stage in repair for homeless women requires that they have the opportunity to embrace alternate mythologies and to construct other conceptions of themselves that offer more promise for creative life.

Bridges of Return

Naomi Goldenberg, the feminist theologian, in her book *Changing of the Gods* employs the metaphor of building bridges in her discussion of the process whereby an individual returns from a life of emptiness and meaninglessness to one of authenticity.[1] Goldenberg postulates that a sense of existential meaninglessness derives from an individual's being alienated from his or her own inner experience, living a life in which the public self is very different from the inner, private self. The process of repair and reaffiliation for homeless women similarly will require the building of connections, bridges that will span the distance between their external and their internal realities. For many homeless women who have become identified publicly with our shadow projections, their external life is fused with the aspect of the archetype they have come to embody. Publicly, they are victims, exiles, predators, and rebels. In identifying with these collective projections, many women have lost sight of their own unique individual selves. The bridges that once connected the personal, inner self to the external, public persona are in a state of disrepair; some have become un- crossable.

For many homeless women their sense of disconnection from a personal sense of identity is paralleled by a sense of disconnection from other people. The distorting impact of carrying projected content serves to isolate them from others as well as from them- selves. Jean Baker Miller discusses the profound sense of discon- nection that an individual experiences when the interpersonal world ignores or denies his or her emotional reality.[2] Many of us would gladly pretend that the intense pain, anger, and loneliness that many homeless women experience does not exist for them or for us. In so doing, however, we only serve to confuse and further alienate these women. If their feelings and experiences are so bad and disorganizing that we can hardly bear to look at them much less hear their stories, then they must be unworthy and different from the rest of us. This sense of personal shame not only renders the homeless woman disconnected from relationships in the present, but disinclined to seek new relationships in the future.[3]

The first step for many women in reconstructing these bridges and reinstating a dialogue between the inner and the external self is to "repersonalize" the individual. So many homeless women have become anonymous, unrecognizable people, cut off from their personal histories and from their personal identities. In the same way in which survivors of a natural disaster must at some point identify and reclaim the bodies of their dead relatives, so, too, must homeless women identify and reclaim their own lost or damaged personal identities. Without familiar faces, familiar routines, and familiar mementos, it is easy for an individual to lose sight of who he or she is.

In discussing his experiences in the death camp at Auschwitz, writer Primo Levi makes mention of the importance small trinkets had for camp survivors.[4] Anything that reminded an individual of his or her past life became a link to the personal self. Without these personal markers, individuals became anonymous and in- terchangeable. Clues were needed to remind oneself that one had a unique and personal identity prior to Auschwitz. In a similar way, without the existence of personal mementos, personal posses- sions, and even personal memories, it is difficult for many homeless women to maintain a connection to their unique personal selves.

To forget who one is and to be unable to remember the specific and unique events of one's life is to experience a death of the spirit.[5] Our memories root us in a personal past and a personal identity. Some memories are not solely objective, but they are also the creations of our imagination, at times reflecting our deepest desires and fears. Consequently, we may read in our remembered past not only a record of what has happened to us, but also a history of our own emotional and psychological development at the time that events occurred.

Part of the process of repair for many of the homeless women involved either retrieving personal and meaningful possessions that had been left behind at shelters or with relatives or investing new possessions with some personal significance. One woman made several crocheted pillows for her apartment while others spent time selecting pictures and decorations for their new homes. Another woman, whose habit it had been to own only one outfit of clothing at a time, wear the garments until they were rags, and then discard them, began to value some items enough to have them cleaned and to keep them as part of her permanent wardrobe. Again and again women were encouraged and assisted in developing a sense of personal ownership, first for concrete things, but eventually for thoughts, feelings, and hopes.

Individuals who experience a disconnection from their own recollections are especially susceptible to identifying with a collective projection. Lacking a personal identity and thus standing naked and unprotected, an individual may be eager to take on whatever persona, whatever outward covering, is available. Once wrapped in an external and collective identity, an individual may obscure even further his or her own inner self, finally forgetting completely those last remnants of a past life.

The process of recapturing one's personal self often begins with the telling of one's story. Initially, when women told their stories for this book, the stories were brief and sketchy. Some women told the stories of their lives in five or ten minutes. With some prompting and encouragement, women expanded their stories in length and developed them further. Some women told their stories several times, finding that with subsequent tellings some of the inessential details of the story disappeared, leaving a woman with a version that reflected her core self.[6] Women who have lost sight of their unique individuality must have a forum in which they can have their stories heard, a forum in which they can rediscover the women that they were. For only in knowing from whence one has come will individuals be able to forge a new direction for themselves.

As part of her recovery from psychological homelessness and interpersonal disconnection each woman was invited to participate in a women's group of from six to ten members. The group was a place to share stories of homelessness and to applaud sagas of survival. Eventually, however, the focus of the group shifted from an emphasis on homelessness to a more general discussion of issues that concern women everywhere: how to be in a loving relationship, how to survive alone, how to repair relationships with family and friends, and how to feel good about oneself. These groups, plus meetings that each woman had individually with a counselor, provided the opportunity for what has been termed a "growth enhancing relationship."[7] First, the women were provided with a safe forum in which to share their experiences. Counselors spent time assuring the women not only of the physical safety of the space, but of the psychological safety of the group itself. Women were allowed to share their experiences, knowing that they would not be cut off or rejected because their stories were too frightening or painful for others to hear. They also knew that they would not be blamed or shamed for what they thought or felt. Finally, women could expect that their honest stories would be met by the genuine responses and experiences of other women. Such an interpersonal experience serves not only to validate and affirm the individual's sense of self but also to encourage connections and affiliations with others.

The process of reconnecting to one's personal history also allows women to rediscover lost family members, friends, and associates. When people remember who they were, they also remember the people who were important to them. If an individual feels sufficiently secure in his or her rediscovered identity, he or she may find the courage to contact people from the past, thus building or rehabilitating interpersonal bridges.

When they begin to work with profoundly disaffiliated homeless women, social workers and counselors often make the mistake of assuming that these women are totally without human connections. In part because homeless women guard the names of friends and relatives like top secrets and in part because they have such difficulty trusting and connecting even to benign helpers, clinicians conclude that the address books of homeless women must be empty. This is rarely the case, however. As women begin to trust both their memories and their relationships, they may begin to reveal large and extended family networks. As they ceased to feel so ashamed of themselves and began to feel more personally whole, many women contacted sisters and brothers about whom they still cared; one woman found and visited a foster family that had cared for her when she was a child. While some of these reconnections held the promise of future relationships and mutual support, others were purely symbolic as in the case of one woman who made a pilgrimage to a Midwestern nursing home to say goodbye to her ninety-year-old demented mother.

In the process of remembering one's history, many women also go through a process of mourning in which they lament the loss of past relationships, past dreams, past identities. For some women, opportunities, once available, are no longer viable; these opportunities are lost forever. Part of reconnecting with one's personal history is to reconnect not only with one's successes, but with one's disappointments as well, and to mourn properly and to bury lost and battered dreams.

Finally, the process of reaffiliation also involves the individual's reconnection to a prevailing spiritual or mythological reality. In becoming disaffiliated from society and disconnected from families, many women lost connections to powerful mythological and religious traditions as well. In reclaiming one's personal identity, one also reconnects to sources of mythological and religious identification, a reconnection that may help heal the sense of meaninglessness brought on by the alienation from one's personal identity.[8] To be part of a community is to participate in the mythological life of that community, and, in fact, a number of the homeless women who were interviewed did eventually choose to reconnect to the churches of their childhood, churches that at one time had held a powerful significance for them.

Mythologist Joseph Campbell uses the myth of the hero's journey to help understand the psychological experience of schizo-phrenic individuals who break with reality and subsequently turn their attention inward.[9] Without implying that homeless women are psychotic, we may similarly use the mythology of the journey to understand their break with society and their subsequent reaffil-iation as well.

The myth begins with the hero's separation, often with a dra-matic break, from the existing social order. Some event results in his or her abrupt departure from society. Many women experience their descent into homelessness as a radical break or departure from the life that has gone before.

The myth continues with the hero's journey downward and inward, turning attention and energy into the self. As the individual spirals downward, he or she encounters bizarre, frightening, and dangerous creatures. Again, one might argue that as part of the isolation and separation they experience, many homeless women do indeed retreat inside themselves. And while some of them do encounter dark and terrifying psychological realities, all of them encounter, on the streets, terrifying, frightening, and disturbing real monsters.

The myth of the journey concludes, if the hero is fortunate, with a centering experience in which the individual is returned to his or her previous life with a new inner strength and contentment. At the point of deepest descent, the individual reorganizes his or her own psyche, often aided by the intervention of a guide or a magi-cian. From this reorganization comes a new self, similar to the person of the hero who descended, but also different, for he or she has grown and matured from the experience of the journey itself. While not all homeless women will experience a heroic return from their exile and disaffiliation, the process of reconnecting with their own unique and personal identities might increase the number who cross the bridge from the realm of anonymity and homelessness to a life of greater personal meaning and social affiliation.

While the reconnection of individual homeless women to their own personal identities is an important part of the repair of women who have functioned as carriers of archetypal images, it is not, however, the only element in that repair. For the spell of the collective archetype to be broken, nonhomeless women must be able to look beyond collective projections and see the real women who live behind the image.

Curse of the Beast

Folklore is replete with stories of a prince or princess who becomes enchanted and is transformed into a monster, a beast, or some nonliving creature. In these stories, the curse persists until the prince or princess wins the love of someone who is able to see beyond or beneath the grotesque exterior and love the prince or princess who lives within. A similar process is required if the curse of the collective archetype is to be broken for homeless women. Other women must be able to see beyond the rags and the often monstrous exterior and find the good and beautiful woman who lies beneath. Only in this way will the collective images fall away, allowing the real women underneath to emerge and to rediscover their own personal identities.

One of the most memorable stories of transformation through love and acceptance is the story of Beauty and the Beast.[10] The beast in the story had been a handsome prince before he was cursed by an old hag who appeared one day at his palace. The old woman, a fairy in disguise, approached the prince for charity and shelter. The prince, seeing only her crippled and ugly exterior, turned the woman away. As she was leaving, she cast a spell upon him. The prince, despite his riches and his powerful position, was cursed to be alone until someone found the beauty inside the beast. Gradually, the prince was transformed from a handsome prince into an ugly monstrous beast.

As the story proceeds, the beast encounters a merchant who trespasses on his property. Initially, he is tempted to kill the merchant until the merchant tells him the story of his daughter, Beauty, who is waiting for him at home. Beauty had asked her father to bring her one red rose from his travels.

The beast agrees to let the merchant go but only on the condition that he will send his daughter Beauty in his stead. Despite much lamenting within the family, Beauty returns to become the mistress of the beast's palace. Once ensconced in the palace, Beauty grows fond of the beast despite his frightening exterior; however, when he asks her to marry him, she refuses, saying that she does not love him. Beauty's love is quite literally reserved for the man of her dreams. She is enchanted by dreams of a handsome prince, a prince who is charming and wonderful. During her dream, however, Beauty is haunted by the voice of a woman who says to her, "Look deep into the other's beauty to find your happiness."[11] Initially, Beauty does not understand the meaning of this injunction and she continues to reject the beast, seeing only his exterior form. Eventually, when he is near death, Beauty realizes that she does indeed love the beast, and she consents to be his wife. Once she agrees, his beastly visage disappears, and he is transformed into the handsome prince of her dreams.

At several points within the story, one of the characters must define his or her relationship to the shadow. The first such encounter involves the handsome prince who meets the shadow in the form of the old hag. He fails to treat her with compassion and to welcome her into his home. Rather, he is cruel and arrogant, dismissing her and sending her away. Unable to accept the shadow in a loving and respectful way, the prince is cursed with becoming the shadow himself. He must now look and behave like an uncivilized beast.

The prince not only fails to acknowledge the shadow, but he also fails to see beyond the shadow. He accepts the outward appearance of the hag as being representative of her inner self as well, and he misses the opportunity to see the powerful magician who hides beneath the impoverished exterior of the hag. Fittingly, the punishment for failing to acknowledge and respect the humanity in another is for the prince to become less fully human himself. To be fully human, each individual must be willing to embrace not only that which is acceptable, presentable, and beautiful, but also that which appears to be crippled, ugly, and unwanted.

Although the prince has been cursed by a suprahuman magical being, he can only be restored by another mortal, one who is able to love him. Similarly, the love and compassion of other men and women may be necessary if the total repair of homeless women is to occur. While the causes of homelessness are many and varied and the solutions require a concerted effort on social, economic, political, and human fronts, a principal element in the reclamation of homeless individuals will be the caring and love of other humans who are willing to see beyond the rags, the lice, and the odors and discover the person who hides beneath.

In the story the transformation of an individual is an interpersonal rather than a purely individual event. The individual is incapable of bringing about his or her transformation alone; another person must mediate the transformation. It is the task of the man or woman who has been cursed and dehumanized to convince one other person that he or she is worthy and valuable. If one other person believes in and sees the inner self of the individual, then transformation will be possible.

This theme of looking beneath the surface to find the inner worth of an individual appears in slightly altered form in many mythologies. A Zulu myth about the marriage of a goddess, for example, has such a message.[12] In this story the goddess is about to marry a young man, but before taking him as her husband, she desires to test his compassion and his authenticity. The test she devises challenges him to see beyond outward appearances. The goddess disguises herself as a disheveled, ragged, beggar woman, putting on rags and discoloring her hair and her skin. In this transformed state, she presents herself to her prospective bridegroom. She also arranges to be accompanied by one of her handmaidens who is dressed in fine robes and jewels. The prospective bridegroom must decide which of the two women is in fact the goddess, a difficult task since outward appearances suggest that it is the handmaiden who is divine.

In the myth the young man looks deep into the eyes of both women. Through the eyes he can see to the true and inner self, and in the eyes of the goddess, he sees a strong and powerful woman who resonates an inner goodness. Seeing beyond the external appearance, the man in the story chooses the woman in rags to be his wife. Once the choice is made, the rags fall from the goddess, and she is dressed in robes and jewels as a beautiful princess. Only by his ability to see beyond the outward appearance is the young man in the story rewarded. If he were to be distracted solely by exterior presentation, then he would lose the goddess as his bride.

I am reminded of a story that I heard several years ago when traveling in the Far East. The story concerned a famous statue of the Buddha that had been encased in concrete, disguised to hide its true value and to protect it from theft should the capital city be invaded. Over the years, however, many individuals forgot that underneath the discolored and unattractive concrete was a statue of pure gold. Because it was disguised in this way, many individuals treated the statue with disrespect, carting it from place to place in a haphazard manner. During one of these moves, the statue fell, causing part of the concrete casing to fall away and reveal to the startled workers a statue of gold.

Often, if one is willing to look beneath the surface, one finds an unexpected treasure hidden there. It would, however, be foolhardy to imply that beneath the rags and the outward appearance of homelessness, all homeless women are goddesses or wonderful, good people. These women, just as other women, are complex and complicated, possessing within themselves a range of human possibilities. What is certain, however, is that if one looks beneath the surface, one will find what is real and genuine. When the kernel of authenticity within the individual is found, that kernel is free to be nurtured and to grow, enabling the woman in question to become that which she might were she not constrained by the limits imposed when one identifies with projections of the shadow.

Disrobing

The next stage in the release of homeless women from the bonds of archetypal projections requires their own active rejection of collective projections. After homeless women rediscover their personal histories and personal identities and after they have experienced the transforming power of other people's genuine concern and acceptance, they must still consciously cast off unacceptable and inappropriate projections. These women must challenge the roles into which they have been cast, demanding that others deal, on a psychological level, with their own unwanted baggage.[13] As homeless women stop foraging for their food in actual garbage cans, they will also have to stop foraging for identities in psychological garbage cans, becoming less available to own others' unwanted shadow selves. While a woman's initial separation from shadow projections may require an active rejection of those characterizations that no longer fit, subsequently she can step aside and allow the projection to go past her, declining to provide a convenient hook to snare the projection and make it her own.

One woman's personal story of casting off a shadow projection may make it clearer how this process unfolds. Joyce first became homeless after the death of her common-law husband, a man over twenty years her senior who encouraged Joyce's belief that she was a dependent and helpless child. Despite a chronological age of almost forty, Joyce dressed in short shorts and a halter top, wore her hair in two pony tails and cried pitifully when she was left alone. Joyce was so desperate to find a man to replace her dead husband that she had never fully mourned him. She spent her days going from emergency room to emergency room, collecting prescriptions and samples that she guarded in a shopping bag like a child hoarding Halloween treats. Both as a homeless woman and in her relationship with her husband Joyce played the helpless victim, unable to care for herself and at the mercy of forces beyond her control. She believed her only rescue would come at the hands of another male protector.

In the course of telling her story to other women, Joyce came to hear what parts of her pain were genuine expressions of her personal mourning for her husband and what parts were mere rote and impersonal expressions of fear and powerlessness. As she allowed herself to and received validation for mourning her lost relationship, Joyce felt both more alone in a real sense but also more connected to other women who were able to recognize and share her pain. As she shed some of her acquired helplessness, Joyce began to remember past competencies as a homemaker and as a caretaker that she had forgotten she had. Indeed, toward the end of his life Joyce had nursed her husband, helped him move to Washington to be near better medical services, and kept his family informed of his condition.

As she became less identified with the role of victim, Joyce's appearance began to change as well. She bought stylish but modest skirts and dresses, had her hair cut and styled, and discarded her bag of medical charms. She eventually made contact with some relatives in another state, and after careful planning, a trial visit, and several months to say goodbye to the people who had shared her recovery with her, Joyce moved on, an adult woman, aware of her vulnerabilities but no longer so identified with them that they formed the core of her self.

New Mythologies of Personal and Communal Power

In order to feel empowered to reject these disowned collective personalities, homeless women will need to feel stronger and more powerful in general. Some of the requisite strength may derive from the creation of new mythologies and new role models with which homeless women can identify. Many of the homeless women whose stories are reported in this book identified strongly with mythologies of powerlessness. Most of them contained within themselves and within their life experience elements of the exile and the victim. Those who were able to create a defiant or aggressive stance for themselves as predators or rebels often did so at great cost to their personal and psychological safety. None of these women had an example from her own life or from the collective mythology of her culture of a strong and powerful woman, a woman who was able to dig deep within herself and access creative life force.

These women need a new set of stories, a new set of heroines with whom they can identify and from whom they can draw strength. At first it may seem naïve and unrealistic to assume that we can reconstruct an individual's mythological, archetypal heritage. Yet, if some of the despair homeless or disenfranchised women feel comes from their inability to access positive images for growth and development and if the damage to their self image is in fact at the archetypal or mythological level, we may have no choice but to address the void of positive mythologies.

While it is beyond the scope of this book to present all of those stories that might be incorporated in a new mythology for homeless women, the presentation of a few such stories might suggest positive and fruitful directions to those working with homeless women.

The first story, taken from the Bantu tribe of Africa, concerns the Great Mother goddess Songi.[14] As the protectress of the tribe, Songi resented the mistreatment of the women within Bantu society. Tribal women were routinely denigrated and abused by their husbands, a situation that Songi sought to remedy. The goddess chose as the instrument of her intervention a young daughter of the tribe whom she encountered one day as the young woman was running through the woods. In a ceremony that included a ritual bonding with the Great Mother, the young woman of the tribe incorporated some of the power of the bountiful goddess, Songi. As part of the ceremony, the goddess notched the teeth of the young woman. The ritual completed, the young woman was sent home and told to gather together her mother and her grandmother, constituting three generations of tribal women, and thus united, these women were to sing the praises of the goddess. As they proceeded to sing, bounties and gifts spilled forth from between the notched teeth of the young woman; from deep inside her came all the riches and worldly possessions that the tribe might need to survive. Upon seeing the riches that came forth from the young woman, the men of the tribe became even more abusive toward their wives because their wives did not have the power to bestow similar gifts upon them. The young woman who had been honored by the goddess then called together all the women of the tribe, and she proceeded to file and notch each woman's teeth. From between these sharp teeth now came similar riches and bounties. The myth concludes with the men of the tribe being told that they may participate in this new wealth only if they honor and respect their wives, refraining from abusing them ever again.

The story provides a model of feminine power on several levels. The women learn that they contain within themselves all of the riches and treasures that the tribe needs. They need only to find a way to bring forth that which exists deep inside of themselves in order to flourish. When the women gain access to their own inner strength, they not only provide for the material needs of the tribe, but they also put an end to the abuse and victimization that has characterized their lives. They are empowered when they realize that their own inner core is worthy and valuable. Moreover, these women combine their inner strength with an outward display of power. Their teeth, the gateway to the riches within, are sharp and notched. These women are no longer passive and docile, rather they are powerful and potentially dangerous. Through this newfound aggressiveness and power, the women are able to bring forth nurturance for the tribe.

The story is not only about individual power, however. The women are able to actualize their inner resources when they unite with the goddess, a symbol of natural and universal feminine power. Unlike the Amazons who became powerful by imitating men, the Bantu women celebrate their feminine selves. The strength that the tribal women experience does not only come from their connection to the primordial Great Mother, but also from their more personal and immediate connection to other generations of women. Each woman feels her bond with her mother on one side and her daughter on the other, thus participating in an accumulated heritage of feminine power.

In the Grimm brothers' story "The Girl Without Hands," the heroine's path to transformation is more introspective and lonely.[15] In this story a young woman is sacrificed to the Devil because of her father's shortsightedness. The Devil offers to trade her father great riches in exchange for whatever stands behind the poor man's mill. Thinking that only an old apple tree will be sacrificed, the man readily agrees. When he arrives home, however, he finds that his own daughter and only child has been standing behind the mill and now must belong to the Devil.

When the Devil comes, after a period of three years, to claim his prize, he finds that the young woman has fortified and strengthened herself, lessening the Devil's power over her. Even when the Devil orders that the young woman's hands be chopped off, she is able to keep herself pure, crying cleansing tears over her maimed arms. Because of her own virtue, she survives and is spared having to go off with the Devil.

In the beginning of the story, the young woman's calm and inner strength are contrasted with her father's rash and greedy behavior. He is panicked for his daughter, and for himself, when he realizes what he has done; yet he is unable to change the situation. His daughter is saved by her own strength of character and her pious actions that make her immune to the Devil's power.

The young woman's story continues with her decision to leave home and make her own way in the world, refusing to remain with her parents who have agreed to care for her as an invalid. She wraps her handless arms in bandages and goes out into the world on her own. In the course of her travels, the young woman enters the garden of a king. She attracts his attention with her devotion, piety, and simple beauty, and he asks her to be his wife. The king makes his new wife a pair of silver hands to replace the hands that she has lost. For a time the couple lives happily, and the young bride gives birth to a son. Through a series of deceptions and malevolent maneuvers, however, the young woman and her baby son are separated from the husband and father. Once again the young woman is forced to make her own way in the forest. This time she wanders alone and lives alone with her child for a period of seven years. During that time, through her own efforts and as a result of her own inner strength and determination, her natural hands grow back. Subsequently, she is reunited with her lost husband, who at first does not recognize her because he is searching for a young woman with silver hands. She tells him that by virtue of her good deeds and her prayers, her own hands have been restored to her. The myth ends happily with the family's being reunited.

While the heroine of this story is victimized and abused by her father's thoughtlessness, the Devil's cruelty, and the evil intentions of others, she is not a passive victim. She does not run from adversity, but she draws on her own inner strength to triumph over adversity. She chooses to make her own way in the world, despite an obvious handicap, and refuses to be weak and dependent on her parents. In this manner she provides an example for women who feel defeated by circumstances and past abuses. Rather than succumbing to hopelessness and despair or raging at her father's thoughtlessness, she assumes responsibility for her own life and draws on the strength within her.

In the story, the young woman suffers the loss of her hands, symbols of one's worldly competence and the instruments of one's constructive action. She is thus without the tools to care for and do for herself. She must discover her own inner strengths and skills and become a truly self-directed woman. While she uses the silver hands made for her by another for a time, she must eventually generate her own competence and rely more fully on her own inner reserves. During a period of prolonged isolation and separation from loved ones, she does indeed regenerate her own hands. She is the instrument of her own success. As in the story of one of the homeless women, the young woman in this story "birthed herself"; she created herself as an independent woman. Homeless women, many of whom have felt incompetent and devalued, may also need the opportunity and the encouragement to regenerate their own metaphoric hands and thereby reconnect with lost skills and competencies.

The final story, taken from Australian folklore, involves communal and group power rather than purely individual strength. The story begins as a young maiden, Lia, descends from heaven to help the people of the Goanna tribe.[16] The men and women of the tribe live in a parched and dry land where they must forage and dig each day for their food. When Lia joins the tribe, she finds that the daily lives of the men and women are quite different. The women spend the day laboring under the hot sun, parched and weary from digging for roots. The men, however, leave the village and return in the evening, cool and refreshed.

Each day the men provide the women with one skin full of water. Not only must the women share the meager provision, but they must make it last all day. Lia is troubled by the disparity between the lives of the men and those of the women, and she is curious how the men manage to refresh themselves each day. Lia begins to tell the women that they are entitled to the same comforts the men enjoy. She arouses their dissatisfaction by pointing out that one skin of water is not enough for a whole tribe of women, and she nurtures their growing belief that they deserve to have more.

One day the women leave their task of digging for roots and go into the mountains to search for water. They wander close to the source of the stream, although they do not find the water itself. When they return home, their husbands notice that they have been away and that they have come close to discovering the secret of the water. Consequently, the men chastise and berate their wives, threatening them with violence. The men frighten the women, hoping that they will be intimidated into staying in their place and not venturing forth and challenging the men's authority and sole access to the water.

The threatening behavior of the husbands is enough to cow all of the women except for Lia. On a subsequent day, she goes into the mountains by herself in a further search for water for the women of the tribe, but she is unsuccessful. The spirits of the mountain tell her that water will be found only if all the women join together and come as one, a united force, into the mountains.

Lia goes back to the village and tells the women of her discovery. United, they go forth and discover not only the mountain stream, but also the source of a great river. The women share their success with one another. They rejoice in the water that they have found, splashing each other and playing with one another in a way that has been previously unknown.

When they return to their village, the women discover that a new river now flows into the village, dividing the town into two parts and bringing much-needed water and fertility to the land. When their husbands return to the village, they find themselves separated from the women by the wide river. The women smile to themselves and rejoice with one another because they know that never again will they be subject to abuse and violence at the hands of their husbands. The myth ends with the women founding their own village, their own society, safe from the men who must remain on the other side of the river.

Only through their combined strength, by joining with one another and discovering the sisterhood and fellowship among them, were the women able to change their situation. Their joint effort not only freed them from the victimization of their husbands but also enabled them to rejoice in a new and fertile life. Many of the homeless women have found similarly that in joining with one another, in sharing their stories with each other, and in forming new families and new communities with one another, they are able together to find a strength and a level of competence that none of them had known as separate individuals.

In each of these three myths, then, we are presented with images of women who are strong and powerful. Either alone or as a group they are able to find within themselves hidden reserves and strength that allow them to go forward. Such mythologies are positive replacements for the stories of abuse and victimization that homeless women live out on a daily basis.

Paradoxically, as homeless women become stronger and more personally competent, they are better able to accept care and nurturance from others. When individuals feel personally bereft of inner resources, they may experience envy and anger at a bountiful caregiver, believing that the caregiver has everything while they have nothing at all. Because of debilitating envy, some women actually reject help when they need it the most.

In their discussion of Cinderella and her envious sisters, Ann and Barry Ulanov postulate that the individual who has been interpersonally and materially deprived and who consequently experiences a sense of inner hunger may be the most envious of others.[17] Needing to destroy the good they see in someone else, these individuals often denigrate and dismiss the very help they need. Some of the homeless women, especially those who were identified with the predator or the rebel, were especially vicious in their attacks toward caregivers, whom they perceived as having everything while they themselves had nothing. Moreover, the homeless women insisted that these caregivers had been successful because they were lucky, not because they had worked hard; consequently, they doubly envied these individuals.

Only when an individual feels that she has received nurturance, that she has substance inside of herself, and that she has personal strength with which to meet others in a reciprocal relationship is she able to accept the good things that others have to offer without being overwhelmed by her own envy. In reality, many homeless women are better able to receive help and care from others as they begin to feel stronger and more personally alive. When they are able to absorb nurturance, they feel stronger still, allowing them to take even more. Once the first drop of psychological food is absorbed, the individual's capacity to be nurtured grows quickly.

The preceding discussion of repair for homeless women has focused exclusively on attempts to ease the destructive projections that encumber them. These interventions intend to repair the psychological damage that is done when homeless women are confused with the collective projections that they have come to embody. Repair at the archetypal or mythological level is not the only remediation that homeless women need, however. Efforts must be made to repair the economic and social conditions that contribute to homelessness. Additionally, those women who have been psychologically damaged in a personal way by the traumas of their lives or by the experience of homelessness may require competent psychological counseling. I am suggesting, however, that when women have come to identify with destructive collective projections they may continue to be disabled even after social, economic, and psychological conditions have been changed. For these women, repair at the archetypal level is critical. Only when they are free of the burden of carrying other people's unwanted psychological baggage will homeless women have the freedom and the energy to actualize their own inner selves.

Chapter 11

Repair for All Women

While women who live on the streets are homeless in a literal sense, women who are disconnected from fundamental aspects of feminine possibility are homeless in a psychological sense.[1] These women, too, must find a way to come home, a way to reintegrate and welcome back those aspects of themselves that have been cast out. While the effects of this psychological estrangement are less immediately obvious than the consequences of homelessness, they may be no less damaging to the women who experience them. Women who label large aspects of human experience as unpleasant, ugly, and unacceptable and proceed either to deny or to cast out those unwanted possibilities cut themselves off from the totality of human options. Such women live authentically only half of the time. The other half they must engage in repressing, denying, or projecting unwanted feelings and behaviors. Try as we might, we cannot construct a world for ourselves that contains only those elements of society or those aspects of human development that we like. We must either accept all of the parts of our human condition or split unwanted parts off, denying ourselves full participation in the range of human possibilities.

Edward Whitmont, the Jungian analyst, maintains that ugliness, darkness, destruction, and terror are as much a part of the human condition as beauty, love, nurturance, and joy.[2] Indeed, these negative qualities and feelings are the reverse side of our positive virtues. In our quest for personal wholeness and psychological integration, we must accept these shadow sides of human possibility and, as Whitmont suggests, accept them respectfully if not lovingly.[3]

Repair for all women involves the awareness and realization that evil and ugly tendencies, these socially unacceptable urges, desires, and possibilities, are as much a part of our essential humanness as are those valued and socially approved aspects of ourselves. Moreover, when we affirm the full range of our human possibilities, we are able to transform certain denied behaviors and desires into constructive actions.

When we cease being afraid of our shadows and allow ourselves to look clearly at that which we have hidden and denied, we can begin the process of transforming and rehabilitating the shadow. Perhaps an analogy will clarify the process of repair. When we take an unwanted object, a piece of luggage, perhaps, and store it in a damp corner of the basement, the object often deteriorates and becomes even less desirable. It may warp, become mildewed, or become covered with spider webs and a layer of dust. Standing thus in the basement, the once unwanted suitcase now looks even more undesirable. When we first retrieve it from the basement, we may be repulsed. Similarly, when individuals bury or deny parts of who they are, they run the risk of inventing monsters. Many patients in psychotherapy come to fear that if a split-off part of the psyche is brought into the light of consciousness, tears will flow forever or rage will lead to murder. In contrast, when we actually bring our psychological cast-offs up from the basement, we often find that they are not as bad as we imagined. A little fresh air and a little repair may soften an unpleasant image. After all, even though the luggage was unwanted and has become somewhat dilapidated, it is still only a suitcase.

Moreover, when we demystify and de-energize the unwanted parts of our psychological makeup, we are able to see those parts of ourselves more clearly, recognizing perhaps a previously unknown possibility. Every psychological state has the potential for positive and negative actions. Anger can lead to assertiveness, just as compassion can lead to smothering. Only when we recognize and acknowledge a part of ourselves are we free to experience its positive transformation.

The victim is not only a woman who is abused, she is also a woman in touch with her own vulnerability, aware of the fact that she is dependent on others and that she needs human relationships and human interaction in order to survive. She acknowledges her own mortality and the finitude of her own life; consequently, she is better able to use the time and resources that she has constructively. Her vulnerability and her awareness of her potential for victimization empower her and allow her to make healthy and constructive choices.

The exile is a woman who wanders at the periphery of society, but she is also a woman in touch with her own aloneness, comfortable with herself and her separateness and distinctness from other people. She is not afraid of being alone and may be able to draw strength and transformative energy from the time she spends in isolation. Just as the women in societies that isolated women once a month during the time of their menstrual cycle, the woman who is comfortable with the exile inside her knows how to use her time alone. Time alone allows a woman to reflect and to re-evaluate priorities, finding her own center in the midst of a busy life and external demands.

The predator is a woman who can be violent and destructive. She is also, however, a woman who can be aggressive and competitive. She is a woman who can stand her ground and fight for those things in which she believes. She is not intimidated by those who appear to be stronger than she is, and she is able to concentrate her own power and strength to move forward in constructive directions.

The rebel is a woman who says "no" to that which infringes on her autonomy. She is defiant and sometimes angry, but she is also a woman who knows what she wants and what she needs in order to be a whole individual. She protects her autonomy and shields the unique aspects of herself from the impingement of collective influences.

A woman who owns her shadow side, who is willing to embrace and accept those parts of herself that have been cast out, opens herself to the possibility for new and constructive actions. Whitmont comments that the realization of one's unacceptable and undesirable urges does not necessarily mean that one will act on those urges in the most terrifying and despicable way.[4] One appreciates the full range of human possibility; one then acts reasonably, transforming shadow energy in positive directions. Indeed, it is not an awareness of the shadow that brings about devastation and problematic action, but it is a denial of the shadow and a projection of the shadow outward that results in catastrophe for all men and women.

If, for example, a woman has a strong rebellious side, but represses that side of herself because of the lifestyle she has chosen and the pressures of her particular social group, she may find that her rebellious self makes an unexpected appearance in the life of her son or daughter. The mother consciously denies her own rebelliousness; she leads a traditional and conformist life, fearing that if she ever acknowledges her own scornful and defiant self, she will be unable to control her behavior and will go about challenging and attacking the rules of her social world. Her daughter, however, begins to act out even as a young teenager. She breaks rules at school, she breaks rules within the home, and she says "no" to those expectations that her mother and society have of her. When she is old enough, she leaves home, runs off, and joins a rock band much to her mother's and father's conscious dismay. One might conjecture that this daughter has acted out her mother's rebellious side. The rebel has found a home in the impressionable teenager. If the mother had been able to allow her own rebelliousness to come up from the dark basement, she might have found a way to convert her rebellious energy into constructive action. Instead, the rebel stayed underground, only to be retrieved and used in less thoughtful ways by her daughter. We often find subsequent generations living out those repressed aspects of ourselves that we are unable to own.

In Jungian analyst Ann Ulanov's words, women must become "receiving women," capable of receiving into themselves all those parts of feminine possibility that have been cast out.[5] Ulanov maintains that women have much to gain from taking back in or receiving that which belongs to them. When an individual projects much of her own unwanted personality into the atmosphere and onto others, she psychologically pollutes the interpersonal atmosphere, forcing others to act out that with which she is personally uncomfortable.[6] As a result, individuals who deny much of themselves and who project their own disliked and unwanted parts onto others often experience chaotic relationships.

Other people always seem to be doing those bad, nasty, and undesirable things that the individual so assiduously avoids. As a result, relationships are characterized by blame, disappointment, and betrayal. The individual may feel an inordinate need to control other people, spending energy manipulating and distorting relationships just to keep the shadow projections in check. When we free other people of having to carry psychological projections for us, we enable our relationships to become both less traumatic and less problematic. Moreover, we free others to be more genuinely themselves, allowing us to discover, in those closest to us, attributes that have been disguised or ignored while we have been busy controlling and manipulating undesirable shadow content.

The benefit to an individual from receiving back his or her own psychological parts also comes in areas other than interpersonal relationships. When one projects, one expends a great deal of psychic energy in ridding oneself of undesirable possibilities.[7] Without the need to control, deny, project, and repress aspects of ourselves, we find that we do indeed have more energy for creative, active possibilities.

Reintegrating aspects of the shadow also affords individuals the opportunity to see the world more clearly. People and events are no longer colored or distorted by psychological projections. For example, a woman who is afraid of her own anger and destructiveness may project those affects out indiscriminately. She sees everyone as angry and dangerous; consequently, she fails to assess accurately situations in which violence and aggressiveness are real possibilities. She also misses opportunities for relationships with people who are benign or gentle.

When we allow ourselves to feel terror, pain, destructiveness, or evil within ourselves, then we can allow ourselves to be aware of those possibilities in other people. This awareness serves to help us in making informed and constructive choices in our relationships with other people and also allows us to empathize more fully with others. If someone believes that she has no evil inside herself, it may be difficult for her to empathize with and to acknowledge the evil in others. We become not only more empathic but also more generous listeners when we acknowledge the full range of human activity within ourselves.

Finally, an individual who allows diverse options within herself knows herself more fully and totally. Consequently, she is less likely to absorb projections from other individuals.[8] Rather, she can step aside when others attempt to project their own unwanted affect onto her and can return to the sender his or her psychological baggage. If we do not know what belongs to us and we are unaware of our own varied possibilities, we are more likely to absorb that which belongs elsewhere.

The process of reintegrating one's shadow side is not as simple as embracing a long-lost sister.[9] The conscious personality has feared the shadow, has denied it, and has denigrated it. Consequently, for the conscious public self to acknowledge and appreciate the shadow will take time. It has been suggested that one will need to reabsorb the shadow slowly, just as the Israelis reabsorbed the long-lost Falashas in a slow and conscientious process. One must confront one's underside bit by bit, absorbing, assessing, and making personal that which has been denied.[10]

We may ask if any models for this kind of reintegration exist. If the public self is to confront and to accept or reaccept the shadow side, how do we proceed with this difficult journey? The ancient Sumerian myth of the goddess Inanna offers us a prototype for the confrontation between the conscious public self and the dark shadow who dwells within.

The Story of Inanna

Inanna was the queen of heaven.[11] She was many-faceted, containing within herself a range of feminine possibilities. Inanna lived where the sun shone, a goddess of light whose province was the upper world. One day Inanna decided that she would descend into the underworld, the kingdom of her sister Ereshkigal. Despite the fact that she was the queen of heaven and felt powerful and strong in her decision to descend to a world from which others did not return, Inanna told her servants that if she was not back within three days they should search for her. Even the powerful goddess must take precautions when she decides to go underground, to go deep inside to an unknown and dark world.

When she arrived at the gate to the underworld, Inanna announced herself as the queen of heaven. Her position in the upper world, however, was not sufficient to gain her access to the realm beneath, and she had to follow the same rules as anyone who chooses to descend; she was brought naked and bowed low.[12] At each of the seven gates through which she had to pass in order to fully descend, Inanna removed one piece of her queenly attire, leaving it behind. When she finally confronted Ereshkigal, her sister of the shadow, Inanna was bare and unprotected.

If one is to confront the shadow, one must remove one's public identity. The process, moreover, is not a thoughtless disrobing but rather a slow and gradual process where, step-by-step, one leaves behind illusions and aspects of the public personality.[13] That which identifies one in the upper, public world has no relevance when one confronts the shadow underneath.

Ereshkigal, herself a goddess, is in many ways the opposite of Inanna. She represents a powerful energy, but hers is a powerful negative energy, one that has been disowned and denied, surviving only underground.[14] Before her exile to the underworld, Ereshkigal, too, resided in the sunlight. She was raped repeatedly, abused, and victimized by her husband. As a result, she was cast out from the human community and came to live in a world underground. She is described as an isolated, bitter woman who is rageful, spiteful, and greedy, containing within herself primitive unsocialized affect.[15] Ereshkigal is the death-bringing goddess whose eyes are cold and impersonal, and she evinces no pity for her victims.

The shadow goddess Ereshkigal represents those aspects of woman that have been cast off. She is the suffering victim, despairing, bitter, and rageful, and she has turned her victimization into a predatory anger that now wreaks destruction on those who come near her. She is also an exiled woman; she is no longer part of the human community and she suffers alone, hungry and lustful for human companionship. When Inanna finally confronts her sister, Ereshkigal condemns her to be impaled on a stake. While this act seems cruel and inhuman, authors have suggested that in her merciless punishment of Inanna, Ereshkigal acts out the female rebel.[16] By impaling Inanna on a stake, she enacts raw, female power, that power that does not need a man to be expressed. Together, Ereshkigal and the impaled Inanna contain all elements of the disowned female shadow. They are victim, exile, predator, and rebel.

When Inanna does not return to the upper world after three days, her servant proceeds to enlist aid in securing Inanna's release, not knowing that the goddess has been killed. One of the gods agrees to help Inanna's maidservant, and he creates, from the dirt that has accumulated under his fingernails, two little mourners to be sent to the underworld on Inanna's behalf. These two figures are anonymous, otherworldly creatures. They are made from seemingly insignificant refuse, from that which is normally cast out, washed away, and eliminated. By creating powerful, magical beings from seemingly insignificant dirt, the god recognizes the value of those aspects of the self that may appear to be irrelevant and undesirable.

These two little creatures are able to slip unnoticed into the underworld, where they find Ereshkigal mourning and wailing. As she cries and laments over the tragedies of her life, these two proceed to mirror her cries, she saying "Woe unto me," and they responding "Woe unto you."[17] The goddess is at once moved and is brought to a level of consciousness by this empathic mirroring. She is touched and humanized because someone has heard her pain and has been able to reflect back to her the sound of her own anguish.

Because she has been heard and understood, Ereshkigal feels human and generous. She is able to be giving toward these two who have felt her pain. When she asks them what they want, they respond that they want the body of the goddess Inanna. Inanna is thus returned to the upper world and restored to life; however, she comes back a changed woman. She is surrounded now by the demons of the underworld who are instructed to accompany her until she chooses a scapegoat to return to Ereshkigal in her stead. Inanna proceeds to search for one who will take her place. She is angry, rageful, and selfish. She has incorporated into herself the shadow sister. Inanna behaves as if she has swallowed the shadow whole, and the shadow elements, rather than being integrated into her personality and interwoven with those characteristics of lightness that marked Inanna before her descent, remain as an encapsulated whole within the goddess.

Inanna finally decides that she will choose her lover to take her place in the underworld, and she proceeds to condemn him to exile. At this point in the story, a third woman enters the drama. Inanna's lover has a sister, Geshtinanna. Geshtinanna is not a goddess; she is a mortal woman and she is characterized by her wisdom and her integrity. Geshtinanna feels compassion for her brother who is to be condemned to a life in the underworld, and out of compassion, she offers to share his punishment with him. Geshtinanna's act is not a rash and thoughtless one. Consciously aware of what she is doing, she agrees to spend half of her life in the underworld and half of her life above ground.

Geshtinanna has been described as a whole and integrated woman.[18] She is a woman who takes a stand, she is clear about what she wants to do, and she pursues a course of action out of knowledge, not out of ignorance. She is aware, moreover, that she is a woman of value. She does not agree to assume her brother's place out of self-denigration. She is clear that she is a worthy woman, and she makes this choice out of human compassion and love. It has been suggested that Geshtinanna is the whole woman who emerges from the union of the shadow and the public self.[19] She is a fully integrated woman.

The story of Inanna, Ereskigal, and Geshtinanna thus contains all the essential elements of the individual's confrontation with the shadow: there are two opposing personalities, one of lightness, one of darkness; there is a descent marked by a series of necessary losses; there is a painful confrontation between the two forces; there is repair or restoration through compassion and love; and finally, there is the creation of a new, more fully human woman who symbolizes the union of the two opposites. It testifies to the timelessness of these themes as well as to the universality of the process of integration that we find these same themes in a story from the mythology of Sumeria, a lost and ancient civilization, and from the struggles and reports of modern women as well. The question remains, however, how should modern women proceed in the reintegration of their personal shadow selves?

Two Opposing Personalities

Often individuals are unaware that they have split off and denied part of their personality. They are only aware that they feel uneasy or uncomfortable in particular situations. One woman in therapy, for example, knew that she became angry whenever she heard or read of battered wives or abused children; she did not know, however, that she disowned her personal sense of vulnerability, her internal victim. Another woman knew that she hated to watch or participate in any competitive sports; she was unaware, however, that she had rejected her own aggressive and predatory side. At times, individuals will be able to name the part of the self that has become shadow, but be unfamiliar with the real substance of that part of the self. For example, a woman might say at the beginning of therapy, "I have trouble with anger," a statement that usually translates into "I do not feel angry when I and others think I should, and I am afraid that if I do get angry I will be unable to control myself." Such a statement indicates that the individual suspects that a part of the self has been split off and denied, but is uncertain how to reown that lost part of the personality.

For all women, the process of reintegration must begin with the recognition that a part of the self is missing, forgotten, and denied. Gradually, one must be able to name the parts of the shadow, to explore and become familiar with them, and ultimately to become comfortable in their presence. It is important that the personality of Ereshkigal, the shadow sister, be just as developed and articulated as the personality of Inanna, the goddess of lightness.

Necessary Losses

One cannot grow and take in new possibilities unless one eliminates other possibilities. Those aspects of the public self that have become outmoded need to be left behind as one moves toward psychological development and integration. Often one fills one's psychological space completely with the activities and trappings of one's public life. A woman is so busy being a good mother and a conscientious homemaker that she pushes out the part of her that feels isolated and lonely, the exile within her. If she is to reintegrate the alone and alienated part of herself, she will need to put aside some of her public self, making room for the outcast sister. At each stage of her descent, Inanna must leave part of her public identity behind, this disrobing being necessary if one is to take on and reown previously cast-off parts of the self.

Even when a woman willingly descends to encounter the shadow, she may still experience the changes in her public self as a loss. She may need to say good-bye properly and mourn parts of the public self that are being left behind. Moreover, she may need time to adjust to her psychologically stripped-down self. Friends and family members may be similarly disconcerted as they discover that old behaviors and response patterns have disappeared.

Confrontation

When the confrontation with the shadow finally occurs, individuals often feel overwhelmed. People will cry, tremble, and shake as they look for the first time on the face of the self they have hidden for so long. Sometimes individuals will feel flooded with a wave of deep sadness; other times they will feel pierced with a sharp pain, like the stake that impales Inanna. Regardless of the particular affect, individuals experience deep feelings when they meet the shadow in themselves and they need to respect the power of those feelings.

Repair Through Compassion

The individual's ability to empathize with his or her own denied shadow self is critical to psychological growth. One must cease being hateful and disparaging towards one's own vulnerabilities and weaknesses. While a person may certainly decide to change certain aspects of the self, he or she must embrace all of his or her possibilities and must do so without scorn and derision. The ability to accept and to feel compassion and empathy for one's most despicable, undesirable side, is a necessary part of any growth. Indeed, when the mourners empathize with Ereshkigal's pain, she feels understood, opening her to be more generous and more compassionate herself. We thus humanize and transform our dark side when we are able to accept it and empathize with it.

The process of accepting the shadow often begins when an individual sees compassion, empathy, and acceptance of the unwanted self in the eyes of another. So often I have heard patients recount with tears in their eyes the relief and love they felt when a lover, a friend, or even a therapist saw them at their worst and did not turn away. If someone else, someone outside the immediate family and someone who is valued, can see and accept the shadow, then maybe the individual herself can begin to incorporate that sense of acceptance and even compassion toward the dark side of the self.

A New Woman

In receiving the shadow sister and in integrating previously cast off possibilities into her conscious life, a woman may indeed find that she is not the same, but that a new woman has been created. This movement toward a new integration may initially require some vacillation and balancing between various parts of the self. When Inanna first returned from the underworld, she was overly identified with the shadow, and many individuals find that when they first give the shadow expression, it seems to dominate for a while. One woman, for example, found that when she first acknowledged her own defiant and rebellious side, she was saying "no" everywhere and to everyone. Eventually, she exercised her assertiveness only when she felt it important to do so, and she expressed her legitimate objections in a more temperate manner. In the psychological space between timid conformist and defiant rebel a new woman had emerged.

In the myth, neither Inanna nor Ereshkigal remains the central figure at the end of the story. Instead, a new woman emerges, combining within herself the positive and negative sides of feminine possibility. She symbolizes the union of these two opposing sisters, these two aspects of the feminine, by spending six months of her life in the underworld and six months of her life above ground. This rhythm between upper and lower worlds also parallels the rhythm of the seasons. This new woman is not only whole and centered within herself, but she is in harmony with the rhythms of the universe and the psychological processes of others as well.

Chapter 12

Conclusion

It is not uncommon for men and women to record the public events of their lives in photographs. Each photograph is a positive statement of who we are, of who we have been, or of something we have done. What we often forget is that each photograph also has a negative—a reverse image that is as much a part of the process of picture taking as the final positive photograph we put on our mantelpiece. For everything that we are publicly, for every part of ourselves that we are willing to own and acknowledge, there is also a reverse negative image, a side of ourselves that remains hidden, disowned, and unwanted. This shadow side of individual and collective development is as much a part of human psychological reality as that which is publicly owned and displayed.

The content of the shadow does differ, however, across different cultures and across different generations.[1] Since the shadow reflects that which is collectively and personally disowned, differ-

ences in the social milieu, differences in public opinion, and differences in collective philosophy will result in differing shadow
images. Indeed, what is publicly owned at one point in our history
may, for a variety of reasons, be relegated to the shadow at another
point in time. The reverse is also true; that which is shadow and
denied may become public and owned. For example, nations
are often invested in disowning their violent and aggressive side;
consequently, any imperialistic activities are defined as primarily
defensive, or supportive operations, with more overtly aggressive
and violent behaviors being projected onto the enemy. During
times of war, however, governments and citizens need to own
publicly the violent and aggressive self. Soldiers, after all, must be
fearless and aggressive. During wartime then, it is the frightened,
dependent, and vulnerable self who must hide in the basement,
both literally and psychologically, an unacceptable public person
in a society that owns the aggressor. As the social and political
conditions change, so too will the content of the shadow change.

There are also differences in the content of the shadow for
different subgroups within a culture and for different individuals
as well.[2] While it has been the contention in this book that the
victim, the exile, the predator, and the rebel constitute the feminine
shadow in the latter half of the twentieth century, different women
will present a different balance among archetypal images in the
construction of their personal shadows. Some women, for example, who live public lives that are rebellious and fully independent
will not have the rebel relegated to the realm of the shadow. They
will live the rebel publicly, and their shadow will consist of another
configuration of disowned psychological parts. Thus, while the
victim, the exile, the predator, and the rebel constitute the faces
of the collective feminine shadow, the particular balance among
these four will be constellated differently for different individual
women.

What remains constant, however, is that each woman will necessarily have a shadow and that the shadow will be greater or lesser
depending on how much of her psychological makeup she must
deny and negate. While the feminine shadow obviously has most
relevance for women, it is not irrelevant in the lives of men. It has
been suggested that men often project onto women those aspects
of their own psyches with which they are the least comfortable.[3] If

women then project those unwanted psychological dynamics out even farther onto outcast and disenfranchised women, we might conjecture that homeless women carry aspects of the masculine shadow once removed. For example, if women cannot tolerate the victim and must deny their personal and collective vulnerability, men, who have been socialized to be strong, must feel the need to disown weakness even more so. Thus, at least in part, the feminine shadow may contain those parts of masculine personality with which men are least comfortable.

Regardless of the particular content of the shadow, it is always the case that we come to know our personal shadow as it is reflected in the eyes of another. Shadows become apparent and visible as they are cast out and projected onto other people. We read therefore the story of our own unwanted lives in the faces of others. Not surprisingly, our first reaction to seeing embodied in another that which we have denied in ourselves is often to be afraid. Many individuals never get beyond this first response and indeed spend their lives being afraid of their shadows, being afraid of those psychological parts of themselves that are unacceptable, and being afraid of those real men and women who embody or actualize the shadow for them.

To be afraid of one's shadow is to limit actively and consciously one's human possibilities, to build for oneself a rigid and tight world in which only acceptable and public feelings and images are allowed. To move beyond a response of fear, confusion, and disorientation when confronted with the shadow, an individual must be prepared to recognize the shadow as a long-lost sister, as that part of the self that has been cast out and disowned.

Women who grow up in families of many biological sisters often find as adults that they and their sisters have inadvertently divided the range of feminine possibility among themselves.[4] One sister becomes the sociable one, another is competitive and aggressive, and yet a third is artistic and introspective. Taken as a unit, this family of sisters encompasses the range of possible feminine behaviors and feminine reactions. Each sister on her own, however, is only a part of the totality. Similarly, women share with their psychological sisters of the shadow the full range of feminine possibility. The public woman lives out those aspects of her personality and her inner self that are socially accepted and valued. Her shadow sister, however, actualizes the unwanted, disowned, and devalued feminine options. Taken together, public women and their shadow sisters encompass the full range of human possibility. Just as the sisters of one family often need each other to form a whole actualized woman, so, too, do public women and shadow sisters need each other if real integration of the self is to occur.

The process of integration and personal growth must begin with awareness. Women must become conscious of the projections that they have cast out into the environment. By first recognizing those unwanted parts of themselves in the faces of others, they can begin the process of reowning vital parts of their feminine possibility. Personal growth results from this reintegration of psychological projections, not only for the woman who has cast out parts of her essential self, but also for those women who have been burdened with carrying shadow projections who are freed to undertake their own process of self-actualization. When we demythologize and demystify those who have embodied our unwanted selves, we free them to be more truly themselves and to actualize their own diverse possibilities.

The journey toward personal wholeness and growth is a lifelong process.[5] One does not reintegrate aspects of the disowned shadow once and for all, becoming a complete and integrated person, never again to consider that which is disowned and undesired. Rather, one works throughout one's life to take back increasingly that which has been cast out and denied.

It has been suggested that the image of the shadow appears to women at times in their lives when they are undergoing some significant transition.[6] At a point when a previously owned, acceptable public personality comes into question, the individual might be more available to experience and to acknowledge parts of the self that have been denied. Major transitions, which for most women coincide with natural biological changes, force them not only to reevaluate the way in which they have been in the world, but also to create new responses and new public personalities. For example, when a woman moves from being a daughter to being a wife and mother, she must create a new public personality. While some women do indeed try to take the dutiful daughter into their married life, such a bringing forth often results in problems for the woman and for her new family.

Similarly, when women go through menopause, many must move from the position of primary caretaker and mother to the position of independent and single woman. These transitions call into question everything that we have known in the past and force us to redefine ourselves. At those times, it is possible for a woman to reintegrate aspects of the shadow that have been previously cast out because the whole personality is in flux. Because old options are no longer viable and new options must be considered, unwanted parts of the self have the opportunity for new life. For example, a woman who denied her own rebellious independent self during the years of her mothering and homemaking activities, once her children no longer need her and she becomes again an independent and separate woman, might take that opportunity to reintegrate her rebellious shadow, the part of herself that for many years had been disowned and disallowed. This reintegration of previously unacceptable behaviors may explain why women often behave in unpredictable ways at points of transition. The children of a once compliant and staid mother may be surprised to find her taking off for a trip around the world. This trip, however, may be perfectly consonant with the reintegration of her rebellious and independent shadow.

Any time in a woman's life then, whether biologically induced or otherwise, when a personal shift or transition is involved affords an opportunity for the reintegration of aspects of the shadow. In psychotherapy, a process designed to facilitate and enhance the development of the self, the individual and the therapist artificially precipitate a period of transition. The therapy itself brings the woman into contact with parts of her disowned and denied shadow. It is not uncommon for women in psychotherapy to have dreams or images that involve the emergence of the shadow.

As I was completing work on this book, a patient of mine brought me an especially apt dream. In the dream she found herself sitting in her office about to begin the day's activities. She became aware, however, that the office had had a previous occupant, another woman who had worked there before she came. As she became aware of the existence of the other woman, she also became aware that this other woman, the woman whom she had displaced, was now homeless. The other woman was no longer safely in a job and in an acceptable role, but she had become a homeless woman who wandered the streets, lost and disheveled. In the dream, when my patient first became aware of the existence of the homeless woman, she felt frightened and repulsed. She visualized this woman as unattractive, smelly, and crazed. Subsequently, however, her anxiety about this woman quieted, and she realized that if the woman approached her needing a place to stay, she would allow this woman to move in with her, to stay with her in her own home. The dream ended with my patient feeling somewhat reassured that the homeless woman would be taken care of. This dream occurred at a point in her therapy when my patient was contemplating the reintegration of her own aggressive and disowned parts, those parts of her that had been relegated to the shadow. In her dream she confronts her shadow self, that part of her that has been displaced and cast out, and while her initial response to the shadow is to be frightened and repulsed, her eventual response is to open up herself and her psychological home to this shadow.

The more aspects of one's self that an individual can take in, the more he or she can be an integrated and whole human being. While the goal of complete individuation, the taking into the self of all personal and collective possibilities, is one that few if any individuals ever complete, it is a goal that each of us must attempt if we are to lead authentic lives.[7] Moreover, the process of self-awareness and personal integration must begin with the acceptance of the shadow.[8] Without an acknowledgment and a return of those parts of the self that have been cast out, there can be no personal growth or development.

An Old Testament benediction promises the righteous person that his or her "shadow will be as the noonday"[9] Such a blessing will be granted if the individual reaches out to those who are hungry and afflicted. In a similar way, modern men and women can cease to cast a psychological shadow if they, too, reach out to the afflicted and homeless among us and take back from those carriers of the shadow unwanted psychological projections. When we bring home those parts of ourselves that have been unwanted and disowned, we, too, will cast no gloom and our shadows will be as the noonday.

Notes

Chapter 1

1. Kozol, *Rachel and Her Children.*
2. *Ibid.*
3. *Ibid.*
4. Cohen, Putnam, and Sullivan, "The Mentally Ill Homeless" 35:922–24.
5. Levine, "Service Programs for the Homeless Mentally Ill," 173–200.
6. *Ibid.*
7. Weigle, *Spiders and Spinsters.*
8. Collins, "Theology in the Politics of Appalachian Women," 149–58.
9. Plaskow, "The Coming of Lilith," 198–209.

Chapter 2

1. Kaufman, "The Implications of Biological Psychiatry for the Severely Mentally Ill," 201–42.
2. Watson, and Austerberry, *Housing and Homelessness.*

3. Levine, and Stockdill, "Mentally Ill and Homeless," 1–16.

4. Kozol, *Rachel and Her Children.*

5. Roth, and Bean, "New Perspectives on Homelessness," 37:712–17.

6. Watson, and Austerbery, *Housing and Homelessness.*

7. Bachrach, "Homeless Women," 65:371.

8. Ball, and Havassy, "A Survey of the Problems and Needs of Homeless Consumers of Acute Psychiatric Services," 35:917–21.

9. Baxter, and Hopper, "The New Mendicancy: Homeless in New York City," 52:393–407.

10. Cooper, J.C. *Fairy Tales.*

11. Connelly, *All Sickness Is Home Sickness.*

12. Moon, *Changing Woman and Her Sisters.*

13. Wehr, *Jung and Feminism.*

14. Gallagher, and Dodds, *Speaking Out, Fighting Back.*

15. Jones, et al., "Psycho-social Profiles: The Urban Homeless."

16. Bassuk, "Homeless Families," 30:45–53.

17. Kolbenschlag, *Kiss Sleeping Beauty Good-Bye.*

18. Harding, *The Way of All Women.*

19. *Shakespeare's Sonnets.*

20. Sontag, *Illness as Metaphor.*

21. Whitmont, *Return of the Goddess.*

22. Ulanov, *Receiving Woman.*

23. Miller, *Toward a New Psychology of Women.*

24. Sontag, *Illness as Metaphor.*

25. Ulanov, *Receiving Woman.*

Chapter 3

1. Jung, *Psychological Reflections.*

2. *Ibid.*

3. Hillman, *Revisioning Psychology.*

4. Henderson, "Ancient Myths and Modern Man."

5. Campbell, *Hero With a Thousand Faces.*

6. Jung, *Aion.*

7. Claremont de Castillejo, *Knowing Woman.*

8. Jung, *Aion.*

9. von Franz, *C. G. Jung: His Myth in Our time.*

10. Whitmont, *Return of The Goddess.*

11. Evans, and Evans, *Dictionary of Contemporary American Usage.*

12. Hillman, *Revisioning Psychology.*

13. von Franz, *Problems of the Feminine in Fairy Tales.*

14. Moon, *Changing Woman and Her Sisters.*

15. Bleeker, "Isis and Hathor."

Chapter 4

1. Seifert, *Snow White, Life Almost Lost.*
2. Jung, "The Psychology of the Child Archetype."
3. *Ibid.*
4. Campbell, *Myths to Live By.*
5. Sontag, *Illness as Metaphor.*
6. Koltuv, *The Book of Lilith.*
7. Miller, *Toward a New Psychology of Women.*
8. Lerner, *Women in Therapy.*
9. Leonard, *The Wounded Woman.*
10. Bolen, *Goddesses in Every Woman.*
11. Leonard, *The Wounded Woman.*
12. Nisbet, *Emile Durkkeim.*
13. Harding, *The Way of All Women.*
14. Kolbenschlag, *Kiss Sleeping Beauty Good-Bye.*
15. Heilbrun, *Reinventing Womanhood.*
16. *Ibid.*
17. *Ibid.*
18. Miller, *Toward a New Psychology of Women.*
19. Kolbenschlag, *Kiss Sleeping Beauty Good-Bye.*
20. Lerner, *Women in Therapy.*

Chapter 5

1. Wehr, *Jung and Feminism.*
2. Hopper, Baxter, and Cox, "Not Making It Crazy," vol. 14.
3. Jones, et al., "Psycho-social Profiles."
4. Kates, *Murder of a Shopping Bag Lady.*
5. Karlsen, *The Devil in the Shape of a Woman.*
6. Ulanov, A. *Receiving Woman.*
7. Kozol, *Rachel and Her Children.*
8. Bachrach, "The Homeless Mentally Ill and Mental Health Services."
9. Showalter, *The Female Malady.*
10. *Ibid.*
11. Ulanov, *Receiving Woman.*
12. Lifton, *The Nazi Doctors.*
13. *Ibid.*

Chapter 6

1. Keen, *Faces of the Enemy.*
2. Peck, *People of the Lie.*
3. Morris, ed., American Heritage Dictionary, New College Edition.
4. Brown-Miller, *Against Our Will.*

5. Grotstein, J., "Forgery of the Soul," 203–26.

6. Brown-Miller, *Against Our Will.*

7. Schwab, *Gods and Heroes.*

8. Walker, *The Woman's Encyclopedia of Myths and Secrets.*

9. *Ibid.*

10. *The Homeric Hymns.*

11. Miller, *Toward a New Psychology of Women.*

12. Kerenyi, "Kore."

13. Rusk, "The Sexual Abuse of Children."

14. Gallagher, *Speaking Out, Fighting Back.*

15. Schwab, *Gods and Heroes.*

16. Gallagher, *Speaking Out, Fighting Back.*

17. Gallagher, *Ibid.*

18. Brown-Miller, *Against Our Will.*

19. Schwab, *Gods and Heroes.*

20. Bachrach, "The Chronic Patient," 37: 981–82.

21. *Ibid.*

22. Goodrich, *Ancient Myths.*

23. Brown-Miller, *Against Our Will.*

24. Woods, "Victim in a Forcible Rape Case."

25. Berger, *The Goddess Obscured.*

26. Gallagher, *Speaking Out, Fighting Back.*

27. Ward, *Harlots of the Desert.*

28. *Ibid.*

29. Kerenyi, "Kore."

30. Leonard, *Wounded Woman.*

31. Maier, and Seligman, "Learned Helplessness: Theory and Evidence," 105: 3–46.

32. Seligman, and Maier, "Failure to Escape Traumatic Shock," 74: 1–9.

Chapter 7

1. Lipsey, "We are all Witnesses: An Interview With Elie Wiesel," 10: 26–33.

2. *Ibid.*

3. Wehr, *Jung and Feminism.*

4. Baron, et al, "Sudden Death Among Southeast Asian Refugees," 250: 2947–51.

5. Schwab. *Gods and Heroes.*

6. Zaleski, "Living in the Rift," 10: 6–13.

7. *Ibid.*

8. Ward, *Harlots of the Desert.*

9. Caprio, *The Woman Sealed in the Tower.*

10. The Oxford Annotated Bible, Revised Standard Edition.

11. Whitmont, *Return of the Goddess.*

12. Gaster, "The New Golden Bough."

13. *Ibid.*

14. Foderaro, "Neighbors Try to Secede Over Housing Plan," B-1.

15. Wiesel, "Jew, Myth, and Modern Life," 70–77.

16. *Ibid.*

17. Foucault, *Madness and Civilization.*

18. *Ibid.*

19. *Ibid.*

20. Deloria, "Out of Chaos," 10:14–22.

21. *Ibid.*

22. *Ibid.*

23. *Ibid.*

24. Thurman, "Tibet: Mystic Nation in Exile," 10:56–69.

25. *Ibid.*

26. *Ibid.*

27. *Ibid.*

28. Franck, "The End of Exile?" 10:84–89.

29. *Ibid.*

30. *Ibid.*

31. Auel, *The Clan of the Cave Bear.*

32. Wehr, *Jung and Feminism.*

33. Mishima, *Confessions of a Mask.*

34. Whitmont, *Return of the Goddess.*

35. Hwang, Glass, and Siklin, "1000 Airplanes on the Roof."

36. Wiesel, "Jew, Myth, and Modern Life."

37. Watson, and Austerberry, *Housing and Homelessness.*

38. Lamb, "Deinstitutionalization and the Homeless Mentally Ill," 35: 899–907.

39. *Ibid.*

40. *Ibid.*

Chapter 8

1. Morris, ed., American Heritage Dictionary, New College Edition.

2. Keen, *Faces of the Enemy.*

3. *Ibid.*

4. *Ibid.*

5. *Ibid.*

6. *Ibid.*

7. Jones, *Women Who Kill.*

8. Hillman, "On the Necessity of Abnormal Psychology," 1–38.

9. *Ibid.*

10. Jones, *Women Who Kill.*

11. Keen, *Faces of the Enemy.*

12. Grotstein, "Forgery of the Soul," 203–26.

13. Kozol, *Rachel and Her Children.*

14. *Ibid.*

15. Jones, *Women Who Kill.*

16. Brown, "Kali, The Mad Mother."

17. Jones, *Women Who Kill.*

18. *Ibid.*

19. von Franz, *Shadow and Evil in Fairytales.*

20. Jones, *Women Who Kill.*

21. *Ibid.*

22. Prescott, *Princes of the Renaissance.*

23. Corvo, *Chronicles of the House of Borgia.*

24. Jones, *Women Who Kill.*

25. *Ibid.*

26. Neumann, *The Great Mother.*

27. Malamud, "The Amazon Problem," 47–66.

28. *Ibid.*

29. *Ibid.*

30. Schwab, *Gods and Heroes.*

31. Neumann, *The Great Mother.*

32. *Ibid.*

33. Brown, "Kali, The Mad Mother."

34. Neumann, *The Great Mother.*

35. Weigle, *Spiders and Spinsters.*

36. *Ibid.*

37. Walker, *The Woman's Encyclopedia of Myths and Secrets.*

38. Neumann, *The Great Mother.*

39. Moon, *Changing Woman and Her Sisters.*

40. Walker, *The Woman's Encyclopedia of Myths and Secrets.*

41. Weigle, *Spiders and Spinsters.*

42. *Ibid.*

43. Reich, and Siegel, "The Emergence of the Bowery as a Psychiatric Dumping Ground," 50:191–201.

44. Davies, "The Canaanite-Hebrew Goddess," 68–79.

45. *Ibid.*

46. Lorenz, *On Aggression.*

47. Peck, *People of the Lie.*

48. *Ibid.*

49. *Ibid.*

Chapter 9

1. Morris, ed., American Heritage Dictionary, *New College Edition.*

2. Camus, *The Rebel.*

3. *Ibid.*

4. *Ibid.*

5. Weisel, *Legends of Our Time.*

6. *Ibid.*

7. de Beauvoir, *The Second Sex.*

8. Kavolis, "Civilizational Models of Evil," 17–35.

9. *Ibid.*

10. Peck, *People of the Lie.*

11. Weigle, *Spiders and Spinsters.*

12. Rossi, *The Feminist Papers.*

13. Shainess, "Antigone."

14. Heilbrun, *Reinventing Womanhood.*

15. Drake, and Adler, "Shelter is not Enough."

16. *Ibid.*

17. Baxter and Hopper, "The New Mendicancy: Homeless in New York City," 52:393–407.

18. *Ibid.*

19. Rossi, *The Feminist Papers.*

20. *Ibid.*

21. *Ibid.*

22. *Ibid.*

23. *Ibid.*

24. Camus, *The Rebel.*

25. Sanger, "My Fight For Birth Control," 522–32.

26. *Ibid.*

27. Johnson, *From Housewife to Heretic.*

28. *Ibid.*

29. *Ibid.*

30. Lisle, L., *Portrait of an Artist.*

31. *Ibid.*

32. *Ibid.*

33. *Ibid.*

34. *Ibid.*

35. *Ibid.*

36. *Ibid.*

37. Philips, *Eve: The History of an Idea.*

38. *The Oxford Annotated Bible.*

39. Koltuv, *The Book of Lilith.*

40. *Ibid.*
41. *Ibid.*
42. Warner, *Monuments and Maidens.*
43. *Ibid.*
44. *Ibid.*
45. *Ibid.*
46. *Ibid.*
47. *Ibid.*
48. *Ibid.*
49. Schwab, *Gods and Heroes.*
50. Trypanis, *Sophocles: Three Theban Plays.*
51. *Ibid.*
52. Camus, *The Rebel.*
53. Shainess, "Antigone."
54. Shaw, "St. Joan."
55. *Ibid.*, 91.
56. *Ibid.*
57. *Ibid.*
58. *Ibid.*
59. *Ibid.*
60. *Ibid.*

Part Three

1. Kozol, *Rachel and Her Children.*

Chapter 10

1. Goldenberg, *Changing of the Gods.*
2. Miller, "Connections, Disconnections and Violations."
3. *Ibid.*
4. Levi, *Survival in Auschwitz.*
5. Cooper, *Fairy Tales.*
6. Collins, "Reflections on the Meaning of Her Story."
7. Miller, "What Do We Mean by Relationships?"
8. Goldenberg, *Changing of the Gods.*
9. Campbell, *Myths to Live By.*
10. Mayer, *Beauty and the Beast.*
11. *Ibid.*
12. Stone, *Ancient Mirrors of Womanhood.*
13. Miller, *Toward a New Psychology of Women.*
14. Stone, *Ancient Mirrors of Womanhood.*
15. *The Complete Grimm's Fairy Tales.*
16. Stone, *Ancient Mirrors of Womanhood.*
17. Ulanov, and Ulanov, *Cinderella and Her Sisters.*

Chapter 11

1. Connelly, *All Sickness is Home Sickness.*
2. Whitmont, *Return of the Goddess.*
3. *Ibid.*
4. *Ibid.*
5. Ulanov, *Receiving Woman.*
6. *Ibid.*
7. *Ibid.*
8. *Ibid.*
9. Woodman, *Addiction to Perfection.*
10. *Ibid.*
11. Perera, *Descent of the Goddess.*
12. *Ibid.*
13. *Ibid.*
14. *Ibid.*
15. *Ibid.*
16. *Ibid.*
17. *Ibid.*
18. *Ibid.*
19. *Ibid.*

Chapter 12

1. Keen, *Faces of the Enemy.*
2. Perera, *Descent to the Goddess.*
3. Miller, *Toward a New Psychology of Women.*
4. Harding, *The Way of All Women.*
5. Seifert, *Snow White: Life Almost Lost.*
6. Koltuv, *The Book of Lilith.*
7. Jung, "A Study in the Process of Individuation."
8. *Ibid.*
9. *The Oxford Annotated Bible.*

References

Auel, Jean. *The Clan of the Cave Bear.* New York: Bantam Books, 1980.

Bachrach, Leona. "The Chronic Patient: Dimensions of Disability in the Chronic Mentally Ill." *Hospital and Community Psychiatry* 37:981–982, 1986.

———— "The Homeless Mentally Ill and Mental Health Services: An Analytical Review of the Literature." In *The Homeless Mentally Ill.* Edited by H. R. Lamb. Washington, D.C.: American Psychiatric Association, 1984.

———— "Homeless Mentally Ill Women: A Special Population." In *The Myth of Options: Social and Cultural Issues.* Edited by J. Spurlock and C. Rabinowitz. New York: Plenum, 1989.

———— "Homeless Women: A Context for Health Planning." *Milbank Quarterly* 65:371, 1987.

Ball, J., and Havassy, B. "A Survey of the Problems and Needs of Homeless Consumers of Acute Psychiatric Services." *Hospital and Community Psychiatry* 35:917–21, 1984.

Baron, R., et al. "Sudden Death Among Southeast Asian Refugees." *Journal of the American Medical Association* 250:2947–51, 1983.

Bassuk, Ellen. "Homeless Families: Single Mothers and Their Children in Boston." *New Directions for Mental Health Services* 30:45–53, 1986.

Baxter, E., and Hopper, K. "The New Mendicancy: Homeless in New York City." *American Journal of Orthopsychiatry* 52:393–407, 1982.

Berger, Pamela. *The Goddess Obscured.* Boston: Beacon Press, 1985.

Bleeker, C. J. "Isis and Hathor." In *The Book of the Goddess: Past and Present,* by Carl Olson. New York: Crossroad Publishing Co., 1988.

Boer, C., trans. *The Homeric Hymns.* Dallas: Spring Publications, 1970.

Bolen, Jean S. *Goddesses in Every Woman.* New York: Harper and Row, 1985.

Brown, C. M. "Kali, The Mad Mother." In *The Book of the Goddess: Past and Present.* Edited by C. Olson. New York: Crossroad, 1988.

Brown-Miller, Susan. *Against Our Will.* New York: Bantam Books, 1975.

Campbell, Joseph. *Hero With a Thousand Faces.* New York: Pantheon Books, 1949.

——— *Myths to Live By.* New York: Bantam Books, 1972.

Camus, Albert. *The Rebel.* New York: Alfred Knopf, 1956.

Caprio, Betsy. *The Woman Sealed in the Tower.* New York: Paulist Press, 1982.

Claremont de Castillejo, Irene. *Knowing Woman.* New York: Harper and Row, 1973.

Cohen, N., Putnam, J., and Sullivan, A. "The Mentally Ill Homeless: Isolation and Adaptation." *Hospital and Community Psychiatry* 35:922–24, 1984.

Collins, Sheila. "Reflections on the Meaning of Her Story." In *Womanspirit Rising.* Edited by C. Christ and J. Plaskow. San Francisco: Harper and Row, 1979.

——— "Theology in the Politics of Appalachian Women." In *Womanspirit Rising.* Edited by C. Christ and J. Plaskow. San Francisco: Harper and Row, 1979.

Connelly, Dianne. *All Sickness is Home Sickness.* Columbia, Md.: Center for Traditional Acupuncture, 1986.

Cooper, J. C. *Fairy Tales: Allegories of the Inner Life.* Wellingborough: Aquarian Press, 1983.

Corvo, F. B. *Chronicles of the House of Borgia.* New York: Dover Publications, 1901.

Davies, Steve. "The Canaanite-Hebrew Goddess." In *The Book of the Goddess: Past and Present.* Edited by C. Olson. New York: Crossroad, 1988.

de Beauvoir, Simone. *The Second Sex.* New York: Alfred Knopf, 1952.

Deloria, Vine. "Out of Chaos." *Parabola* 10:14–22, 1985.

Drake, R., and Adler, D. "Shelter Is Not Enough: Clinical Work With the

Homeless Mentally Ill." In *The Homeless Mentally Ill.* Edited by H. R. Lamb. Washington, D.C.: American Psychiatric Association, 1984.

Evans, B., and Evans, C. *Dictionary of Contemporary American Usage.* New York: Random House, 1957.

Foderaro, L. "Neighbors Try to Secede Over Housing Plan." *The New York Times* December 5:B-1, 1988.

Foucault, Michel. *Madness and Civilization.* New York: Vintage Books, 1965.

Franck, F. "The End of Exile?" *Parabola* 10:84–89, 1985.

Gallagher, Vera, and Dodds, William. *Speaking Out, Fighting Back.* Seattle: Madrona Publishers, 1985.

Gaster, T. *The New Golden Bough.* New York: Mentor Books, 1964.

Goldenberg, Naomi. *Changing of the Gods.* Boston: Beacon Press, 1979.

Goodrich, N. L. *Ancient Myths.* New York: New American Library, 1960.

Grotstein, James. "Forgery of the Soul: Psychogenesis of Evil." In *Evil: Self and Culture,* by M. C. Nelson and M. Eigen. New York: Human Sciences Press, 1984.

Harding, Esther. *The Way of All Women.* San Francisco: Harper and Row, 1970.

Heilbrun, Carolyn. *Reinventing Womanhood.* New York: W. W. Norton and Co., 1979.

Henderson, J. "Ancient Myths and Modern Man." In *Man and His Symbols.* Edited by C. G. Jung. New York: Dell Publishing, 1964.

Hillman, James. "On the Necessity of Abnormal Psychology: Ananke and Others." In *Facing the Gods.* Edited by J. Hillman. Dallas: Spring Publications, 1980.

——— *Revisioning Psychology.* New York: Harper and Row, 1975.

Hopper, K., Baxter, E., and Cox, S. "Not Making It Crazy: The Young Homeless Patients in New York City." *New Directions in Mental Health* 14:33–42, 1982.

Hunt, M., trans. *The Complete Grimms Fairytales.* New York: Pantheon Books, 1944.

Hwang, D., Glass, P., and Siklin, J. "1000 Airplanes on the Roof." *National Theater,* Washington, D.C.: December 8–10, 1988.

Jacobi, JoLande. *Psychological Reflections: An Anthology of the Writings of C. G. Jung.* New York: Harper and Row, 1953.

Johnson, Sonia. *From Housewife to Heretic.* Garden City: Doubleday, 1981.

Jones, Ann. *Women Who Kill.* New York: Fawcett Crest, 1980.

Jones, B., et al. "Psycho-social Profiles: The Urban Homeless." In *Treating the Homeless: Urban Psychiatry's Challenge.* Edited by B. Jones. Washington, D.C.: American Psychiatric Press, 1986.

Jung, C. G. *Aion.* Collected Works, Bollingen Series, vol. 9, no. 2. Princeton: Princeton University Press, 1959.

———. "The Psychology of the Child Archetype." In *Essays on a Science of Mythology,* by Jung and Kerenyi. Princeton: Princeton University Press, 1963.

———. "A Study in the Process of Individuation." In *Collected Works,* vol. 9. Princeton: Princeton University Press, 1969.

Kates, B. *Murder of a Shopping Bag Lady.* Orlando: Harcourt, Brace, Javanovich, 1985.

Kaufman, C. "The Implications of Biological Psychiatry for the Severely Mentally Ill." In *The Homeless Mentally Ill.* Edited by H. R. Lamb. Washington, D.C.: American Psychiatric Association, 1984.

Kavolis, V. "Civilizational Models of Evil." In *Evil: Self and Culture.* Edited by M. C. Nelson and M. Eigen. New York: Human Sciences Press, 1984.

Keen, Sam. *Faces of the Enemy.* San Francisco: Harper and Row, 1986.

Kerenyi, C. "Kore." In *Essays on a Science of Mythology,* by C. G. Jung and C. Kerenyi. Princeton: Princeton University Press, 1949.

Kolbenschlag, Madonna. *Kiss Sleeping Beauty Good-Bye.* San Francisco: Harper and Row, 1979.

Koltuv, B. *The Book of Lilith.* York Beach: Nicholas Hays, Inc., 1986.

Kozol, J. *Rachel and Her Children.* New York: Crown Publishers, 1988.

Lamb, H. R. "Deinstitutionalization and the Homeless Mentally Ill." *Hospital and Community Psychiatry* 35:899–907, 1984.

Leonard, Linda S. *The Wounded Woman.* Boston: Shambala, 1985.

Lerner, Harriet G. *Women in Therapy.* North Vale: Jason Aronson, 1988.

Levi, Primo. *Survival in Auschwitz.* New York: McMillan Publishing Co., 1961.

Levine, Irene S. "Service Programs for the Homeless Mentally Ill." In *The Homeless Mentally Ill.* Edited by H. R. Lamb. Washington, D.C.: American Psychiatric Association, 1984.

———, and Stockdill, James. "Mentally Ill and Homeless." In *Treating the Homeless: Urban Psychiatry's Challenge.* Edited by B. Jones. Washington, D.C.: American Psychiatric Press, 1986.

Lifton, Robert J. *The Nazi Doctors.* New York: Basic Books, 1986.

Lipsey, R. "We Are all Witnesses: An Interview with Elie Wiesel." *Parabola* 10:26–33, 1985.

Lisle, Laurie. *Portrait of an Artist.* New York: Washington Square Press, 1986.

Lorenz, Konrad. *On Aggression.* New York: Bantam Books, 1963.

Maier, S., and Seligman, M. "Learned Helplessness: Theory and Evidence." *Journal of Experimental Psychology: General* 105:3–46, 1976.

Malamud, R. "The Amazon Problem." In *Facing the Gods*. Edited by J. Hillman. Dallas: Spring Publications, 1990.

Mayer, M., retold by. *Beauty and the Beast*. New York: Four Winds Press, 1978.

Miller, Jean B. *Toward a New Psychology of Women*. 2d ed. Boston: Beacon Press, 1986.

Mishima, Yukio. *Confessions of a Mask*. New York: New Directions Book, 1958.

Moon, Sheila. *Changing Woman and Her Sisters*. San Francisco: Guild for Psychological Studies Publishing House, 1984.

Morris, W., ed. *American Heritage Dictionary, New College Edition*. Boston: Houghton Mifflin Co., 1975.

Neumann, Erich. *The Great Mother*. Princeton: Princeton University Press, 1955.

Nisbet, R. *Emile Durkkeim*. Englewood Cliffs: Prentice-Hall, 1965.

Oxford Annotated Bible, Revised Standard Version. New York: Oxford University Press, 1962.

Peck, Scott. *People of the Lie*. New York: Simon and Schuster, 1983.

Perera, Sylvia. *Descent to the Goddess*. Toronto: Inner City Books, 1981.

Philips, John. *Eve: The History of an Idea*. San Francisco: Harper and Row, 1984.

Plaskow, Judith. "The Coming of Lilith: Toward a Feminist Theology." In *Womanspirit Rising*. Edited by C. Christ and J. Plaskow. San Francisco: Harper and Row, 1979.

Prescott, O. *Princess of the Renaissance*. New York: Random House, 1969.

Reich, R., and Siegel, L. "The Emergence of the Bowery as a Psychiatric Dumping Ground." *Psychiatric Quarterly* 50:191–201, 1978.

Rossi, Alice. *The Feminist Papers*. Boston: Northeastern University Press, 1988.

Roth, D., and Bean, G. "New Perspectives on Homelessness: Findings from a Statewide Epidemiological Study." *Hospital and Community Psychiatry* 37:712–17, 1986.

Rusk, F. "The Sexual Abuse of Children: A Feminist Point of View." In *Rape: The First Sourcebook for Women,* by N. Connell and C. Wilson. New York: New American Library, 1974.

Sanger, Margaret. "My Fight for Birth Control." In *The Feminist Papers,* by A. Rossi. Boston: Northeastern University Press, 1988.

Schwab, Gustav. *Gods and Heroes*. New York: Pantheon Books, 1946.

Seifert, Theodor. *Snow White: Life Almost Lost*. Wilmette: Chiron Publications, 1986.

Seligman, M., and Maier, S. "Failure to Escape Traumatic Shock." *Journal of Experimental Psychology* 74:1–9, 1967.

Shainess, N. "Antigone: Symbol of Autonomy and Women's Moral Dilemmas." In *The Psychology of Today's Woman*. Edited by T. Bernay and D. Cantor. Hillsdale: Analytic Press, 1986.

Shakespeare, William. *Shakespeare's Sonnets*. Edited by Douglas Bush and Alfred Harbage. Baltimore: Penguin Books, 1961.

Shaw, George B. "St. Joan." In *The Collected Works*, vol. 17. New York: William H. Wise and Co., 1931.

Showalter, Elaine. *The Female Malady*. New York: Penguin Books, 1985.

Sontag, Susan. *Illness as Metaphor*. New York: Vintage Books, 1977.

Stone, Merlin. *Ancient Mirrors of Womanhood*. Boston: Beacon Press, 1979.

Thurman, R. "Tibet: Mystic Nation in Exile." *Parabola* 10:56–69, 1985.

Trypanis, C. A., trans. *Sophocles: Three Theban Plays*. Wiltshire: Aris and Philips Ltd., 1986.

Ulanov, Ann. *Receiving Woman*. Philadelphia: Westminister Press, 1981.

———, and Ulanov, Barry. *Cinderella and Her Sisters*. Philadelphia: Westminister Press, 1983.

von Franz, M. L. *C. G. Jung: His Myth in Our Time*. New York: G. P. Putnam's Sons, 1975.

——— *Problems of the Feminine in Fairy Tales*. Dallas: Spring Publications, 1972.

——— *Shadow and Evil in Fairytales*. Dallas: Spring Publications, 1987.

Walker, Barbara G. *The Woman's Encyclopedia of Myths and Secrets*. San Francisco: Harper and Row, 1983.

Ward, Benedicta. *Harlots of the Desert*. Kalamazoo: Cistercian Publications, 1987.

Warner, Marina. *Monuments and Maidens*. New York: Atheneum, 1985.

Watson, Sophie, and Austerberry, Helen. *Housing and Homelessness*. London: Routledge and Kegan Paul, 1986.

Wehr, Demaris. *Jung and Feminism: Liberating Archetypes*. Boston: Beacon Press, 1987.

Weigle, Marta. *Spiders and Spinsters*. Albuquerque: University of New Mexico Press, 1982.

Whitmont, Edward. *Return of the Goddess*. New York: Crossroad Publishing Co., 1986.

Wiesel, Elie. "Jew, Myth, and Modern Life." *Parabola* 12:70–77, 1986.

——— *Legends of Our Time*. New York: Schocken Books, 1982.

Woodman, Marion. *Addiction to Perfection*. Toronto: Inner City Books, 1982.

Woods, P. L. "Victim in a Forcible Rape Case: A Feminist View." In *Rape: The First Sourcebook for Women*, by N. Connell and C. Wilson. New York: New American Library, 1974.

Zaleski, P. "Living in the Rift." *Parabola* 10:6–13, 1985.

Index

DATE DUE

DE 31 01			
GAYLORD			PRINTED IN U.S.A.